A FATAL CONJUNCTION

Two laws
Two cultures

A FATAL CONJUNCTION

Two laws
Two cultures

Joan Kimm

THE FEDERATION PRESS
2004

Published in Sydney by:
The Federation Press
PO Box 45, Annandale, NSW, 2038
71 John St, Leichhardt, NSW, 2040
Ph (02) 9552 2200 Fax (02) 9552 1681
E-mail: info@federationpress.com.au
Website: http://www.federationpress.com.au

National Library of Australia
Cataloguing-in-Publication entry

Kimm, Joan
A fatal conjunction: two laws two cultures.

Bibliography.
Includes index.
ISBN 1 86287 509 X

1. Aborigines, Australian – Wife abuse. 2. Aborigines, Australian – Women – Social conditions. 3. Abused women – Australia. 4. Family violence – Australia. I. Title.

362.849915

Typeset by The Federation Press, Leichhardt, NSW.
Printed by Southwood Press Pty Ltd, Marrickville, NSW.

Contents

To GSD,
without whose encouragement
this would not
have become a book.

Preface

Silence is the language of complicity.[1]

A conversation with two young Aboriginal women was the starting point for this investigation of Aboriginal family violence. Each said that they would not tolerate violence from an Aboriginal man in an urban setting, but that they would do so if they were living a traditional lifestyle: that this was expected and it would be part of their life under customary law. If they could not agree to be subject to this violence then they could not live in that community.

The statements of these women were astounding. Although as a solicitor I had some experience of women who remained in abusive relationships, these were independent young women speaking hypothetically about potential abuse. Their comments raised issues about conflicting human rights, namely Indigenous rights and women's rights to be protected from violence. The status of Indigenous women in Australian law was also in question. In short, if Aboriginal women are expected to tolerate violence, are their rights of less moment than those of other women in Australia?

Radhika Coomaraswamy, as the Special Rapporteur on Violence Against Women to the United Nations Human Rights Commission, set standards for testing legal rights:

> The quality of a system of laws may be better understood by analyzing its effects on society's margins. This involves questions such as who is involved in the law's protection? Who is excluded? Who is privileged? Who is actually punished? – These questions give a sense of the social dimension of a legal system as it actually affects people's lives.[2]

I used these questions as a yardstick to test the rights which judges have accorded to Aboriginal men as perpetrators of violence against Aboriginal women and to women as victims of that violence. In the past the scales of justice were not tipped in favour of women.

Therefore this book is not a statistical analysis of violence, although statistics establish some of the parameters of that violence, but it is a qualitative examination of violence through the lens of the law. It is about the effect on Aboriginal women of two patriarchies and two laws, Indigenous and non-Indigenous, and how present violence to women is affected by a heritage of past violence in those two cultures.

In October 2001 Dr Lowitja O'Donoghue spoke about the responsibility of Australians to act upon Aboriginal family violence when delivering the Hyllus Maris memorial lecture at La Trobe University:

> It is now everyone's business to take the issue on board. ... Indigenous violence has to be understood in ways that take into account culture, history, race and place as well as gender.[3]

When Aboriginal men have been charged with violence against Aboriginal women these factors have frequently been successfully argued on behalf of the accused, often under the guise of customary law "defences". Testing the validity of these arguments on behalf of Aboriginal men involved researching historical and anthropological, as well as legal, sources. As anthropologist Gillian Cowlishaw observed, different disciplines can give insights into the Aboriginal experience, even if the tools used are those of "literary critics, historians, sociologists and lawyers".[4]

Nonetheless, in discussing the law cases dating from the 1950s onwards and their historical and anthropological contexts, it is possible that some of this material will be regarded as offensive because traditional culture has become a political issue with legal ramifications. But without this information it is very difficult to consider the rationale of judicial decisions before the mid-1980s. In justification I can only repeat Elizabeth Eggleston's words, written in the 1960s, about her research into Aborigines and justice:

> The lawyer's concern for such matters as part of his effort to establish the rule of law has been recognised by the International Commission of Jurists. The lawyer's involvement in this field stems mainly from his position as a citizen, but his expertise in relation to legislation casts on him a special responsibility to act.[5]

This professional concern for rights, but particularly in relation to Aboriginal women's rights, was expressed in 1989 when the anthropologist Diane Bell and her Indigenous colleague, Topsy Napparula Nelson, wrote about the frequency of rape within Aboriginal society:

> Although it could be said that this is "not my business', it is very much my business. I hold to the position that, no matter how unpleasant, feminist social scientists do have a responsibility to identify and analyse those factors that render women vulnerable to violence. The fact that this is happening to women of another ethnic or racial

group cannot be a reason for ignoring the abuse. But it is cause to look carefully to the cultural context, to heed the silences.[6]

Many Aboriginal women met Bell and Nelson's disclosures with hostility. However, since then, public debate and concern about Aboriginal family violence have been openly expressed. In 1999, the Queensland Domestic Violence Task Force of Indigenous Women concluded that the levels were such as to "threaten the continued existence of Australia's Indigenous peoples".

The intensity of this violence needs to be understood by non-Indigenous Australians. When working as a solicitor with non-Indigenous clients, I encountered infanticide, homicide, suicide, betrayals, violence, incest and other child abuse. These were tragic cases but in none was the violence equivalent to the horrific circumstances of Aboriginal violence. An Aborigine said to me that the film about Maori violence *Once Were Warriors* was equally true of Aboriginal violence.

Abuse of all women usually occurs in a private relationship; unlike other assaults, this discrete space can secure immunity from the scrutiny of the law. However, the abuse of Indigenous Australian women is a social paradox. Even in comparatively urban settings domestic violence can be part of an Indigenous cultural tradition of public violence,[7] so it can be more visible than non-Aboriginal abuse. But it seems that, whatever the actual visibility of the incidents and the severity of the injuries, Aboriginal women are disadvantaged in that Aboriginal culture has become an inviolate space in our society where abuse of women often occurs with impunity because of distorted views of the respect which must be paid to Indigenous rights. It appears, that whatever the significance of the claims of gender "equality" in traditional society, the violence inflicted on Aboriginal women fits Coomaraswamy's paradigm that women are *universally* vulnerable to violence.

[F]irst a woman's sexuality makes her susceptible to sex related crimes which are "fundamentally connected to a society's construction of female sexuality and its role in social hierarchy'; second, a woman's relationship to a man or group of men makes her vulnerable to types of violence which "are animated by society's concept of a woman as the property and dependant of a male protector"; third, violence against women may be directed towards the social group of which she is a member because, for example to "rape a woman is to humiliate her community"; finally there is a strong connection between militarisation and violence against women.[8]

Aboriginal family violence should not be ignored just because it is culturally (and even socially) more comfortable to do so. Coomaraswamy views feminism as a useful tool that gives "insight into society as it actually exists as opposed to how it appears to exist". If we do not seek truth a chimera is guiding us. In her 1999 Boyer lectures, Inga Clendinnen said the good history of a nation is made by true stories:

> And nations, … especially democratic ethnically and religiously diverse nations like our own, cannot hold together unless they share a common vision as to … what behaviour is worthy of respect, what behaviour is shameful.[9]

LR Hiatt and Peter Sutton present anthropologists' perspectives on the importance of arriving at truth, if we can, about the cultures in our nation.

> [I]n contemporary Australia the dialectical quest for truth about the indigenous culture, by open argument and counter argument, is no less important than about the culture of the invaders and oppressors.[10]

Peter Sutton in 2001 in his Inaugural Berndt Foundation Biennial lecture, said:

> Critics may suggest that I have played into the hands of those with interests hostile to those of Indigenous Australians, simply by saying certain things that, while possibly true, might be hijacked for purposes opposite to my own. What is most likely to trigger such a response is my unqualified position that a number of serious problems Indigenous people face in Australia today arise from a complex joining together of recent, that is post-conquest, historical factors of external impact, with a substantial number of ancient, pre-existent social and cultural factors. Here I focus, in particular, on violent conflict.[11]

Nonetheless, I have also taken account of Aboriginal historian Jackie Huggins' warning that, "We cannot translate other's history into our own – we can merely juxtapose them".[12] Therefore I have attempted to record the Aboriginal and non-Aboriginal perspectives of two very different, legalistic societies. It was also important to do so because constantly Australian general law, which has assumed dominance over customary law, decides legal issues arising from Aboriginal culture. If offence has been caused I again join with other women in their justifications and repeat Clendinnen's apology spoken when she broached the sensitive issue of Australia's two cultures and two histories:

To Aboriginal listeners I say: you have lived your history, while I have only retrieved what I can from books. I must ask your tolerance for the liberty I am taking – a necessary liberty, because it is through reading that most of us come to understand our fellow humans better.[13]

I am aware that there have been polarised reactions to my conclusions that Aboriginal family violence is caused by factors within, as well as outside, Aboriginal culture. Positive responses were received from people with actual experiences of Aboriginal communities in South Australia and right across Northern Australia. But the criticisms require a brief response. It is not my intention to denigrate Aborigines. Some seemed to have mistaken the thrust of the argument. It is about women's rights to be immune from violence, and the conflict between valuing these rights and respecting Indigenous cultural rights.

One critic said that references to Aboriginal practices would need to be specifically referenced "right around the country". This is akin to the criticism by anthropologist Sandy Toussant of historian Bain Attwood in *Phyllis Kaberry and Me* in which Toussant claimed Attwood "homogenised" Aborigines. However, the use of "Indigenous", "Aborigines" and "Aboriginal" is contemporary practice amongst many Indigenous people, historians, lawyers, as well as the Australian Law Reform Commission, criminologists and sociologists. Even though it is now understood that there were many diverse practices and hundreds of different languages in classical Aboriginal society, there was, as the anthropologist Basil Sansom has said, an "Aboriginal commonality", a "bundle of features" which he describes as being "pan-Aboriginal".[14] Male initiation ceremonies, whatever the actual ritual, and customary law marriage are examples of these "features". I have, however, where possible, made specific references to particular tribal affiliations, but this information was not always recorded in case reports or other sources. In discussing Aboriginal attitudes of course I do not mean all Aborigines, in the sense of each and everyone. There are frequent qualifications such as "some" etc, but to do so every time an Indigenous viewpoint is discussed makes very tedious reading.

Unless otherwise indicated, both the accused and the victim are Aborigines. It is impossible to determine how "traditional" the lifestyles of those concerned are in these cases. In 1986 the ALRC report on Aboriginal customary law concluded that there was no need for a restrictive definition and that a flexible approach to the idea of a traditional Aborigine was preferable.[15] The influence of traditional lifestyle can be strong even though the precise structures of traditional law and the language in which it was embodied have often been destroyed by European depredations.[16]

The two cultures have very different concepts of law. Aborigines living traditionally venerate the law. When they have used the term "sacred law" I have repeated it. Otherwise the terms "customary law" or "traditional law" mean Indigenous law, "general" or "common law" mean Anglo-Australian law. The technicalities of various criminal defences are discussed very briefly. In criminal law there are common principles, but Aborigines live in different jurisdictions amongst which there can be different constructions of crimes, depending on whether the common law or different, or similar, criminal codes are in force. The majority of the cases discussed come from Queensland and Western Australia where the "Griffith Code" is in force, the Northern Territory, which has its own criminal code, and South Australia which is a common law jurisdiction.

Joan Kimm
Melbourne
May 2004

Chapter 1

"No safe places"

> Violence is a thing that I notice amongst my relatives … my nieces and nephews and their current relationships. For me it is hurtful to see my nephews' wives with black eyes and fat lips, and I feel so powerless to help them. … So we go around accepting in part that sort of violence as a natural occurrence in my family.[1]

In 1999 the Aboriginal and Torres Strait Islander Women's Task Force on Violence (Task Force Report) reported that the degree of violence suffered by Indigenous women "cannot be adequately described".[2]

In November 2001 anthropologist Peter Sutton who has lived in, worked in and visited an Aboriginal community since the mid-1970s, published an article on a critical malaise within Indigenous society. He wrote that the reality of the endemic violence, the suicides, the homicides and the spousal killings, is almost beyond the comprehension of those outside this environment.[3] The 1997 Australian Bureau of Statistics found that in 1995-97 in Western Australia, South Australia and the Northern Territory Indigenous people under 65 lost more than 51,000 years of potential life.[4]

Memmott et al (Memmott) in a 2001 report on *Violence in Indigenous Communities* found that many Aborigines and non-Aborigines see violence as a major problem, that the rate of this violence is disproportionately high in comparison to that of non-Indigenous Australian violence, that violence is increasing, and the types of violence are worsening in some areas.[5] The judiciary, Aboriginal women and social scientists have all made similar observations.[6]

The physical and emotional trauma suffered by women and children and indeed the whole community is in reality incalculable. Aboriginal women including Lowitja O'Donoghue, Chair of ATSIC from 1990 to 1996, academic Marcia Langton and Judy Atkinson – who was one of the first to publicise endemic violence to Indigenous women – have written or spoken of the death of women, the constant assault of sexual and physical violence upon women and children, and the great cost to the community of this "cancerous disease" that perpetuates "cycles of abuse and self-abuse". Research conducted under the auspices of the Queensland DPP reported that the "most frightening trend" was the resignation of many Aboriginal women to "their lot".[7] Atkinson found that in some communities violence is so accepted "that women expect to be bashed and, in fact, do not think their 'bloke' loves them unless he belts them".[8]

Between 1 January 1980 and 31 May 1989 the level of homicide by men of their Aboriginal female relations exceeded that of all Aboriginal deaths in custody.[9] More women have died in Queensland and the Northern Territory through violence than all the deaths in custody.[10] Yet Aboriginal deaths in custody were the subject of a 1991 Royal Commission Report. (RCIADIC).[11] In 1990 Langton and other researchers compiled a report *Too Much Sorry Business* on the circumstances of Indigenous violence and dislocation for RCIADIC. Both she and Atkinson place Aboriginal men's violence to women in the context of deaths in custody. Fifty-three per cent of the men whose deaths were examined by RCIADIC were in prison because of violence, 9 per cent for homicide, 12 per cent for assault and 32 per cent for sexual assault.

Aboriginal deaths in custody remain a public issue,[12] but the reason for which the majority of the men were confined is not usually mentioned. For instance a RCIADIC recommendation led to the establishment in 1992 of the Aboriginal Justice Advisory Committee which was superseded in 1994 by the Aboriginal Justice Council (AJC). The terms of reference of the AJC embraced general welfare policies and specifically addressed "the design and delivery of programs that reduce Aboriginal offending, arrest and imprisonment rates". The AJC did identify three critical social issues "family, education and policing" and its pronouncement that "family is central to the fabric of society and critical to its wellbeing" may well have been a veiled reference to family violence. But this should have been a central issue in the terms of reference because in itself it leads to such a high rate of imprisonment. The AJC was dissolved and ceased operating in June 2002. It was criticised not for its failure to address the specific reasons for violence, but because it had not effectively dealt with issues which although of vital importance were external to the Aboriginal community; namely implementation of RCIADIC recommendations and its failure to have "Aboriginal injustices heard and coordinated in a strategic way".[13]

Yet statistics from different sources all create a composite picture of horrific violence in Aboriginal society where women are at particular risk. Categorised quantitative figures of Indigenous violence from many sources covering 1987 to 1997 by types of crimes, of injury (of which domestic violence is the most common) and by analysis of communities establish that in every area the rate per population is much higher for Indigenous offenders.[14]

Aboriginal women suffer more as victims of murder, attempted murder and sexual assaults than do any other group of Australian women. Jenny Mouzos' research into "femicide" in the period from 1989 to 1998 found alarming figures in relation to fatalities for Indigenous women.[15] Women, indigenous and non-indigenous, suffer most violence within intimate relationships. Indeed, 58 per cent of female homicides occur within intimate relationships. But the proportion of Aboriginal/Torres Strait Islander women killed by an intimate partner (74%) is higher than the proportion of Caucasian (54.2%) and Asian (51%) women. Less Aboriginal/Torres Strait Islander women (15%) are killed by a stranger in homicides than are Caucasians (17.2%) and Asians (16.3%).

Another indication of the magnitude of this violence is the over-representation of Aborigines and Torres Strait Islanders in total homicide figures. Indigenous women were approximately 15 per cent of all female homicide victims; Indigenous men (aged 15 and over) were approximately 12.3 per cent of all male homicide victims. From 1989 to 1999 "Indigenous persons were on average 8.1 times more likely to become victims of homicide than [were] non Indigenous persons". Indigenous persons accounted for 16.6 per cent (male 13.5%, female 3.1%) of homicide offenders but they are fewer than 2 per cent of the population.[16]

Atkinson found that in 1987 Aboriginal women were victims of 79 per cent of all chargeable homicides in the Northern Territory and that from 1989 to 1999,

> In the Northern Territory, Indigenous persons account for approximately 27 per cent of the total population, although they account for approximately 73 per cent of homicide offenders. In Western Australia, Indigenous persons account for 3.1 per cent of the total population and for 28.6 per cent of homicide offenders.[17]

Memmott reports 1992 findings that the comparative rate of homicides is worse where Indigenous communities are still able to live a semi-traditional life in remote Australia.[18] The figures compiled by the Australian Bureau of Statistics (ABS) reports on Indigenous health and welfare and mortality in 1996, 1997 and 2000 indicate endemic despair and disadvantage in these areas. The ABS found that in 1995-97 about 23 per cent of all homicide deaths in Western Australia, South Australia and the Northern Territory were Indigenous. Deaths from suicide and self-inflicted injury for Indigenous women and men were respectively 40 per cent and 70 per cent more than could be expected when compared to general Australian rates. Ferrante et al found similar patterns in their 1995 study of domestic violence in Western Australia:

> [C]ountry Aborigines (ie, those living in rural areas or regional centres) are one and a half times more likely than Perth Aborigines and about 45 times more likely than "country" non Aborigines to be victims of reported domestic violence.
> Aboriginal victims living outside Perth accounted for 38.3% of *total* reported cases of domestic violence, 80.5% of the total number of Aboriginal cases of domestic violence, and 71.2% of the total number of domestic violence cases reported from the "country".[19]

The grossly disproportionate nature of these figures is apparent when placed in the context of Western Australia's total population – where Aboriginal women account for less than 1 per cent. In Queensland, fewer Aborigines in Brisbane (24.8%) thought violence was a problem when compared to Aborigines in rural areas (56.5%).

Memmott found that a constant monitoring of statistics is useful in evaluating programs dealing with violence, however, sustained spousal abuse can cause deaths which are not officially listed as homicide, the immediate cause of death might be recorded as liver or renal failure. Hence some researchers consider that qualitative evaluation is more useful because statistics can never "give the full picture".[20] Audrey Bolger, a sociologist who has examined Indigenous violence in the Northern Territory, suggests the quality of the violence is a more important indicator of the level of violence at present, as so much of it is hidden.[21]

Court cases illustrate how legal interpretations of the circumstances in which fatalities occurred mask homicides. Women's deaths are not always attributed to the beatings they have suffered and this pattern goes across Aboriginal Australia. For instance in the 1977 South Australian case of *Young*[22] the accused, a Pitjantjatjara man and his wife were both drunk. Young struck his wife around the head; she died from inhaling vomit while unconscious. It was found that the death was not a homicide and Young was acquitted of murder. Young was then charged with assault occasioning actual bodily harm. The judge described the assault as "reasonably serious" and sentenced Young to nine months' imprisonment. *Pat Edwards*, a 1981 Northern Territory case, is almost identical. In that case it was found that "[m]edical evidence did not clearly establish whether her [his wife's] death had resulted from [the] blows to the head". Mrs Edwards' death was not recorded as a homicide. Atkinson, records five cases in 1989 in the York Peninsula in Queensland where after severe assaults a secondary infection caused women's actual death, no charges were laid against the men.[23]

The qualitative research of the Task Force Report on Aboriginal women's experiences in Queensland does give an idea of the scale and intensity of the violence which otherwise could more easily be envisaged in the context of enemy brutality against women in war. For instance a 17-year-old girl was tied to a bed within reach of her three-year-old child and raped repeatedly by three men. She did not press charges either through fear, or through being inured to this violence, which is "accepted as normal behaviour because they have not been able to get help when they have tried". A 14-year-old girl was charged with shoplifting, her mother when contacted said that she was concerned her daughter had the "pox". On being examined at the Sexual Health Service it was reported that:

> I have never seen a girl so red raw inside. She screamed all the way through the consultation. Turns out she had been sexually assaulted since the age of three. It [sic] is the first person I have ever seen where I thought "there is no hope for you".[24]

The Indigenous women of the Task Force Report commented that these young Aboriginal women had grown up in an "environment where there were no safe places".

Reported violence, which occurred throughout the Northern Territory during just one January weekend in 2002, illustrates a pattern of sickening assaults. In separate incidents Indigenous men broke a woman's hand with a fence post and punched her six-month old baby so violently in the face that its nose was broken, allegedly burned down a house and stabbed a woman with a screw driver, and stabbed a man nine times.[25]

This violence is not new. Aboriginal and non-Aboriginal women have drawn public attention to it since the 1980s. Court cases establish that non-Indigenous lawyers and judges have been aware of the present form of violence since about the 1970s, which is seen as the result of drink, deprivation and dislocation, and since the 1950s, a pre-existing traditional violence to women.

In 1982 criminologist Paul Wilson summarised the repetitive chaotic terror of one Aboriginal woman's life as part of the profile of the Northern Queensland family of Alwyn Peter, an Aborigine charged with murdering his girlfriend.

> Alwyn's brother Sidney stabbed a girl, Geraldine, with whom he was living. Geraldine, although seriously wounded, survived, and Sidney was sentenced to jail for committing grievous bodily harm.
> Geraldine then began a relationship with another man, who had previously killed his wife. This man later killed Geraldine by stabbing her with a knife. The subsequent police investigation revealed an earlier death in the family. Geraldine had previously given evidence to (sic) the murder by her father of one of his two wives.[26]

Geraldine's role as a repeat victim can be seen as either apathy caused by the traumatic circumstances of her life or else as a realistically low expectation about what the lifetime experiences of some Aboriginal woman might be. It is symptomatic of non-Indigenous attitudes in the law two decades ago, that Wilson's profile was prepared for Peter's defence. Geraldine's sufferings were described with the aim, which succeeded, of exculpating Peter from a charge of murder.

The cases before the courts, particularly from the 1970s when alcohol was almost invariably involved, detail other horrendous injuries of the level of violence discussed in *Imitja Panka* later. Ferrante et al found more Aboriginal women suffered serious injuries requiring hospital treatment than did non-Aborigines: 24 per cent of Aborigines with serious injuries (including death) compared to 11 per cent of non-Aboriginal victims. Aborigines (13%) were more than twice as likely as non-Aborigines (6%) to use weapons in domestic violence.[27] Both groups use sharp instruments to about the same extent but Aborigines have a greater tendency to use blunt instruments such as bats, sticks or steel stakes. A national survey established that "generally the weapons (used by Aborigines) were crude, but crudely effective".[28] Ferrante et al speculate that the difference in weapon use between Aborigines and non-Aborigines is because of availability and accessibility.[29]

Aborigines' hunter-gatherer and warrior society necessarily entailed both sexes having familiarity and skill with weapons and tools, spears, clubs, digging sticks and nulla nullas. Both women and men are vigorous fighters. Burbank observed that Aboriginal women are strong women who are ready to fight and to use the nulla nulla against each other as well as against men. In the 1960s a bush nurse thought that the missing fingers on the hands of the older women indicated leprosy. She was told, "No, these are my fighting fingers" of the hands which held their clubs or nulla nullas.[30] Langton records the vigour with which women fight today, "the weapons (are) usually ironwood digging sticks, or a man's club".[31] A Tennant Creek doctor commenting on the serious male violence towards women observed that men commonly used knives but also fists and broken bottles, and it was women who use nulla nullas and sticks.[32] Aboriginal women possibly suffer worse injuries than non-Aborigines in family violence because they are prepared to fight men. However, Burbank views much of women's intersexual aggression "as counter aggression, elicited and necessitated by aggressive men". Men perform 57 per cent of all initiating roles in violence, women perform 43 per cent. Men take the role of target in only 39 per cent of the total, women, in 61 per cent.[33] An Aboriginal woman described how violence escalates.

> When you are living with a man and he hits you, you can't do anything. Your family can't do anything, so you have to fight back to defend yourself.[34]

At a health clinic in South Australia the injuries with which the women presented were far more serious than those of the men because of the weapons which the men used upon the women, star stakes, "iron bars, bricks, bottles". It was remarked of one female camp dweller that:

> She doesn't feel it any more. He speared her with a barbed spear right through her arm – another man pulled it out – but nothing was done about it. No one reported it ... She's so used to being attacked with knives, stones, sticks.[35]

Unfortunately alcohol, "white poison",[36] often triggers physical violence. The 1986 ALRC Report on the recognition of Aboriginal customary law,[37] the judiciary, Bolger,[38] Langton,[39] Atkinson,[40] and the 2002 Gordon Report into family violence and child abuse which was commissioned by the Western Australian[41] all identified alcohol as being destructive. Ferrante et al found that according to reported injury level by race in domestic violence incidents alcohol was involved in 24 per cent of those with Aboriginal victims and 10 per cent of those with non-Aboriginal victims.[42] Atkinson considers family violence is related to alcohol abuse but it is a distinct and separate problem.[43] However, alcohol often acts as the physical trigger for a violence that can affect the lives of all Aborigines but particularly women. In the 1986 case of *Bulmer* Justice Connolly said in the Queensland Court of Criminal Appeal:

> The criminal courts have constantly to deal with persons of Aboriginal or Torres Strait Island extraction who, when far gone in alcohol, make violent attacks, commonly with knives on women and children.

Anthropologist Victoria Burbank, who lived in an Arnhem Land Community for 18 months, noted this connection has been made by a "number of Aboriginalists" namely anthropologists, Myers 1986; Reid 1983; Sackett 1977, 1988; Sansom 1980 and Wilson 1982. Further she observed that Aboriginal women in her study at "Mangrove" link alcohol and aggression. "Alcohol makes a man's [chest area indicated with hand] burn. They get really angry".[44]

Aborigines do see alcoholism as a serious problem. The ABS *National Aboriginal and Torres Strait Islander Survey 1994* found that among Aborigines 13 years and over, 59 per cent perceived alcohol to be the main health problem in their area, and 76 per cent said that alcohol was the most serious substance abuse problem.[45] To put the gravity of these figures into perspective the other most serious health problems were considered to be drugs (30.2%), heart problems (22.0%). Of substance abuse the most serious problem was marijuana (52.9%). It may well be now that amongst the younger generation the abuse of solvents will be ranked as one of increasingly serious substance abuse.

Langton's 1991 report to RCIADIC considered that the cause of increased infliction of violence in remote areas is a combination of traditional lifestyles and alcohol.[46] "Many Aboriginal societies in the Northern Territory have never been dispossessed and yet the grog problem is crippling these same Aboriginal people". The result is disastrous. "There (is) uncontrollable violence ... serious breakdown of community and family life and the collapse of authority

structures."[47] Langton's finding is consistent with the statistics considered above which establish that violence is more prevalent in rural
and remote areas where traditional life still exists.

Anthropologist Diane Bell and lawyer Pamela Ditton, writing in
the late 1970s, consider that the interlocking relationship between
the people, the law and the land is critical and must be protected.[48]
Yet since Justice Woodward's reports for the Aboriginal Land Rights
Commission in 1973 and 1974 there has been some form of
recognition in the Northern Territory that complex laws of tribal
land ownership existed and that these rights, which go to preserving
traditional culture, should be protected. Justice Woodward's recommendations that Aboriginal land, including existing Aboriginal
reserves, should be vested in trusts to be supervised by Northern
and Southern Land Councils were generally incorporated into the
1976 Commonwealth *Aboriginal Land Rights (Northern Territory) Act*.
With the exception of Queensland, State land rights legislation
shortly followed. The 1992 High Court decision in *Mabo v Queensland (No 2)* which recognised native title and culminated in the
Commonwealth *Native Title Act* 1993 meant that Aborigines theoretically were able to regain traditional lands where the traditional
connection still existed. Yet it seems that the worst violence exists
where, as Langton reported, there has been no dispossession, or
where attempts to gain land rights have been most successful
because traditional connections with the land can be established.

The possible cause of the higher rate of violence in semi-
traditional communities is that the relationship, the beliefs and
the customary law, which together founded a religious legalistic
society, have been eroded. Even in 1965 Pastor Paul Albrecht of the
Hermannsburg Mission wrote of the "authority crisis" in Aboriginal
communities. Traditional authority had been weakened but Aborigines had not accepted the validity of the control asserted over
them by non-Aboriginal authority.[49]

ABS census figures show that by mid-2001 barely 1 per cent of
Aborigines any longer believed in traditional religion. This does not
detract from land rights but many younger Aboriginal people in
remote isolation might now have a life which for them is mea-
ningless and unstructured, although the shell of traditional lifestyles
can still exist. The possible result now is that cultural attitudes of
violence, particularly towards women, remain but the strict customary law constraints on the infliction of that violence have now

disappeared, and further, traditional society has been corrupted by alcohol.

The way in which traditional life and the law has been subsumed by an alien culture is revealed through the Indigenous perspective in a number of interviews in the early 1990s between Aboriginal elders and Stephen Davis, a political geographer. Felix Holmes, the last senior man of the Limilngan tribe, was born about 1905, he was initiated around 1917 and he was "responsible for the Mordak mortuary song cycle, which connects the sites and territory of several of the tribes in the Kakadu area with tribes around Darwin". At almost any other period over the last 40,000 years Holmes would have been a revered elder in Aboriginal society. Now he said youths rob him of his last two or three pension dollars to buy alcohol. There are:

> [new] Aborigines with new totem ... Grog bottle ... No respect, no law ... no time for country, No time for culture, No time for old people ... New Aborigines don't understand ... They don't know you got to work for country ... Learn ceremonies, sing songs, Visit sites ... I walk back to my country. That way I still know who I am. ... When I die ... It's all finished. No one knows our law ... No one cares. And my spirit will look after the dreaming.[50]

Other Aborigines, across Northern Australia from Western Australia to Queensland, who could recall traditional life, spoke to Davis about their concern for the lack of respect for the elders. They, like Holmes, mourned the loss of the spiritual connection to the law and the land, "That grog is new law for them, and that holding them back from country. Only one sacred site for that mob ... Grog shop".[51]

Yet two paradoxes exist in identifying alcohol as the cause of Indigenous violence. First, commonly Aborigines are more abstemious than non-Aborigines,[52] yet being more visible when consuming alcohol because of public drinking they are often falsely stereotyped as drunkards. A survey of the Kimberley region found Aborigines are more likely to be teetotallers than are non-Aborigines: 46 per cent Aboriginal women consume alcohol compared to 75 per cent European women; and 76 per cent Aboriginal men consume alcohol compared to 87 per cent European.[53] Second, in rural areas, where violence is worse, males (25%) and females (48%) were most likely to say that they had never drunk alcohol, while those in capital cities were most likely to say they had drunk in the previous week.[54]

The answer to both paradoxes might be that Aborigines who drink, do so more desperately, "they drink to get drunk 'fall down drunk'". Any and all alcohol will be consumed in one "binge".[55] Women have described the dreaded "thirsty Thursday" when with their children they have to "make themselves scarce to avoid violence". Women fear completely uncontrolled attacks from male relatives who are *nuggari* (drunk). For instance "in Numbulwar a man severed a limb off his sister while he was drunk. He went at her with an axe as well as a spear".[56]

Of those who drink at least weekly, 79 per cent consumed alcohol at harmful levels compared to 12 per cent of other Australians. This pattern of destructive drinking is reflected in the death rate both from chronic liver disease and cirrhosis. Between 1995 and 1997 the ABS found these diseases accounted for about 3 per cent of all Indigenous deaths, a rate which is about seven times more deaths among males and 13 times more among females than for other Australians. The ABS in 1997 found that alcohol consumption also involves a higher risk of being either a victim or of being involved in self-destructive behaviour. This finding accords with that of the ABS in 2000; the Indigenous death rate from homicide or other purposely inflicted injury is seven to eight times higher than should be expected. Another factor relevant to alcohol and violence is the ABS finding in 1997 that Aboriginal men's "harmful drinking patterns peaked at age 25-34", compared to the 14 to 24 years' peak of Indigenous females and the general male and female population. This later age of Aboriginal men's destructive drinking might well be particularly hazardous for family violence.

In the Northern Territory the death rate in the town camps around Alice Springs is three times that of the whole Northern Territory population, and one-and-a-half to twice the rate of Central Australian Aborigines. This can be directly linked to alcohol consumption. In the town camps from 1974 to 1988 nearly one in six deaths (16%) resulted directly from alcohol induced fights or murders. Women were more likely to suffer such a death: 25 per cent of female deaths were directly from alcohol induced fights or murders.[57]

The 1980 Northern Territory case of *Ivan Imitja Panka* illustrates the kind of death which women can suffer in town camps. The circumstances were a fatal mixture of alleged male rights under traditional law and alcohol. Panka pleaded guilty to manslaughter on the grounds that his wife had offered him provocation in traditional law because she refused to cook him some meat: that is, he was relying on a husband's traditional rights of chastisement.[58] He "decided to punish her for being cheeky". Both were very drunk. After punching and hitting her he "took a piece of rippled reinforcing steel and forced it into her vagina".

There is continuing trauma in those who witness violence as children, among their family or as general brutality in the community. A child having observed a man beating a young girl who was holding her baby commented "He hit the baby on the legs, even though she was trying to protect the baby, the baby got hurt". A young man from Mt Isa said, "Children – young people they had seen the violence. They don't forget it".[59]

Learned behaviour perpetuates violence. "That's the only way I learned to survive; it wasn't until I was much older that I realised violence was not part of everyone's life."[60] These attitudes are not confined to any one community. Aboriginal men in a South Australian workshop on alcohol and violence identified witnessing continuous violent behaviour by their fathers as a precipitating factor in their own violence.

> As a child you witness those things. So violence seemed to be an everyday occurrence ... my use of violence happened, particularly towards a woman, when I was about sixteen to eighteen ... a girl ... refused me sexual favours so I belted her rather severely.[61]

Meredith Wilkie's report *Aboriginal Justice Programs in Western Australia* identified "fundamental issues of poverty, powerlessness and alienation" in Aboriginal criminality so much of which is comprised by violence. A number of young Aboriginal men who spoke to the Indigenous Women's Task Force articulated their feelings of loss and despair. However, Lowitja O'Donoghue said in the Hyllus Maris lecture at La Trobe University in October 2001 that violence has now become an issue beyond the confines of the Aboriginal community and whatever the wounds of a devastated past, "simply excusing violence on the grounds that the perpetrator is a victim too is not on".

Chapter 2

Community silence and denial

> [G]iven Aboriginal experience of white institutions and authority
> agents, it is scarcely surprising that, ultimately, some women
> appear to find a violent spouse less threatening than the agencies
> from which they might seek relief.[1]

Although many Aboriginal women suffer the most severe violence
of any other group of women in Australia their community,
particularly the perpetrators, are frequently not prepared to acknowledge this as very abusive behaviour. Complicated loyalties can also
inhibit Aboriginal women from reporting the violence to the police.
Further the judiciary in the past have not treated the violence as
seriously as they would if it had affected other Australian women.
Court cases show that these patterns have been repeated in every
criminal law jurisdiction.

In January 2002 the Western Australian government appointed
a three-member panel to inquire into the response by government
agencies to complaints of family violence and child abuse in Aboriginal communities. The two Indigenous members were a magistrate,
Mrs Sue Gordon, who was the chair, and Mr Darrell Henry. The
non-Indigenous member was the Honourable Kay Hallahan. Their
report (the Gordon Report) identified Aboriginal "community
silence and denial" about reporting violence: "Many Aboriginal
people will choose not to report on the grounds that they are
protecting their 'own' from the wider society".[2]

Causes for this silence are in part the violence which has been
inflicted on Aborigines by non-Aborigines and the barriers which
have been erected around Aboriginal society by Anglo-Australian
law. The result is that many abused Aboriginal women can be
enclosed in violence by their Indigenous identity. However, another
reason for the violence lies within that identity and culture. Langton
has commented on the autonomy of Aboriginal women in some
areas of traditional life, but she asked: what is the specific factor

which contributes to their "universally oppressed" situation? She concluded that both the internal dynamics of Aboriginal society and the impact of Europeans have affected present violence.

> The determining characteristic of the imbalance in gender relationships is the ability of men to use force, in the final analysis, to preserve male dominance in ideology, in structure and in relationships. This was so in traditional times and remains so, but in vastly changed circumstances.[3]

That the achievement of Indigenous post-colonial status has not emancipated many Aboriginal women from violence is arguably because the twin sources of violence are not addressed realistically or holistically. Coomaraswamy's second indicator of women's vulnerability to violence is where a society is "animated by the concept of a woman as the property".[4] A number of Aboriginal women who are leaders, academics or lawyers, have obliquely referred to Aboriginal men's oppression of women in their society.

Lillah Watson, an Aboriginal activist in the 1970s, warned, "Black women's liberation also must be part and parcel of the whole liberation movement of black people in this country".[5] Jackie Huggins observed that "we are, in fact, women too and not just Blacks. Black women experience a series of multiple simultaneous oppressions continuously". She refers to the "politics of sexism" and to "the oppression they (Aboriginal women) suffer through sexism", but says these matters will not be spoken of "publicly, to audiences of 'others'" until there are "genuine moves towards racial equality".[6] In the 1990s Larissa Behrendt, an academic lawyer, postulated that reality was a social structure in which white society is paramount over black society, and within each racial block, male is paramount over female.[7] Thus Aboriginal women are not only positioned in a subculture, they occupy the position of being a subculture within a subculture. Yet Huggins wrote that women rightly perceive their Aboriginal identity as more fundamental to their construction of identity than their gender, so acting in a way that separates their gender from their culture is not a valid option.

The emotional consequences of this subjugation and violence perpetuate trauma in women that must affect the lives of their children also. Gwen Baldini, a Nyungar woman, the co-ordinator and counsellor at the Yorgum Aboriginal family counselling service has found that women's status within Aboriginal communities means that the sexual abuse and assault are concealed. The victims are silenced by "fear/anger, pain and frustration ... (which) ...

without support can stay with them forever".[8] Queensland women report similar experiences and say further that these feelings of impotent anger can lead to drug or alcohol abuse, which in turn affects families and clan groups.[9] In their national survey in 1986 Aboriginal women Daylight and Johnstone found because there was no catharsis through reporting or counselling for victims of sexual assault the women felt like some sort of "dirty sex machine" and they were "eventually discarded by their men when the truth came out". Many turned to prostitution, alcohol or drugs.[10]

Atkinson considers that much family violence is not reported to "others" because women fear retribution, they are wary of police abuse, and they fear imprisonment for their male relatives.[11] Each of these factors was also identified by the women of the Aboriginal communities of New South Wales and Queensland as a cause of non-reporting. Women have also identified being intimidated in court by the accused or his family, cultural shame, lack of cultural awareness by police, lawyers and the judiciary, lack of information and lack of access to legal services, lack of faith in the court system, lack of Indigenous staff in the Office of the Director of Public Prosecutions and being generally intimidated by court processes.[12]

Fifty-seven per cent of Aboriginal women (nationally) said they did not report the last verbal threat of violence, of which only 18 per cent did not do so because the threat was not serious enough to report. In 1994, 43 per cent (nationally) of Aboriginal women who had been subject to an attack did not report the last physical attack upon them.[13] Of these women only 9 per cent said the attack was not serious enough to report, while 20 per cent said that they did not do so because they had solved the problem themselves, or that they knew the perpetrator.[14]

The 1990 Western Australian case of *Juli* illustrates an attempted solution by a victim who knew the perpetrator and how fear of retribution can be a deterrent to dealing with violence. Both the victim and the perpetrator lived in the one Aboriginal community in the Kimberley. They had known each other for about ten years and were related through the kinship system, but not by blood. Juli, who was 25 years old, raped the 18-year-old victim who immediately reported the attack to a health clinic and then to the police. She asked the police to only warn the applicant and to ask him to keep away from her because "I was frightened for myself and for my family". About 14 days later Juli again raped her and only then was she prepared to make a formal complaint.

Aboriginal women face the real possibility that if they make a complaint, imprisonment of the perpetrator is likely, as criminal charges are laid in a much higher proportion of cases involving Aboriginal offenders than in those involving Europeans in domestic assault cases.[15] Ferrante et al attribute this to the fact that Aboriginal women suffer significantly more serious injuries than do European women. Extensive medical treatment is usually necessary. Therefore it is almost mandatory for charges to be laid because of the severity of the injuries. In this circumstance and in view of the high rate of violence, the claim that the problem had "solved itself" as a reason for non-reporting may be doubted and can perhaps be attributed to "enabling behaviour".

Langton's 1990 report found that the source of "enabling behaviour" by victims to their abusers lies in the expectations about support from family members arising from traditional attitudes about kinship.[16] Atkinson defines "enabling behaviour" which can continue despite family trauma caused by alcoholism or assault:

> What happens usually if a person is drinking they asking their wives or family to go and buy grog, and then they come back and flog the wife and kids, next day wife has got a black eye, and he's got a headache, so the wife gives him panadol and makes sure he's alright. So what's happening is that family is helping that person become an alcoholic … they'll look after him.[17]

For some women this can be a cultural imperative and some will accept responsibility for paying men's fines rather than see them imprisoned.[18] Men also expect this support and ironically will use violence to obtain money from pensioned mothers and grand-mothers if it is not forthcoming.[19] Family support thus denies the aggressor the opportunity of facing the consequences of his actions and in effect "enables" him to continue his destructive behaviour. Hence the reasons women gave for not reporting a serious attack, namely "solution of the problem or familiarity with the perpet-rator", possibly conceals a high percentage of family violence.

Despite the violence they suffer many Aboriginal women plead future reconciliation when making victim impact statements on issues of sentencing. Their motives are either the fear of vengeance, the consequences of imprisonment for the perpetrator, or some issue of self-guilt perhaps induced by cultural expectations of enabling behaviour or men's right to inflict moral violence. Culturally recon-ciliation is also a significant influence on women's actions. Both Atkinson and the Gordon Report found seeking respite from violence is acceptable, but permanent separation is less so. For a variety of these reasons abused Aboriginal women tend to seek crisis care and then to reconcile, irrespective of formal court proceedings.[20]

The attitudes, which induce reconciliation and perhaps forgiveness, mean that in a community where violence is endemic many Aboriginal women are bearing horrific levels of abuse. For instance a woman said that she intended reconciliation in circumstances where her life was imperilled. Her husband had been imprisoned for stabbing her on five separate occasions. He had been released for two months when he again stabbed her.

> They rushed me to ... hospital. I died three times but I don't remember. He gets sentenced next week. I will be waiting for him when he gets out. I love him. It's the grog that does it. It was my fault too. I was drunk.[21]

Two 1994 cases, in widely separated areas, being *Charles* in Western Australia and *Bell* in Queensland, are instances of a common pattern. In each there was extreme violence, repeated rapes of a pregnant wife in one, and stabbings and threats to kill a wife of four months in the other, and in each the victims pleaded reconciliation on behalf of their attackers. In each case the trial judge took into account these pleas in sentencing, the Crown appealed against the sentence and the Court of Appeal refused to accept the weight given to reconciliation and increased the sentence. That is, the courts imposed absolute standards of deterrence against violence whatever the Indigenous cultural imperatives, whether of reconciliation, community pressures upon women or their fear of the possible perils of imprisonment for the male perpetrator. In *Charles* the Court of Appeal underlined the futility from the perspective of the criminal justice system of accepting a plea of reconciliation.

> All that is said by way of excuse in the pre-sentence report is that the complainant confirmed that her relationship will continue ... (this) ... simply serves to conceal the underlying problem.

Two observations should be made about the courts' attitude. First, in *Bell,* because of the victim's plea of reconciliation, Bell was released. The Court of Appeal did not agree with this sentence, but it found that "belated incarceration" was not appropriate. Bell received a suspended sentence, which effectively meant that he faced automatic imprisonment if he was again violent in the next two years. However, within Aboriginal circumstances is a suspended sentence more likely deter the offender, or is the certainty of imprisonment rather a deterrent to a victim or her community from reporting any further violence?

Second, the Gordon Report found that many Aboriginal communities exhibit "widespread dissent about the role of the criminal justice system and its appropriateness in Aboriginal communities".[22] Therefore if the Indigenous right of autonomy is to be respected, can Aborigines say that the courts should accept complainants' pleas of reconciliation at face value? Two Aboriginal women have stated somewhat contrasting views. Atkinson, who certainly opposes violence, nonetheless looks at the issue from the cultural viewpoint; although Aboriginal women want an end to violence, they do not think that prison is an effective means of achieving this end. Baldini, however, apparently opposes pleas of reconciliation, she said at the 1996 Perth National Conference that it is important for Aboriginal women to realise that the blame should be placed on the perpetrator, not the victim, so that women can be freed "of their guilt and pain".[23]

The observations of Justice Moynihan in the 1997 Queensland case of *Daniel* illustrate the judiciary's increasing awareness of, and suspicions about, the cultural and moral imperatives which could be exerted upon Aboriginal women to support the offender.

> [C]are must be taken, especially when the offence involves violence against a woman or child, that there has been no persuasion exerted on the victim and that the community attitude is more than the view of the influential members of the community. It should also be recognised that persuasion might be subtle and indirect; concern at ostracism or disapproval by other members of a community, and even a sense of guilt at criminalising or causing the incarceration of a community member.

Yet if Aboriginal women do not "support" their husbands or partners in court, they can be exposed to violent retaliation from their abuser's family. One woman said, "Extended family came around and get into me. They went for me at the court after he was found guilty of attempted murder on me".[24] The attacker can threaten reprisals either immediate, in a matter of days, or men reportedly threaten revenge after years. O'Donoghue observed that for a woman who has been beaten or stabbed frequently and severely, the terror of waiting for this almost certain retribution upon herself and perhaps her children is almost unimaginable.[25]

Aboriginal men's abusive control of women can extend throughout the wider community. The Gordon report found that:

> [S]ome elder groups or councils are part of the reason why indigenous communities are having little success in creating less violent, more positive communities with male elders hindering prevention initiatives because of their own involvement in violence.[26]

The Aboriginal Women's Legal Issues Conference[27] in 1993 said that male-dominated Aboriginal organisations prevent either the establishment of, or operation of, support services for Aboriginal women.[28] This Conference, the ALRC 1986 report on customary law[29] and the 1999 Task Force report on violence[30] all identify lack of counselling, support services, telephone access and the difficulty of police access to remote reserves[31] as factors that contribute to Aboriginal women's vulnerability to violence.

A confidential submission to the 1986 Australian Law Reform Commission said that:

> Domestic violence laws simply do not work in remote Aboriginal communities. ... Aboriginal women simply have no access to legal information; their children tend to be very young; power in these communities rests squarely with the males; white police do not attend domestic violence situations; there is a serious degree of violence; the community council is male dominated and that council filters complaints to the police; there is, generally speaking, no women's council to represent women; ... women don't get heard. ... [T]he communities are effectively closed. ... Women in these communities are also immobilised. ... Restraining orders will not be enforced.[32]

The general law has, perhaps inadvertently, endorsed the power of Aboriginal councils which are commonly dominated by males. In the 1985 decision of *Gerhardy and Brown* the High Court held the Pitjantjatjara body corporate had the right to exclude all who were not Pitjantjatara from their lands and that doing so would not contravene the *Racial Discrimination Act* 1975. This decision applies to all Indigenous people and their lands. Hence Aboriginal women can be precluded from obtaining outside assistance. In some communities the Aboriginal council's policy is that police can only enter onto reserves by invitation. The women, as victims of violence, might not have the necessary authority to issue an invitation to the police and are therefore prevented from obtaining assistance.[33] Without the permission of councils to interfere in community business, police on settlements may be reluctant to take action. They can fear that Aboriginal men will "gang up on them".[34] An

Aboriginal woman in South Australia observed that the police were "often too frightened to intervene" because of fear of being embroiled in family violence and "payback".[35] "The police, some [Central Australian] women said, worked for the council not the women."[36]

In Western Australia, community violence towards the police in the 1970s led to the appointment of Aboriginal police aides,[37] and there are similar arrangements in other states.[38] Aboriginal women in Queensland feel that the state police "Leave it all up to them (the PLO's) to fix the black problem".[39] Many Aboriginal women do not wish to rely on the police liaison officers for protection because they are without police powers,[40] they can be unsympathetic to other Indigenous people from disadvantaged or distressed communities,[41] and it is difficult to relate to a male officer when the perpetrator is an Aboriginal male.[42] In Western Australia in 2002 approximately one-third of all Aboriginal Police Legal Officers were female and submissions were made to the Gordon Inquiry that more female officers be employed. Other complications can arise. In a South Australian town the attendance of an Aboriginal police aide enraged the male offender because he was "shamed" by the legal intervention of a male from his own community.[43]

The Gordon Inquiry explored the sensitive issue of the access of police officers to Aboriginal communities of which, for instance, there are approximately 290 in Western Australia alone. It referred to three High Court cases namely; *Halliday v Nevill* in 1984,[44] *Plenty v Dillon* in 1991[45] and *Coco v The Queen* in 1994[46]. In the two later cases, which respectively concerned service of a summons and the installation of a listening device, the court held that police officers cannot enter upon land in the absence of the implied or express consent of those in possession. In *Halliday v Nevill*, which concerned an arrest, it was held that visitors might enter for a legitimate purpose where there is an unobstructed entry, that is, an open entrance and no sign forbidding entry.

There is some ambiguity in the law about the legitimate access of police or welfare agencies to render assistance to those who might be seeking aid or need aid but are prevented by those in control of the community from otherwise having access to aid. The Gordon Report did not make any definitive recommendation about access in these circumstances but observed that:

> The solution to this dilemma lies, in the Inquiry's view, through a means other than legal analysis. It appears that there will always be potential, particularly in subtle cases, for arguments to exist as

to whether a government officer is truly entitled to enter upon premises on an Aboriginal community ... The guiding principle, in the interests of government service providers and Aboriginal communities, lies in negotiation, understanding and mutual trust and respect.[47]

In May 2003, after the release of the Gordon Report, the Northern Territory Supreme Court specifically affirmed Aborigines' right to bar outsiders from their communities. *Peach v Toohey* was a Crown appeal against a magistrate's dismissal of a charge against a journalist, Paul Toohey: that he had entered upon Aboriginal land without a permit, contrary to s 4 of the *Aboriginal Land Act* (NT). Toohey's defence was that his entry was necessary in the public interest to report an incident at Wadeye Community in 2002 when an Aboriginal man died after being shot in a confrontation between two feuding Aboriginal clans and three Port Keats police officers. The magistrate found Toohey guilty without recording a conviction and ordered that the charge be dismissed. Journalists who wished to lift the veil of secrecy over violence and repression in Aboriginal communities hailed this outcome. The Supreme Court found that the Magistrate wrongfully exercised his discretion, public interest did not prevail, and that the refusal to grant a permit was for the day of the funeral only. This was case of privacy in the context of family grief. Hence, in view of these cases, the issue of police or welfare intervention to aid those in distress seems to be still open.

For practical purposes there is the difficulty of abused women being able to contact the police. Also there seems to be an inherent contradiction in the Gordon Report's respectful recommendation concerning "negotiation" to obtain entry and the observations, already mentioned, that male elders might not always be acting in good faith if they too are involved in violence and second, and that there is frequently a (justified) but nonetheless inherent mistrust between Aborigines and government officers. The Gordon Inquiry was instigated largely because of the distressing results of failed negotiations, which included the death of an abused child, to obtain entry at the Swan Valley Nyungah Community in the late 1990s.

Perhaps these legal and cultural complexities explain the Gordon Report's finding that rural communities need assistance to develop "an active community-based, rather than professionalised response to domestic violence".[48] If this could be achieved it might address divisions within communities which are inimical to women. However, RCIADIC recognised that "there could be conflict of interests between the rights of the individual and the interests of the Aboriginal community ... (and) ... that such conflict may require separate legal representation for the individual and the community".[49] The "Aboriginal community" is not to be identified with the needs of individual Indigenous women, it is a phrase used in the wider context of a cohesive social unit, the usually predominantly male council, against which an individual woman or women may be pitted.

Over the past two decades formal and anecdotal evidence portrays the circumstances of many women's subordination to councils that control the community. In the 1980s Bell and Nelson commented: "Existing Aboriginal organisations are heavily male oriented". They found that cultural barriers can silence women; in the Aboriginal community at Tennant Creek "there are women on the Julalikari the organisation where each of the town camps has a representative" but they may not be women to whom it is proper to speak "because they do not have the proper kin or country affiliations". Bell and Ditton found that males are dominant in Councils, and that women are often allowed only as observers.[50] A non-Aboriginal with a great deal of experience in dealing with councils in the 1990s said that he had found that the members are always male. He instanced the meeting hall at Docker River in the Northern Territory, which is divided into two. Women can sit in the body of the hall but do not have access to the Council meetings beyond the partition. The tight control, which males can exert over women, is exemplified by the experience of a post-graduate student who wished to work on issues of women's health in a South Australian community. The women all agreed, but the men on the Council, with the support of the Land Council's white male lawyer, said that the study could not go ahead.[51] In 2002 the Gordon Report found that not only did communities prefer recreational facilities to be erected in preference to women's refuges but also that "women's and youths' issues were marginalised at community and regional levels".[52]

A non-Indigenous man who has had frequent contact with Aboriginal communities in the Northern Territory said that "women are confined to reserves".[53] Men often control transport because government funding has usually been given to men for the purchase and control of community assets.[54] Many women resent this impotence, which can prevent them from attending to their own rituals and from visiting their own country. They have asked ATSIC to provide more funding and programs for women to "overcome the inequity for women" and power imbalance in the Aboriginal community.[55] Isolation can make reaching shelters impossible, an Aboriginal woman said, "Where can she go? The nearest refuge is 15 hours away. How can she get there? Who will take her? She has no money".[56]

Women can be isolated also because telephones in remote communities are frequently vandalised.[57] There is anecdotal evidence that at times cables are cut the day after installation is completed. Some communities are attempting to control this destruction. For example, at Docker River large boulders were placed around telephone booths to prevent young men driving through them. In other communities the elders have had the boxes painted with clan signs, which means that the boxes are then integrated into the clan and cannot be desecrated. When telephone communication is unavailable, service might be provided by high frequency radio links only, which are less reliable, particularly in the wet season, and which do not allow privacy of communication. The rights of Aboriginal communities to adequate telephone services and the upgrading of existing services were considered in relation to the *Australian Telecommunications Act* 1989 (Cth) but were not upheld by Justice Burchett in the 1990 cases of *(Daisy) Yarmirr v Australian Telecommunications Corporation* and *Yugul Mangi Community Government Council v Australian Telecommunications Corporation*.[58]

Local councils have prevented some Aboriginal women from obtaining medical examinations after alleged rapes so that even establishing proof of the assault can be an insuperable hurdle. Bell and Nelson give examples of the difficulty Aboriginal women have in going to European women doctors both in Tennant Creek and in another "town in the Northern Territory" where the local boards (of Aboriginal males) "resist acting on information from a white woman". One European doctor who tried to help victims of an alleged rape was "refused entry to the premises" (by the local board).[59]

Yet Indigenous women face multiple cultural obstacles if they go outside their own community for assistance. Some Aboriginal communities can condemn those seeking to permanently escape a violent relationship. When the abused tries to leave, the perpetrator can figure as the wronged partner.[60] The Task Force Report found that this is when women are most vulnerable to being killed.

The dangerous nature of this period should be recognised as "separation assault". Tragically, the women who remain in dangerous relationships are also frequently in grave danger. Unfortunately so are the children.[61]

"Separation assault" and the difficulty of leaving an abusive situation are problems for any woman, but many Aboriginal women can have particular cultural and emotional barriers about separation. Leaving could entail farewelling their particular community and identity.

[H]er family is here. Her children too. This is her country. She fought for this country… [To go is to lose f]amily, home, land ties, everything.[62]

The Gordon Report and the Task Force Report made substantially identical observations on the cultural attitudes of Aboriginal women in Western Australian and Queensland, "[t]he Aboriginal approach is to make the violence go away not the victim",[63] "they want the violence to stop and they want the man to be part of the healing process".[64] These are women's cultural values. Until many Aboriginal men acknowledge their culture of violence against, and repression of, Aboriginal women, healing will be difficult because this violence is intra-cultural.

Chapter 3
A failure of law

> The Inquiry finds that cultural sensitivity is imperative for effective service delivery to Aboriginal communities.[1]

Despite the strong cultural forces and loyalties which can prevent, or dissuade, many Aboriginal women from reporting violence to the police, their desperate situation as a "sub-culture within a sub-culture" often causes them to seek external protection. But this help is not always forthcoming because of a disjunction between black and white expectations about normative behaviour for women in abusive situations, particularly with relation to reconciliation and women's responsibility to spouses.

In the 1991 report for the RCIADIC, Langton commented on a basic cause of Aboriginal women's conflict between cultural loyalty and self-preservation:

> [M]any women are hesitant to speak about it ... that Aboriginal Law does not help with domestic violence and that, for the women, the police are the only answer ... In a number of communities women have gone as groups to police stations to request their assistance to prevent violence.[2]

For example, nationally in 1994, of those Aboriginal women who were physically attacked, or those who were verbally threatened, only 9 per cent and 10 per cent respectively said that they did not report incidents to the police because they either did not want to involve the police or feared or disliked the police. In 1994, Aboriginal women nationally actually reported assaults to the police at about the same rate as European women. Aboriginal women reported 57 per cent of physical attacks and 42.6 per cent of verbal threats.[3] In Ferrante's Western Australian survey on reported violence to the police, the reports of Aboriginals and Europeans are more for non-domestic (31%) than domestic violence (20%).[4]

Indigenous social cycles of abuse, separation and reconciliation can impede external assistance for Aboriginal women seeking protection from, or redress for, violence.[5] Cynicism has been identified as one cause of alleged police indifference when they are called to attend repeated intra-familial domestic violence incidents. This is because many Aboriginal women view police intervention as crisis management, stopping the abuse at a critical point, rather than seeing this intervention as many non-Aboriginal women do, as a crisis that precipitates departure.[6]

Similar issues arise with restraining orders. The Gordon Report found that victims of violence could be "unwilling, or unable" to complete the processes necessary to obtain an order. It noted that the Western Australian Police Force was evaluating a pilot project of the South Australian Police Force whereby police had obtained 90 per cent of restraining orders.[7] While the Gordon Report recommended that the South Australian initiative be examined, it noted that some Aboriginal communities are sceptical about restraining orders and that they are only as effective as a permanent police presence in communities. In Queensland the Task Force Report found that protection orders are difficult to enforce in remote communities.[8]

In Western Australia the Department of Housing's policy is to give priority to victims of domestic violence. However, this assistance is based on the premise of a permanent separation of previously co-habitating couples. If there is subsequent reconciliation, the applicant may be removed from the priority housing list. The Gordon Report noted that this policy fits ill with the family violence interactions commonly seen in Aboriginal communities. It can cause great difficulties for women in remote areas where public housing stocks might be limited.[9]

Depending on State or Territory legislation, women who are victims of violence potentially have a claim for crimes compensation payments. A non-Indigenous female barrister who worked for the Central Australian Aboriginal Legal Service (CAALAS) in Alice Springs in the late 1980s thought that it was so imperative that women know about compensation that after court she would go around the town camps trying to find the women who were victims of violence so they could be told about their rights.[10]

Compensation might be women's only available avenue for escape.[11] Its importance for women who are confined in remote communities without resources is illustrated by the following case. A young woman was trapped in desperate circumstances on an

Aboriginal reserve in Cape York Peninsula. At five years of age she had been rejected by alcoholic parents and left in her grandmother's care. At six years of age her uncle had sexually attacked her. He was sentenced to 10 years' imprisonment for this attack, but he had now returned to the community. At 15 years of age, three men from the community attempted to rape her. During this attack her collarbone was broken. After imprisonment they had also returned to the community. In order to make her longed for escape she was absolutely dependent on an anticipated crimes compensation payment.[12]

The pattern of repeated violence, reconciliation and separation is not necessarily a bar to compensation. For instance in 1996 in Darwin a young Aboriginal woman interviewed for the ABC *Law Report* had made six applications for compensation involving assaults over two years, and her husband appeared to be seeking yet another reconciliation.[13] However, in Queensland in 1997 the Justice Department reportedly queried an Aboriginal woman's right to claim compensation when she had been in a relationship of recurrent assaults, injuries and reconciliations. She had an initial award of compensation because of her de facto husband's knife attack. Upon being released from two years imprisonment he again savagely attacked her. At issue was whether her alleged complicity in the violence would be a bar to successive claims for compensation arising from abuse by the one offender. Had the victim "facilitated" the earlier, and then the subsequent, attack by associating with a dangerously violent man?[14] It was impossible to discover the outcome of this case. But if the ground was upheld it is another cultural barrier for Aboriginal women to overcome when exercising rights.

For Aborigines, the police have in the past been the instrument of government policies that separated children from their families. The Queensland DPP's investigation into *Indigenous Women Within the Criminal Justice System*[15] (Queensland DPP's Report), published in 1996, found that reluctance to report rape was compounded by the difficulty of communicating sexual assaults to non-Aboriginal police officers and being intimidated by the legal system and "shame", which has a particular meaning for Aborigines. The word denotes more than being ashamed; it has overtones of being humiliated, of being debased.[16]

Aboriginal women have been persecuted themselves when they have reported abuse to police. In 1992 Amnesty International reported on *Rape and Sexual Abuse: Torture and Ill Treatment of Women in Detention*:

In countries around the world, government agents use rape and sexual abuse to coerce, humiliate, punish and intimidate women. When a policeman ... rapes a woman in his custody, that rape is no longer an act of private violence, but an act of torture or ill-treatment for which the state bears responsibility.[17]

Report of incidents and cases establish that these practices have also existed in Australia. Some Aboriginal women have been humiliated and made to feel sexually and racially devalued by some police, and their rights to protection from violence have been ignored. Some women claim that it is useless to report sexual assault to the police, or that to do so is only to open the possibility of further abuse.[18] An Aboriginal woman is quoted as saying: "(They'll) ... either do nothing at all or they'll keep you there and rape you themselves".[19]

In 1973 Mr Ward McNally (who had been Press Secretary to Senator Cavanagh, one time Minister of Aboriginal Affairs) submitted to a Senate Standing Committee that police in Brisbane had no regard for the rights of Aboriginal women and gave particulars of their experiences, including allegations about a rape. The Queensland Police Union President in response to McNally's allegations said, "People make these exaggerated allegations to gain sympathy for the Aboriginal cause".[20] But about 20 years later three cases between 1993 and 1996 illustrate Aboriginal women's feelings of being powerless in the face of existing abusive police behaviour. The positive outcomes in these cases hopefully indicate that gender and racist abuse by police will no longer be tolerated.

In the 1993 Western Australian case of *Johansen v Billing, Commissioner of Police and Police Appeal Board*, Johansen, a police officer at Kununurra, regularly had sexual intercourse with, exposed himself to, or indecently assaulted, female Aboriginal women prisoners in the cells. When the women complained, their veracity as witnesses was accepted. Johansen was dismissed from the force and did not succeed in obtaining reinstatement on appeal. In the 1994 South Australian case of *Tilley*, an off-duty policeman raped an Aboriginal woman. Although he was subsequently convicted, and did not succeed on appeal, the woman had initially delayed in reporting the assault "because nobody would believe her because he was a police officer and she was an Aboriginal girl".

In the Northern Territory in January 1996 an Aboriginal woman complained to the police that she had been the victim of a multiple rape. The police response was to hold her in custody for more that 12 hours on a minor arrest warrant for drinking in public before being taken to court for bail. Langton described the incident as a "glaring example of racism".[21] In June 1996 the Northern Territory Ombudsman condemned the actions of the police and the Northern Territory Police Commissioner apologised. "We clearly made mistakes. I acknowledge we did not view this person as we ought to – as a victim".[22] Nonetheless, there are two other recent instances where Aboriginal women, victims of sexual assault, have been locked up for four and six hours respectively.[23]

The State has started to acknowledge that it does bear a responsibility to Aboriginal women to ensure that they are confident of being safely heard and of having their complaints properly investigated. The 1991 National Inquiry into Racist Violence found some police have abused some Aboriginal women through assault, sexual assault[24] or sexual harassment.[25] Generally, women's claims about this abuse have been substantiated by the findings in 1994 and 1996, respectively, of the reports of the Western Australian Chief Justice's taskforce on gender bias and the Violence Against Women unit of the Queensland Director of Public Prosecution's office. Both reports recommend cross-cultural and gender training programs for the police.[26]

Once Aboriginal women enter the actual processes of the law the Office of the Status of Women and the ABS found that they are more disadvantaged than any other group in Australia".[27] As women they are generally denied the legal advice and representation that Aboriginal men now expect from the Aboriginal Legal Service. Other legal services and the system itself can be alien and intimidating. Aboriginal Legal Services were founded in the 1970s[28] to fill a vacuum in legal representation for the Aboriginal population.[29] As the preponderance of offenders is male, these services have come to mean the championship of masculine rights.[30] In the 1980s Bell and Ditton had found that Central Australian women felt astonishment that Ditton, a lawyer with the CAALAS, could be interested in women's affairs. Ditton had actually been appointed to work "primarily with Aboriginal women who had legal problems but ... she spent most of her time defending Warrabri men in court".[31]

Although RCIADIC commented on "appalling levels of domestic violence, rape and even murder [which] have been cited as failing to attract the due attention of police and the criminal justice system",[32] it has effectively exacerbated this situation. Its recommendations, consistent with the terms of reference, were that imprisonment should be "a last resort" and the role of Aboriginal Legal Services (ALS) in achieving this result was emphasised.[33] ALS says there is a conflict of interests in acting for the accused and the complainant.[34] ALS generally does not support women seeking legal protection against family assault and many Aboriginal women have criticised it for this reason.[35]

Incidents in two country towns in Queensland and Victoria are microcosms of the power that violent Aboriginal men receive from the support of ALS. In Queensland in 1994 a non-Indigenous man intervened to stop an Aboriginal man beating an injured and screaming young Aboriginal woman. The abuser then turned upon him:

> When his threats of violence, because I was intruding into what he called "his rights" failed to get rid of me, he resorted to the threat to get Legal Aid against me.[36]

In Mildura in 2000 when police interviewed an Aborigine, Bowden, immediately after his arrest for a horrific assault on his de facto wife, a member of the Aboriginal Community Justice Panel was present. However, Bowden refused to even state his name, and apart from a stream of obscenities said only "I want my solicitor to talk to man, I got rights".[37]

The situation is ironic because, as discussed above, 53 per cent of the deaths in custody were men imprisoned for assaults, including rape and murder, on Aboriginal women. One woman said "Legal Aid should take a hard line – why defend men who murdered before? They say it's human rights – but what about *her* rights?"[38] Jenny Hardy, the policy solicitor at the Northern Australian Aboriginal Legal Aid Service (NAALAS), in commenting upon infringements of the rights of sexual assault victims said: "we don't get to hear about it". This is because NAALAS acts for the perpetrator of the assaults.[39]

However, in viewing the role of the ALS from Aboriginal women's perspectives the cultural division between Indigenous rights and women's rights is again apparent. Pat O'Shane, as a New South Wales magistrate, in a published essay, concentrated on racial injustice to Aborigines, the issues of deaths in custody, and the reasons for establishing legal services. She emphasised "continuing racism, discrimination and injustice".[40] O'Shane did not discuss intra-cultural discrimination on the basis of gender. Yet for Judy Atkinson this is a major issue. She condemned the damage done by

ALS to Aboriginal women, who have suffered violence and sexual abuse, as a result of the services' partisan attitude to male offenders.[41] Aboriginal Women's Legal Services have now been established in every State and Territory.

Aboriginal women can be further disadvantaged by other cultural barriers.[42] Aborigines can often feel uncomfortable using any legal service other than ALS where although the solicitors are often non-Aborigines the support staff are usually Aborigines.[43] A survey by the Victorian Aboriginal Legal Service found that few Aborigines use alternative legal services,[44] and Aboriginal women have said that there is not enough information available on how to approach other legal services.[45] When women have been refused advice by ALS because of a conflict of interest in violence cases, they often have not been advised about other legal services.[46] In 1994-95, Indigenous women received only 27 per cent of the 5,280 approvals applications for legal aid to Indigenous people.[47] While 21 per cent of Aboriginal men used legal services, the majority (15%) chose to use an Aboriginal Legal Service. Male offenders are usually represented and sentences can be discounted.[48] Therefore Aboriginal men as perpetrators of violence appear to be advantaged by access to intra-cultural legal advice, while women, either as potential complainants or as applicants for intervention orders, have been more distanced from legal redress.

For men, then, court procedures can enhance their power relationships with women because they are able to use legal representation to escape the consequences of rape[49] or to enforce their perceived rights in family law matters. Conversely, women have confirmed that it is futile to seek protection from violence, and indeed doing so can lead to further attacks by the enraged partner.

> He has breached the Apprehended Violence Order eight times ... but he was never put in prison once. Court just increases his sense of power. He always turns up with the best barrister.[50]

Women, on the other hand, can be intimidated by facing court proceedings or cross-examination without any representation other than the police prosecutor.[51] Many Aboriginal women are suspicious or frightened of providing the requisite information to government or welfare services. In the past, this information has been part of a threatening process of control. Russel Goldfam identifies language as a "primary manipulative tool".[52] He likens the difficulties of

Aborigines who face the legal system without interpreters or assistance as being drawn into a "cone of silence".

Aboriginal women unable to find a haven from violence and without legal protection can finally kill their abuser in desperation.

> My only option was to kill him … that resulted in me getting six years but it got me away from the violence. Being locked away was the first peace I'd had in years.[53]

Prison is a hard won and pitiless refuge and possibly Aboriginal women are only being convicted because of their disadvantaged position in the legal system. The cases of *Gadd* and *Kina* suggest that this might be so.

Glendina Gadd[54] was tried for the murder of her de facto husband in April 1995. He was the father of her two children. She pleaded not guilty because of the violent assaults she had suffered from the deceased over the preceding two years. An Aboriginal health service doctor gave evidence on behalf of the defence. That doctor's evidence is a window on the attitudes and experiences of many abused Aboriginal women. She said Gadd had suffered severe injuries, and that only when Gadd was in prison was she free of injury. Further many women felt "shame" about injuries incurred because of domestic assaults and did not want these entered on medical records. Her views are supported by Daylight and Johnstone who had found that "with very few exceptions, Black women avoid consulting a doctor on their own behalf especially in regard to abdominal or sexual complaints".[55] The doctor's evidence was also that Aboriginal women could not get representation from the Aboriginal and Islander Legal Service, and that very few women took out restraining orders because they thought it futile to have court proceedings for orders, which they doubted, would be effective.

The *Koori Mail*, the source for this case, did not give particulars of Gadd's defence, that is, whether or not she relied on the Battered Woman's Syndrome, and there was no further report about verdict and sentence. However, a search of unreported cases revealed a 1994 appeal case concerning Gadd and also something of her disturbed and underprivileged life, which can involve escalating conflict with the law. In 1992 Gadd was arrested for using insulting words, she then kicked in the window of a police car. Although the prosecution did not seek a custodial sentence she was sentenced to one month for one count of wilful damage.

On 8 June 1994 her appeal against this sentence was heard. By then Gadd had already been in custody since 1 April 1994, on the charge of murdering her former de facto husband. She was 21 years old, mother to a 12-month-old child and was 30 weeks pregnant, being due to have a caesarean section at 38 weeks. Gadd was released on bail on 17 June 1994 in respect of both the murder charge and the appeal. The appeal was allowed, the sentence of one month for wilful damage was set aside, and Gadd was placed on six months probation.

Gadd's life as described by the Court was one of deprivation and lack of opportunity. From the age of 16 years she had a series of convictions, none involving violence or dishonesty, and generally had not received custodial sentences. Gadd had an alcohol problem and she was described as a "nuisance to her community at Murgon". Gadd is the feminine counterpart of the young, violent and alcoholic males like Alwyn Peter, Leo Juli and Maynard Daniel who have committed violent abuse of women. Aboriginal women too suffer "culture stress", but they also become victims of men's violence.

Similar issues arose in *Kina*, a case that has caused general criticism of the rights available to Aboriginal women in the legal system.[56] Kina's life was also one of deprivation and violence, although in her case she was abused by a non-Aborigine whom she stabbed. In 1988 she was convicted of murder. Like Gadd she had been unable to reveal the extent of her abuse because she was constrained by cultural considerations and "shame". Kina appealed unsuccessfully on the ground that the trial judge erred in withdrawing provocation from the jury, but again evidence of her abuse was not presented to the appellate court. In 1993 the Queensland Court of Criminal Appeal set aside her conviction as being a miscarriage of justice on the grounds of the exceptional difficulties of communication compounded by Kina's Aboriginality, the Battered Woman's Syndrome,[57] and Kina's intense shame about the abuse to which she had been subjected.[58] *Kina* may well be a significant advance for Aboriginal women if their cultural situation can now be recognised by the judiciary when they present as victims of abuse.

Chapter 4
The oppression of being "civilized"

> We are indeed a civilizing race ... when we came here the
> aborigines covered these wide plains in thousands. Where are they
> today? We have "civilized" them – they are dead.[1]

The fourth index of Radhika Coomaraswamy's indices of women's
universal vulnerability to violence is the "strong connection between
militarisation and violence against women". In the context of present
violence to Aboriginal women "militarisation" arose from the British
defeat of the Aborigines in the battles for control of the Australian
continent. A collateral of victory was the contemptuous attitude of
many of the victors towards traditional culture and their concomitant abuse of Aboriginal women.

For Aborigines, British killings, dispossession and disease
began in 1788 and marched with the frontiers of settlement so that
by 1877 even Central Australia was affected. The devastation of
Northern Aboriginal society then began. Between the 1920s and the
1940s anthropologists like Elkin, the Berndts and Mountford were
writing of cultural disintegration. This does not mean that there was
acceptance of European culture; there was both denial and
resistance.

The degrading descriptions of Aborigines by the British are
well-known, Aboriginal reactions less so. *Captain Cook, Related by
Percy Mumbulla,* is part of an oral history tradition around Ulladulla
that has preserved Aborigines' utter rejection of the British.

> When they were pullin' away to go back
> to the ship, these wild Kurris
> were runnin' out of the scrub.
> They stripped right off again
> They were throwin' the clothes an' biscuits
> back at Captain Cook
> as his men were pullin' away in the boat.[2]

This verse has symbolic meaning, and is one example of the many versions of the "Captain Cook story", which appear inland even in the north.[3] From their first arrival, "as the ships were sailing in", the British noted the Aborigines' defiant rejection, their pointed spears and calls of "wara, wara" or "wooroo, wooroo", meaning "go away".[4] Aboriginal attitudes may have remained unchanged. In 2001 a non-Aborigine who has worked and lived for many years in the western desert said "Every Aborigine views non-Aborigines through the veil of dispossession".[5]

Invasion fractured customary law, but present Indigenous society is not necessarily divorced from that of the past. However, the nexus between land, religion and the law, which was fundamental to classical Aboriginal society, has been transformed in many places.[6] The situation has become open for customary law to be applied and interpreted in contexts foreign to that law.

The corrosive nature of power on a subordinated culture is implicit in Foucault's analysis of "the different modes by which human beings are made subjects".[7] The power of defining "Aboriginality" has been regarded, almost without question, as a prerogative of those who became dominant. This means that definitions of "Aboriginality" accepted in Anglo-Australian society do not have their origins in Aboriginal culture but rather have derived from European culture. The difficulty then for many Aborigines in acknowledging intra-racial violence outside their own community is that until the recent past the usurpers of their country have demeaned them as the "Other".

A popular scientific theory in the latter part of the 19th century was that Aborigines were directly linked to "orang-otang [sic] and other apes". Some scientists even regarded Aborigines as non-human.

> The blacks are never called men and women and children; "myalls" and "niggers" and "gins" and "picaninnies" seem further removed from humanity.[8]

Through seeing Aborigines as something other than human, non-Aborigines remade Aboriginal identity by massacre, by dispossession, by aggregation in reserves, and by classification on the basis of colour. Massacres meant not only slaughter but also that many remnants of tribes, or individual survivors could no longer lead structured traditional lives. They were dispersed to become beggars and pariahs in their own land. In 1869 the *Port Denison Times*,

Queensland, entitled an article "Shall we admit the Blacks?" and referred to:

> [a] complete war of extermination. One person is reported as having tied two gins together and having made one ball serve for both: and the sole survivor of a mob of twenty three aborigines is located on a station in the North. Another has often boastingly exhibited his revolver covered with notches each representing a murdered gin or blackfellow.

On the Queensland frontier Aborigines were referred to as "black game", "troublesome wild animal(s), to be shot and hunted down whenever seen in open country". "Snipe hunting" was thought to be great sport. Dogs were set on Aborigines.

> It was no unusual thing to hear these ruffians ... boasting of the blacks they had slaughtered and when relating the particular qualities of a savage brute of a dog, say he would pull down a blackfellow, or seize a blackfellow and tear his entrails out.

It is difficult now to have an account of the Aborigines' side of this slaughter. Their bleached bones, their visible desolation and starvation, living on ants, on caterpillars, were physical records in themselves and were described by non-Aborigines. But their feelings and thoughts have vanished with little trace. However, the following two descriptions when opposed to each other reveal something of the callous indifference to suffering on one hand and on the other a factual yet piteous record of agonising deaths.

Forced to rely on handouts of food because their land and hunting sites had been taken, Aborigines were prey to those squatters who dealt out strychnine-laced rations. The first comment was made in 1842 after the mass poisoning at Kilcoy Creek, when 60 Aborigines died, the second in 1908. The chronology of these comments makes it apparent that in Queensland dealing out "death pudding" continued for over half a century.

> That blackfellow been eatim damper. Then plenty jump about all the same fish, when you catch im, big mob been die – him dead all about.

> Why, if you give the blacks phosphorous in their flour it only makes their eyes water, but if you mix arsenic with the flour, that'll stretch them out.

These vile cruelties occurred in Queensland, but identical behaviour is replicated in contemporary accounts of killings and other atrocities elsewhere, for instance in the southern Eden-Monaro in New South Wales.[9]

Possibly the inhumane treatment of Aborigines was partly the consequence of the brutalisation of colonial society by the convict system and a subsequent contempt for the law. By comparison in South Australia, the sole free colony, lawyer Greg Taylor has noted that Justice Jeffcott in charging a grand jury in 1837 said that:

> [A]ggression against the natives or any "infringement on their rights", would be "visited by greater severity of punishment than would otherwise be inflicted" … This would [be] in … contrast to the convict colonies to the east, at whose treatment of Aborigines, his Honour said, "humanity shudders".[10]

Throughout Australia dislocation and dispossession were other weapons against living Aboriginal tradition. "There was a concerted effort by pastoralists to make clear to the Aboriginal people that if they stayed in the bush they would be hunted down and shot."[11] The following pragmatic account of alienation is by a Walmatjari elder whose people moved out of the Western Desert into settled areas near Fitzroy Crossing in northwest Western Australia. These bare facts are yet a lament that tells of the relinquishment of ancient ways. Work on the squatters' stations, usually meant a miserable and undernourished life without pay or respect. "Plant food" there meant flour only.

> In the sandhills they lived like this
> the people lived in the former time in the sandhills.
> They were eating meat and plant food.
> Plants that they ate were various, various.
> They were eating all kinds of plant food,
> All kinds of plant food they ate,
> Until what they ate was finished,
> A finish to eating plant food and meat.
>
> Well, they ate meat only,
>
> Then that finished.
> And the people they went this way
> To other kinds of plant food, Whiteman's tucker.
> Well, those people too, they went north to the stations.
> Then they gave them plant food,
> The people from the sandhills.
>
> Those people went for good,
> Never to return.

> Well, they went on a journey for plant food,
> Whiteman's tucker.
> Then they stayed there, those people,
> So they ate the plant food of the Whiteman,
> And so they stayed there, the people, never to return.[12]

In 1895 on the Annan River, Queensland, a small group of ill and starving Aborigines, no longer able to be traditional family groupings, explained why they could no longer depend on their usual sources of food:

> White-fellow along a yarraman [horse] too much break him spear, burn yambo [humpies] cut him old man with whip; white man too much kill him kangaroo ... we like our own country; only white man no good. The young gins said, "I think altogether we die soon."

The Walmatjari lament about forsaking the sandhills is a direct translation. The other comments have been filtered through non-Aboriginal voices and records; nonetheless the three accounts provide a coherent record of desolation and despair.

So Aborigines were divorced from the heritage of their sacred sites and their country. They sold their revered tjuringas, the most sacred objects, for alcohol, tea, sugar and food. Having been dispossessed, Aborigines were then gathered on to reserves, which, as Justice Woodward noted in the 1973 report of the Aboriginal Land Rights Commission, were established for "the protection of Aborigines. The larger reserves consisted of land either unsuitable or not then required for white settlement. The small reserves were established for particular needs". Reserves were controlled by missions such as those of the Methodists at Yirrkala, 1935, and Millingimbi in 1945, the Church Missionary Society at Anunguru in 1908, the Catholics at Santa Teresa in 1935 or were "medical, control and trading centres" such as Maningrida established in 1957. Justice Woodward noted that the reserves meant that traditional life was being depleted because:

> Mission and settlements, with their assured food supplies, medical attention and other material advantages, have attracted Aborigines to settle, more or less permanently, in one place. Very often this is miles from their own country and, as older men die, accurate information becomes harder to obtain. Rituals are observed less often and not at traditional sites.

On reserves Aborigines could be mixed indiscriminately with other Indigenous peoples to whom they previously may have been antagonistic. An instance is Warrabri, "locally known as Yalikorangu", now known as Ali Curang. At Warrabri in Kaititj/Alyawarra country, Kaititj, Alyawarra, Warlpiri, Warramunga and some Arrente lived in unhappy association. The last four groups were viewed as interlopers. Bell describes the formation of this artificial settlement:

> In the 1920's many Warlpiri (Walpiri) fled from their own country in the Lander River area, where Aboriginal people were savagely massacred, to around Tennant Creek and what is now Hooker Creek.[13]

This may be a reference to the 1928 massacre of the Warlpiri at Coniston where about 60 to 70 Warlpiri, including women and children, were brutally killed over two weeks by Northern Territory police. This killing finally caused such revulsion among Anglo-Australians that it became the last recorded massacre of Aborigines.

Relocation caused enormous tensions, not only severance from country. The Warlpiri country is about 116,000 square kilometres around the Tanami desert. Hooker Creek south of Wave Hill is actually Gurundji land. The Warlpiri and Gurundji were hostile to each other. The Warlpiri were numerous, powerful and good warriors who had already been pushing the borders of Arrente (Arranda) lands. The Gurindji are a much smaller group.

The Warlpiri and Warramunga were for a time at the Phillip Creek mission north of Tennant Creek but because of severe drought in the 1920s they were trucked to a new site at Warrabri. Then Kaititj and Alyawarra moved in from nearby cattle stations where they had been living. Hence at Warrabri people who were formerly living in a society of small groups, rarely interacting, some coming together once a year, were forced into living in large conglomerates.

In the 1960s there were about 650 to 700 people at Warrabri. In 1979 Bell put the number at 750, so the numbers remained fairly stable. Warrabri is hemmed in by cattle stations hence there was little chance of establishing outstations or supporting land claims which would relieve tension although seasonal employment at the cattle stations provided some outlet.

In the 1960s although fully-traditional life was no longer operating, there were family groups of, say, two old men, and their wives and children. The men formed hunting groups, and many rituals and ceremonies were still performed, although here was some indication that the Warlpiri men had a sense of the passing of some rituals. The Aborigines were trying to accommodate to new situations but there were inherent difficulties. For instance, breaking skin taboos means dire consequences, but at Warrabri there were fundamental incompatibilities between different tribes. The skin system of the Warlpiri was divided into four male groups and four female groups. That of the Arrente comprised only six in total.

This disparity could lead to difficulty and violence. For instance a very attractive young Arrente woman came to Warrabri to marry a young Warlpiri man from an incompatible skin group. Her skin name in the Arrente meant that she was given a Warlpiri skin name which precluded marriage to this man. The outrage of this situation is analogous to that of incest in European society. The resulting pressure arising from the continual verbal abuse from the community was too difficult to handle. The young man finally attacked the young woman with a shovel.

The change in environment and social degradation meant that traditional culture was fast failing and the force of customary law was breaking down. At Warrabri an authoritarian government imposed structure and enforced order. But in a microcosm of the future for Aborigines there was neither a real social structure nor employment prospects to replace disintegrating traditional society. Past social values were destroyed. Aborigines who had not "come in" like the Pintubi or who had just "come in" were regarded as "myalls", bush Aborigines by those already established in the settlement. The traditional Aborigines classified people as "black belly", "yellow belly" or "white belly". The people of mixed ancestry, "yellow belly", had no place in the clan structure and were generally collected together at Emily Gap. The fringe dwellers around Alice Springs were those who for one reason or another had fallen out of traditional society. By the early 1960s substance abuse had already started. Taxi drivers were dropping off flagons in the bush around Alice Springs, and women were prostituting themselves for alcohol. Sniffing intoxicating substances commenced, supplies of Fordiograph fluid were stolen and Avgas had to be locked away.

An observer at Warrabri in the 1960s, who has since seen the later further degeneration of this settlement, said that if a people are at the bottom end of society there is a desire not to conform. Commissioner Elliott Johnston in the RCIADIC report made the same point, "Decisions were made about them and for them and imposed upon them. With loss of independence goes loss of self esteem".[14]

Finally, legislation and administrative action also constructed "Aboriginality", of which there were 67 separate legislative definitions, whereby Aboriginal peoples were seen as objects within a system of caste, not culture.[15] In the reserves set up by governments and missionaries, the Protection Acts and Welfare Ordinances determined the status of Aborigines as a subject people in the Colonies, Territories and States from 1869 to 1972.[16] Part of this policy was the removal of children from their families, to be placed in institutional care so the stain of Indigenous identity and culture could be eradicated. Pat O'Shane says the derogatory classifications of "half-, quarter-caste and coloured mean only one thing – rejection of people classified as blacks!"[17]

The National Committee on Violence identified these factors as contributing to cultural disintegration, alcoholism and despair which precipitate violence.[18] Both the National Committee on Violence and Commissioner Johnston of RCIADIC make the point that only recently have non-Aboriginal Australians recognised the brutality with which they have destroyed Aboriginal society. Parallels can be drawn concerning the experience of other Indigenous peoples under British colonisers. Of equivalent Canadian legislation it is written: "The imposition of legislative distinctions upon Canada's native population has been harshly criticised both for its arbitrariness and for its disintegrative effects".[19]

In a community that has been so fragmented, issues of culture and descent are very important in establishing Indigenous identity. Aboriginal culture in itself is difficult to define as it did embrace, and still does embrace, diverse social organisations and beliefs.[20]

Historically, Aboriginal culture was constituted by subtle and complex amalgamations of kinship groups, but "on a regional or language basis" there was no "encompassing political structure".[21] There are many variations in traditional society and different customs, laws, social and totemic groups and matrilineal and patrilineal descent. Tim Flannery remarks on the observation of Edward John Eyre writing in 1845 "that Aboriginal culture was so varied in detail and so similar in general outline and character" and goes on to note:

> Despite many partially successful attempts, there is still no complete overview of Aboriginal life style and cultures. These cultures are the result of over 40,000 years of coadaptation with Australian ecosystems.[22]

The fine tracery of Tindale's map of Aboriginal Australia is visual confirmation of the complexity of hundreds of different societies. For each, their beliefs and lore were centred on their local identity, their country. Yet there is a body of practices common to many Aborigines that can be seen as constituting themes of traditional society. Generic beliefs are the sacred relationship with the land, observance of kinship moieties in arranging marriages, and the sanctity of totemic birds or animals for people of that totem. Other practices have specific applications within particular areas. Generally initiation for boys marks their passage to manhood, but there could be, or can be, a particular ritual, circumcision, sub-incision or knocking out a front tooth.

The ALRC 1986 report on recognition of Aboriginal customary laws variously characterised Aboriginal lifestyles as traditionally oriented, "fringe-dwelling" and urban.[23] It is Langton's opinion that now there cannot be a "totally closed Aboriginal experience",[24] and some anthropologists have said that "no Aboriginal society today is autonomous".[25] The ALRC 1986 report concluded that there was no need for a restrictive definition and that a flexible approach to the idea of a traditional Aborigine was preferable.[26]

In general law Indigenous identity is not affected by Aborigines' place of origin – whether it be from remote or settled regions. In 1983 Justice Deane in the High Court case of *Commonwealth v Tasmania* defined an Aborigine "(as) ... a person of Aboriginal descent, albeit mixed, who identifies himself as such and who is recognised by the Aboriginal community as Aboriginal". In 1990 Justice French referred to the discussion about laws protecting cultural heritage and commented that this definition was perhaps not representative of the contemporary context of the term Aboriginal. However, the High Court substantially adopted this definition in 1990 and followed it in 1995.[27] It is Langton's view that Aborigines prefer this "social" definition to that of a "racial" definition. The latter has connotations of the "'half-caste', 'quarter-caste' categories of the Assimilation era".[28]

In the 1998 Federal Court case of *Shaw v Wolf* the question of Aboriginal identity arose in the ravaged Indigenous society of Tasmania in relation to eligibility to stand for election as ATSIC regional councillors. Justice Merkel applied the established criteria of descent, self identification, and community acceptance. He found that two of the 11 candidates could not be described as Aboriginal persons under the *Aboriginal and Torres Strait Islander Commission Act*

1989 (Cth). Nonetheless, his Honour considered (in the context of Tasmanian Aboriginal society) that the culture was virtually paramount in defining "Aboriginality" and said that this is now "accepted as a social, rather than a genetic construct".

He commented on the difficulties of trying to implement statutory definitions of Aboriginality which included descent in a situation where:

> The European colonial deconstruction of Aboriginality in the 19th century is now sought to be rectified, in part, by post-colonial statutory reconstruction of Aboriginality at the end of the 20th century.[29]

Chapter 5

Violence to women in traditional society

> Aboriginal law is still potent ... [and it] sanctions a level of violence that most Australians would find difficult to accept. Men can discipline their wives by striking them or family members may retaliate on victim's behalf by spearing the offender.[1]

From the mid-1960s Aborigines have entered an era of post-colonial politics in which the law of the dominant government has been challenged. In doing so, identity and culture have become important as the basis for establishing rights.[2] Peter Sutton has found that in fact there has been a "persistence of distinctive pan-Aboriginal cultural values and shared underlying principles of social organisation" in post-classical Aboriginal society.[3] Now both the notion of culture, and culture itself, may have become sacrosanct. This is understandable when culture is the vehicle whereby identity is preserved, and racial unity established, for survival in the face of oppression.[4] Therefore an appreciation and understanding of their place in traditional society is important for many Aboriginal women when addressing the issue of family violence. If gender equality and non-violence can be authoritatively claimed as traditional values, contemporary violence is authenticated as un-Aboriginal and the product solely of European invasion.

Doubtless European disruption of classical Aboriginal society and the concomitant violence are some of the causes for present Aboriginal violence, but if traditional society is examined it is apparent that there is a heritage of permissive violence towards women. Further, these attitudes are more likely to persist in traditional and remote communities where, as discussed, the rate of violence is worse. However, in the Gordon Inquiry's report ("the report") the evidence of a "widespread perception that violence and sexual abuse were an integral part of customary law" was considered in the category of "cultural facts and fallacies". The Inquiry had referred the evidence about customary law violence to the Centre for Anthropological Research at the University of Western Australia ("the Centre") for an independent evaluation of the "extent to which conduct amounting to Family Violence and Child Abuse in Aboriginal communities can be said to be traditionally sanctioned". The report quoted the Centre's findings as:

> Our review of the anthropological literature reveals examples of what, on the face of it, might be taken as instances of family violence or abuse. But the literature also shows that such actions are invariably within the sphere of traditional practice, ritual or the operation of customary law. We have found little material that suggests that violence or abuse per se are condoned, or took place with impunity, outside traditionally regulated contexts.[5]

The Centre's findings were similar to those made in 2001 by Memmott et al in their review of violence in Indigenous communities:

> Contemporary Indigenous violence *in some respects* (italics added) contains elements and structures that appear to have evolved in recent decades and has no counterpart in classical Aboriginal societies of the early contact period.[6]

The Gordon Inquiry treated the finding of the Centre as proof that violence is not cultural *per se*, and supported this view with some selective quotations about traditional society which it found establish that the "extent that family violence which occurs in traditional societies appears to be no different to any other societies in the world". In doing so, it ignored the Centre's conclusions that violence in classical Aboriginal society was confined "within the sphere of traditional practice, ritual or the operation of customary law". Ritual or customary law violence is something quite other than family violence, although the former may well be a cultural heritage from classical society, which endorses and thus has contributed to the present violence of Aboriginal men to Aboriginal women.

The Australian Law Reform Commission (ALRC) 1986 report into Aboriginal customary law found three types of physical sanctions which were mentioned in mythology and which were perpetuated in traditional life:

> wounding or killing a person of either sex with a spear to secure revenge; wounding or killing a woman with a spear or a knife, as a means of controlling women, usually wives; and ... ritualised revenge.[7]

Contemporary anthropologists, Eric Venbrux,[8] Sutton,[9] and Victoria Burbank,[10] concur about innate violence in Aboriginal society. Burbank noted that many customary law practices were inimical to women. Women were vulnerable to "traditionally regulated" violence; first, for infringing male law for which there was strict liability, the punishment was usually death; second, for alleged misbehaviour which anthropologist Basil Sansom has described as "moral violence". Court cases establish that "moral violence" could also lead to death. Third, there were violent expressions of generally inimical social attitudes towards women such as group sexual use. Four, customary law marriage which is now seen as an abrogation of women's rights, but this also could entail a great deal of associated violence.

Evidence of Aboriginal women being controlled by severe violence exists in the earliest written records. From 1788 the British, and later the French maritime explorer de Bougainville, noted head wounds and scars on Aboriginal women, the evidence of the "great cruelty" and "savage barbarity", commonly inflicted by Aboriginal men on Aboriginal women.[11] Captain Tench, in 1789, and ex-convict Lingard, in the 1830s, respectively wrote of practices that although identical, were separated by time and place within the colony of New South Wales.

> When an Indian is provoked by a woman, he either spears her, or knocks her down on the spot; on this occasion he always strikes on the head, using indiscriminately a hatchet, a club, or any other weapon, which may chance to be in his hand.

> If a black man kills his wife, they have no law to punish him. I scarcely ever saw a married woman, but she had got six or seven cuts in her head, given by her husband with a tomahawk, several inches in length and very deep.[12]

In the 1880s, in the new frontier of northern Western Australia, the pastoralist Brockman recounted incidents of severe violence from Aboriginal men to women. A woman was beaten and then in a further attack she was so seriously wounded with a hammer that 12 days later she was still unable to walk, and a month later "she was (still) very lame". Another woman was speared.[13]

The work of paleaopathologist Stephen Webb in 1995 establishes that these contemporary observations of traditional life are neither distorted nor biased. Sutton, in analysing the despairing disintegration of Aboriginal violence, has written of Webb's work in some detail.[14] Webb analysed signs of traumatic injury on 6,241 adult post-cranial samples and 1,409 adult cranial samples from prehistoric sites throughout mainland Australia. The "commonest cranial injury was a depressed fracture of a kind that can 'usually be regarded as the result of deliberate aggression'". The incidences varied within regions, the highest being in northern Australia. In all, there were significantly more incidences involving women averaging at more than five times the number of incidences involving men. Defensive wounds on arms consisting "predominantly of parrying fractures, which indicate defence against attack from a right-handed person" were also apparent. The highest frequency for this injury was amongst East coast women, the incidence being "almost one in five".

Some of these injuries might have been inflicted in fights between women. However, men were warriors, and for this reason alone, apart from individual male-to-male violence, it can reasonably be assumed that they would have suffered a comparable, if not greater, rate of intra-gender violence. But the facts are quite contrary. Juvenile skulls examined by Webb were not injured. This physical evidence also accords with historical observations of the affection for Aboriginal children and the great tenderness with which they were treated. From the first contact between Aborigines and Europeans this behaviour was particularly noted among the men.[15] Both the rate of injury to women and the lack of injury to children in pre-historical Indigenous society are consistent with behaviour in present society. It is cultural practice for Aboriginal children not to be disciplined harshly[16] and Aboriginal women still suffer severe and fatal injuries.

Although many of the practices might now seem abhorrent, traditional violence to women must be seen from the perspective of a highly-structured legalistic society existing in an often harsh environment that created tough standards. Many past practices were necessary both for survival of the group, and the continuation of an ordered society in a nomadic culture. Recorded memoirs and observations of Aborigines and contemporary observers of tribal life establish that there was infanticide and that the old and ailing could be left to a lonely death.[17] Customary law sanctions were rigorous. The *kurdaitcha* man, the executioner who was the instrument of the law, inflicted ritualised revenge, "the killing of the law" upon men and women who transgressed the law either in error or on purpose.[18] "In olden days, you know if one breaks down, one little thing, he's dead, you know speared, just like that".[19]

Traditional society was one of hunters and warriors, although tribes displayed varying degrees of aggression.[20] Inter-tribal conflict could rage for years over absorption of territory when patrilineal lineage might have ended or over women.[21] Lingard noted:

> One tribe is very much afraid of another, and they have sometimes great wars ... they go on till one side gives in, and then the battle is over. Should any of the black men be killed, the winning side takes the women belonging to them. If the women refuse to go, they kill them.

The tradition of strength and aggression remains part of Aboriginal women's self-image also.[22] However, despite Aboriginal women's undoubted strengths, a crucial point in discussing violence to women in classical society is whether there was, or was not, a gender imbalance of power. The view that women did not enjoy equality of religious or physical power or reciprocal rights of punishment has been criticised as one which originated with male anthropologists, who were precluded from knowledge of women's particular culture, and hence they were ignorant of the full significance of women's role in traditional society.

Since the 1970s, Fay Gale and Diane Bell, among others, have made important contributions to revaluing women's status. Women's religious autonomy, their role in caring for country and their economic contribution as food gatherers in a subsistence economy have been stressed. This has been viewed as indicating equality and thus it has been argued that there was mutual respect between men and women in classical Aboriginal society, and hence there was not cultural violence.

But although women's roles were viewed anew through feminist perspectives, Phyllis Kaberry had already addressed many of these issues in her seminal book *Aboriginal Woman Sacred and Profane* that was published in 1939. Kaberry refuted an earlier draconian view of Aboriginal women's status as being "utterly degraded". She established the importance of women's sexual, economic, procreative and mythic religious role, and the "reciprocal gender obligations" which maintain the equilibrium of traditional society. Kaberry also observed, "delegated responsibility amongst the older men and women in the kinship groups", but she concluded that:

> There are, however, aspects of public life in which she [Aboriginal woman] has a subordinate role. Warfare and judicial functions in

cases of death are the prerogatives of the men. Political control is vested in the hands of the headman and the elders.[23]

The real external and internal power in any society resides in the control of these powers, which are commonly male prerogatives. Those outside this authority are vulnerable to its exercise. In the case of Aboriginal women, this is exemplified by their lack of defences to men's violence because ultimately tight control was exerted by initiated men, the senior law men of the community, who knew the most sacred law.[24] In 1990 David Mowaljarlai, in referring to his initiation marks, described his authority as a senior law man:

> Well it's like a crown, you depend on the governor, you depend on him for everything. So all the Aborigines they depend on this man who is the governor. Now he governs his own land – yes, authority, and that's why it's important ... those rules, laws, to control everybody straight all the time. It doesn't happen now.[25]

Further, in most societies power is also indicated by the strength of affiliation to land. Women have complementary roles in ceremonially caring for country, but as Sutton has noted:

> Patrilineal descent was generally the privileged mechanism in assigning land rights; although people also enjoyed rights in their mother's countries, there were no matrilineal land-holding groups, and there are none today as far as I am aware.[26]

Bell also confirms, "land ownership flows through the patriline".[27] Both Bell and Sutton say that the often quoted complimentary rights of *kirda/kurdungurlu or nimarringki/jungkayi* cannot be seen as patrilineal/matrilineal division.[28] They concur that *kirda* (etc) derive from patrilineal descent, and *kurdungurlu* (etc) derive from the senior women for the patri-clan, thus:

> [This] status is conferred through the matrifiliation to one's mother's patrilineal estate, or to a connection she has to land through patrifiliation. ... [C]onfusion seems to have arisen from political factors, and from a desire to stress parallelism between patri- and matri- principles.[29]

However, Sutton notes evidence before Justice Maurice, Aboriginal Land Commissioner in 1988, that Aboriginal women's intermarriage with European men has affected traditional practices. In land claims cognatic descent has emerged, namely descent from a common ancestor. Justice Maurice observed of these "all-embracing groupings" which were advanced in land claims that they "must have something to do with the researchers' own preconceptions of egalitarianism in Aboriginal society which does not exist".[30]

The force of men's power was also expressed in powerful religious connections to the land. For instance women and children were not allowed to enter the ochre pits of the western Arrente in central Australia. Men provided ochre to women, and they were usually confined to using white or yellow for ceremonial decoration. The red ochre, symbolising the sacred blood of the ancestral beings, was used for boys' initiation.

Aboriginal men's authority in classical society therefore appears to fit almost universal indices of power, nonetheless, the dialogue about Aboriginal women's status has been intense. Ultimately, the majority of women anthropologists' views have accorded with those of Kaberry, women enjoyed qualified power. Catherine Berndt, a strong proponent of women's autonomy, whose work dated from the 1960s, found that women did have independence within their own spheres, but men held ultimate authority "in the religious sphere". She observed that men's physical advantages were the basis of one disparity of power. Men had greater fighting resources, they were stronger, and had access to more threatening weapons, such as spears, if a "man was in a bad temper about something his wife had done".[31]

Jan Pettman, a sociologist, has noted the critiques of anthropologists Merlan and Hamilton of Bell's theories.[32] Merlan sees rather than a gender and ritual division which is "independent, parallel and equivalent", a separation of sexes which is "absolute and immutable".' Hamilton queried Bell's feminist and political agenda; she argued that "Aboriginal women are still entrapped in a world of men". Bell herself says, "Looking to the general anthropological literature on sex relations in Aboriginal society, one finds references which evoke images of women as property".[33] Bell is here enunciating a fundamental disparity of power, which is something quite other than the concept of "reciprocal interaction" in ceremonies and food gathering.

Berndt found that men alone derived power from acting as a group, "if necessary drawing on secret sacred sanctions" and through their access to sorcery of a life threatening nature.[34] Women were not allowed to see the sacred tjuringas, which embodied the sacred law. Burbank found that women today still fear men's ability to attack through supernatural means and some women fear it more than actual physical attack.[35]

Women were killed when they committed offences against the law by glimpsing sacred objects, sacred events, trespassing upon sacred ground or profaning the law by a word. These were lawful executions. However, there was disparity in that women did not have an equivalent power of punishment over men. Even if Aboriginal women unwittingly trespassed against male rituals or law, their families would not protect them. For instance, in 1978 at Ernabella a man spoke of how he had caused his mother's death. He was still suffering from this although it must have occurred over 35 years previously. When he was very small he had crept out, without his mother's knowledge, to watch a corroborree, which as a young boy he was forbidden to see. Because he had done so, the next morning his mother was killed and he was brought into the mission at Ernabella.[36]

Men could invoke the power of religion to inflict "sacred rape" or "sacred coitus" upon women. Men were thus authorised to inflict multiple sexual penetrations on a woman, or group of women, in punishment for offences against the law, or in some societies to prepare a female child for marriage, or to penetrate girls upon puberty.[37] Men could use the pretext of sacred rape to bluff and scare women into sexual intercourse (which is rape under general law as there is lack of true consent). In the 1984 Northern Territory case of *Willie Gudabi*, a traditional Aborigine who was approximately 70 years of age coerced a woman into having sexual intercourse with him on a number of occasions by saying that, as she had been touched by a sacred ceremonial object which she was not permitted to see or touch, she was bound to have sexual intercourse with him. Eventually the woman told her husband, the matter was reported to the police, and Gudabi was convicted on one count of rape, but effectively only suffered the threat of prison if he should ever transgress in the future. Gudabi was sentenced to two years' imprisonment, but his immediate release was ordered upon him entering into a recognisance to be of good behaviour for two years.

Group sexual relations also occurred during certain ceremonies, the purpose being to make the rites more effective, such as in the Gunabibi fertility mother ritual or as an expression of common unity when warriors were setting out, or after an initiation ceremony one woman would stay behind to be used by the men.[38]

Older women were used to sexually service young initiates as part of the secret law.[39]

In addition to the precepts of sacred law other sexual uses of women were sanctioned in traditional society. Women were offered in conciliation to raiding warriors. If their sexual services were accepted it signified there would be no fighting.[40] Grant Ngabidj of the Gadjerong, who lived from 1904 to 1977 in the East Kimberley, recounted how women were offered to visitors to the camp, a woman would be sent over for the sexual use of the whole group of men.[41] At times group sex took place when all incest laws were suspended, for example, when a peace was being sealed between two groups.

It is now difficult to establish to what extent this use of women by men was consensual, or indeed whether there could be a true consent in that social context. Kaberry notes that the women of the East Kimberley did not appear to mind sexual relations within the group, but that when they were sent to appease otherwise hostile men, "Some of the women seemed to regard this particular practice with dislike and disgust".[42] This practice is of course consistent with the use of women as a sexual commodity both in traditional and colonial times. Violence is concomitant with Aboriginal men treating Aboriginal women as sexual property. Bell and Nelson found that in traditional society:

> Man the hunter partakes of sex after a successful kill: an aggrieved man may be appeased by access to the wife of the offender, sexual licence at times of male ritual gives men access to otherwise prohibited women; a young girl is made a woman by multiple penetrations by men other than her husband. None of these appear to require a woman's consent, yet none speak of rape.[43]

If absolute "rights values" are considered, women were subject to severe punishments for lesser offences in absolute terms, and they were more vulnerable to severe punishments. If men were offended by women punishments other than beatings could occur which would be regarded in general society as sexual assaults of the most grievous kind. For instance, in the Kimberley if a woman was thought to be "running around", a group of men would take her into the bush, and so cut her genitals that she would be incapable of ever again having sexual intercourse.[44]

In the community observed by Burbank, the behaviour pattern for women to be careful of men's sensibilities is established within a family by *mirrirri*. A male attacks his sister with sticks or spears if the etiquette involving the brother/sister relationship is violated. It is the woman who has to bear the responsibility of avoiding giving offence.[45] Women are likely to be the victims of displaced aggression for men's convenience. That is, the target shifts from a male culprit to a female scapegoat.[46] The threat of aggression can limit women's autonomy in any general aspect of behaviour.[47]

Ashley v Materna, the 1997 Northern Territory appeal case alleged in the Gordon Report to be the only case "where it was argued that customary law sanctioned the assault",[48] seems to be based on custom analogous to *mirrirri*. That case was an appeal against a sentence of 18 months' imprisonment imposed in a magistrates' court for a plea of guilty to a charge of aggravated unlawful assault. The ground for the appeal, which did not succeed, was that the magistrate "failed to give due weight to the cultural context in which the offence was committed". Drink was also a factor in this case; further, the appellant had a proven record of violence, five previous convictions for assault and two for breach of domestic violence orders. The circumstances of the case were that a man, his wife and her brother were sitting around a camp fire, drinking. The husband said something to his wife, the victim, which according to Aboriginal customary law he was not supposed to say in the presence of her brother, the appellant. He then hit her over the head with a 1.3 metre by 10 centimetre stick. She suffered a massive fracture of the skull and was in hospital for about four weeks. A senior elder of the Ngukurr gave evidence that this was customary law, which usually would not be observed now, but was in:

> the 50s to the 60s ... a man swear ... to someone else's sister and the fellow gets up and hits her (sic) sister ... in our ways, that – that woman who that man swore to and she get hit from her brother – that's her punishment – you know. She got to take that.

A coda to this repressive gender violence is that women suffered sanctions even in common pleasurable matters. Women were, and still are, not allowed to play the didgeridoo. Women did, and still do, beautiful and sacred weaving. Germane Greer comments about the Yirrkala, "Men did art and women did craft, as was usual in Europe".[49] This assumption is Eurocentric and belittles thousands of years of Aboriginal tradition, and it is a clear example of how European assumptions "construct" traditional Aboriginal culture. The ceremonial body painting of both genders was quite obvious to anthropologists and other Europeans, both sexes did ground drawings, but in Aboriginal culture the right to do rock paintings was a usually male preserve. These sites enhanced men's power.[50]

However, to temper this harsh picture there are historical and anthropological accounts of happiness and family tenderness in traditional life. Early observers noted both men and women enjoying song, dance and music, and also the "levity" of both sexes. Anthropologists like Phyllis Kaberry and Ted Strehlow, who were familiar with traditional life in the 1930s, both write of the happiness and laughter in the evening camps. It is worth quoting Ted Strehlow's views about the then nomadic Pintubi at length, because he illustrates so clearly how the constraints of a legalistic society enabled order and happiness to flourish, and how ravaging that society has transmuted it into anarchy. In 1978, in recalling the past Strehlow wrote:

> It should not be imagined from what has been said so far that Aboriginal people in the pre-white days lived in an atmosphere of [complete and unmitigated] terror caused by the grimness of Aboriginal law.
>
> On the contrary, the heavy punishments meted out to lawbreakers and the easy elimination of insubordinate and vicious men (a charge of sacrilege readily removed from the community anyone who continually defied the warnings of the local group elders) meant that the members of a local group enjoyed a great sense of security.
>
> In addition, Aboriginal law ensured that in droughts as in good seasons all hunted game and gathered vegetable foods had to be shared equitably among all members of a local group according to rules resting on classificatory kinship.
>
> It must therefore be emphasised that ready laughter was once the most noticeable feature in then pre-white Aboriginal communities. They were essentially a happy people ... whenever the food gatherers had returned to camp, cheerful laughter filled the air.
>
> Their descendants, now gathered mainly in Government controlled settlements like Papunya and Yuendumu, rarely laugh, and under the added influence of white man's grog, drunken orgies, according to reports, have replaced the old entertainments.
>
> Despite the white man's welfare handouts, the old sense of security and intra-group human dignity appears to have been almost lost. The young people have become, it seems, virtually a lawless community, with all the horrors which that term implies.
>
> The old "law" has largely lost its force, its remaining guardians can no longer control the younger generations, and the new "whiteman's law" has not taken any real root among the young people either.[51]

Chapter 6

Moral violence

[A]ll men deserve what the law does to them. Those men will just have to accept what's happening to them now by the women, like myself, because that way they'll see that we're beginning to stand for our rights as traditionally we couldn't, because they were the dominated people, by the men.[1]

Judy Atkinson asked her fellow Aborigines, "Why are men violent to women?" Their replies established that many Aboriginal men apparently see this violence as the masculine duty of physically punishing insubordinate or undutiful women. In the Northern Territory two women replied to Atkinson, "Men feel they own women", "They think that they can control us". In Western Australia a man commented, "Men who aren't drunk and are violent, are the worst. And the grog isn't an excuse. Only that man can put his fist up".[2] Palm Islander Ester Illin, a career public servant and at times a State ministerial regional adviser, said of her second husband:

He tried to break every bone in my body, he wanted to lead and me to follow. He'd bash my eyes, split my lips. Nothing has changed. Aboriginal men still want to lead the way. I think it's about insecurity; they don't like women upfront. But being beaten didn't put me down, it made me stronger.[3]

A Northern Territory Aboriginal man said to Atkinson, "We have to punish her – sometimes – little bit if she does something wrong". A Northern Territory Aboriginal woman who had endured six violent assaults by her husband, in one of which she suffered a broken arm, said this customary violence was inflicted if:

women or a wife was actually being lazy, not feeding the kids or running off with another man, things like that. People would then agree "Oh she needs that beating".[4]

Basil Sansom, an anthropologist, calls Aboriginal men's severe beatings of women, who have offended men's sensibilities as "righteous" or "moral" violence. He described a particular attack in a fringe dweller's camp which probably occurred in the late 1970s as a rather ritualised process in which the man's "wrongs" were publicly proclaimed and the victim remained passive, as was customary, under the beating. The assembled onlookers who observed this extremely brutal attack did not interfere. A woman finally intervened when death seemed a possibility.[5]

> W]hen somebody "Bin take hidin/floggin/ thrashin" ... the essence ... is in the victim's passivity. The victim takes it and suffers the flogging or beating or hiding to happen without fighting back. More remarkably, the victim does not cringe, cover up, protect head with arms or cover soft parts with hands. And the victim is not restrained with bonds ... For the infliction to occur, the victim must first be totally awed into passivity.[6]

This violence to women was apparent even when first contacts were being made between Aborigines and the English. In about 1790 Phillip had formed, to some extent, friendly relations with an Aborigine, Bannelong. After observing the beatings given to women by both Bannelong and another Aborigine, Colebe, Phillip remonstrated with Bannelong "who [had] beat his wife twice very severely in a short time ... [he] laughed when he was told that it was wrong to beat a woman".[7]

There is evidence that these attitudes among men were widespread in early post-classical Aboriginal society. Indeed traditional law practices against women were so proscriptive that the anthropologist Annette Hamilton considers that rather than women suffering more as a result of colonial exploitation:

> an equally cogent argument for the opposite view could be put: ... [that] the presence of white authority figures may have prevented outright violence from occurring as frequently as it might have done before. These are hypothetical arguments which cannot be substantiated now in any case, since we lack adequate data referring to pre-colonial times and are unlikely to obtain them from living informants.[8]

However, the extreme and spontaneous brutality, of which there are numerous examples from the times of virtually traditional lifestyles, needs to be understood so that the strength of its influence within Aboriginal culture in turn can be comprehended. In about 1953 the following incident was witnessed among the Myeelee, a sub-group of the Gagadju, living in the South Alligator river area. A group were sitting around a camp-fire when the older wife of a leading elder came up and interrupted him with a request when he was speaking.

> Without saying a word he reached forward to the fire and took hold of the unburnt end of large, thick stick. Then with one smooth arcing movement up and across his body, he lifted and swung the stick with great force, its burning end swooshing and flashing as it flew through the air, to be brought with a resounding thump against the side of [his wife's] head ... [He] casually placed the stick back in the fire; ... and said quietly ... "She bin gettin' little bit cheeky ... Might be I bin gunna belt her a little bit ... til she show me fella little bit more respect".[9]

Aboriginal men accused of killings and assault have claimed the "right" of violence against women for being "cheeky" by not cooking meat,[10] being disobedient by not coming into a room when called,[11] playing cards with other women, not minding the children who were with a baby sitter, and refusing to come home when ordered to do so,[12] adultery, being suspected of adultery, and deciding to separate from a de facto spouse. Kaberry observed of traditional society in the East Kimberley that:

> [T]he entire psychic relationship of the sexes is one of great social significance: there is much distrust, hostility, and insinuation of misconduct between them; jealousy, suspicion of infidelity and endless quarrelling with and over women.[13]

The circumstances of a killing for suspected adultery in the late 1920s or early 1930s in the Kimberley, recounted by Grant Ngabidj, fleshes out Kaberry's academic observations. Immediately before this story begins Ngabidj refers to the fact that the men had been singing "that secret law".

> I lay down amongst those blackfellers. And three women came along following the same road that the blackfellers had come on earlier. One was named Wudjingarri. The man who was with her looked around, and because they had come on the same road as the other men that bugger became jealous, "Ah, they bin might be fuckin about long all about woman, that lubra longa middle." He went back and got a shovel spear and sharpened it, singing out in language to us, "I'm goin for kangaroo". "All right", I said to him. That same lot of lubras took up their billy cans and went down hunting for water, and that blackfeller chucked one shovel spear, a

big long one too, and hit that lubra right in the kidney on the back left-hand side just under the shoulder blade. It shot her like a rifle, knocked her out, took the heart and killed her, poor bugger.

The woman was buried, the Wyndham police were contacted through a local missionary, and the killer was arrested. The police took evidence from the women, but Ngabidj did not want to get involved. "I was sitting there but I took no notice. I had nothing to do with those people, asking and asking and asking."[14]

The matter of fact way in which Ngabidj recounts this incident is remarkable. The dead woman was a "poor bugger", but it does not appear that the killer was to be punished by the other men. The police arrived because of the missionary's intervention. The refusal of Ngabidj and the other men to co-operate with the police is understandable as Aboriginal resistance to the incursions of pastoralists in the Kimberley was valiant and fierce, and under leaders like Jandamarra continued well into the 1890s. Conversely, it is interesting to note that the women, possibly because of gender as opposed to cultural solidarity, were prepared to give information to the police.

Over 50 years later both Burbank and the Task Force Report noted that a high degree of jealousy can still be closely linked with aggression.[15] Within the "Mangrove" community, neglect of duties proper to a partner's role or a refusal to have intercourse can be taken as a signal that there is preoccupation with another sexual partner. These signals can operate for either sex, but both Burbank and the Berndts found that it is only the man who has the physical power to give a devastating beating.[16] Jealousy can even lead to violent assaults on pregnant women by punching or kicking, at times leading to death of the foetus. A Queensland woman said to the Task Force:

> Alcohol is not the only problem here ... My ex, he was real violent. When I was eight months pregnant with my last, he kicked me in the stomach to try to get rid of the baby because he said it wasn't his. It was but he wouldn't believe me.

Generally, behaviour that causes suspicion of adultery is often not the type of conduct that would give rise to any concern in most non-Indigenous societies. Men now will punch women in the head or hit them for talking to another man, even if they are in their husband's company.[17]

Jealousy surfaced as a motive again and again in cases from the 1950s to the 1990s where men had inflicted "moral" violence on women. These psychological attitudes and the claimed sanction for severe violence in punishing women together constitute the factual circumstances and "cultural defences" of many of the court cases in which an Aboriginal woman has suffered serious injury or death. The argument is that punishment is merited because the woman has been provocative through her misbehaviour. Even in Victoria, where Aboriginal culture has been so disturbed a similar attitude persists. In the 2000 case of *Bowden*, the defendant had previously frequently assaulted his de facto wife. But after a horrific beating that led to his arrest she said to the police:

> I did not give Raymond permission to give me a flogging. While Raymond was flogging me he didn't seem to care about our unborn child. I am prepared to go to court.

In many of the court cases, men claimed "righteous violence" by stabbing or cutting but there were other forms such as beating women's heads with wood or rocks, or attacks with iron bars. There are traditional cutting sites on the body. Arms and legs are the accepted targets in ritualised fighting. In Burbank's study, stab wounds in men's assaults on women, although numerous, were confined to the limbs. This pattern was so frequent that non-Aboriginal nurses who treated the women called these "punishment places".[18]

Two cases widely separated in time, and only examples of the many that could have been recounted, illustrate the endemic nature of this violence to women. In both the pleas were guilty of manslaughter after de facto wives had died after severe beatings. In the mid-1960s a Department of Aboriginal Affairs welfare officer in giving character evidence said, "The practice of these people in punishing their wives or 'de-facto wives' is to give them considerable beatings". The judge in sentencing the prisoner to 12 months' imprisonment for killing his wife said, "I propose to make allowance for your racial customs".[19] Similar comments were made in the 1982 case of *Jacky Jadurin*. Evidence was given in explanation of his actions, that "in Aboriginal society it is not unusual for women to be beaten if they do not obey their husbands". The court noted that this is often after a great deal of alcohol has been drunk but remarked further this "also ignores the very complex web of relationships between men and women in Aboriginal society".

In some communities it is not proper to interfere when a man is inflicting violence on a woman within a relationship. This does not mean that families do not intervene, or retaliate in cases of violence, but bystanders generally refrain from doing so.

> I've seen women on the ground being kicked in the belly and in the head and no one went to help her. You just didn't do that. You could watch, but you weren't allowed to butt into people's fights.[20]

In remote communities, if moral violence is regarded as being solely between the parties, it is not seen as a matter for the police.[21]

> You see it's not a white man's problem. May be the husband hit his wife. That's a problem on the Aboriginal side.[22]

Two instances from different sources in Queensland cite how Aboriginal women were being beaten on the street, in each case they had suffered recent injuries because of previous violence; a broken collarbone and a broken arm, but no Aboriginal person tried to stop the thrashings.[23] Bolger, in examining Aboriginal violence to women in the Northern Territory, recounted how:

> A woman in an Aboriginal organisation related … [how she found] … a half drunk Aboriginal man standing over a woman and kicking her in the ribs with big boots. Three male field officers were standing by watching. She told them to stop him, whereupon they replied: "You can't interfere, it's Aboriginal Law." Retorting that it was NOT Aboriginal Law to kick a woman like that with big boots, when drunk, she told the man to stop and get out. He was so surprised that he did![24]

However, in some areas, in fights between men and women, or in "morally justified beatings" for domestic transgressions, there can be a cultural restraint on the level of violence.[25] For instance, in *Mungatopi's* case at Bathurst Island other men stopped Mungatopi's first attack upon his wife. When he took her with him in his car he was able to kill her without interference. As Aboriginal society becomes more urbanised, or westernised, however, there is less outdoor living and the protection of public scrutiny might decrease.

A case study by Burbank examined a man's stabbing of his wife, which although on a "traditional [punishment] site" was seen as an assault, as it was committed without any "provocation", he was in a drunken rage. His wife did not accept this violence, and she had community support in refusing to do so.[26] This accords with the findings of the anthropologists cited in the Gordon Report that there can be family intervention and that if the abuse persists the woman can return to her family.[27]

However, culturally-sanctioned violence affects present behaviour because it absolves men from responsibility; women are made the scapegoats for the very violence that is committed upon them.

> Men are of the opinion that they are being somehow forced to commit domestic violence because they are being pushed by their women, in that the women are not doing what they are told.[28]

There are indications that some Aboriginal women will no longer accept customary violence. A 1996 interview in Darwin between a young Aboriginal woman and Susannah Lobez for the Australian Broadcasting Commission's *Law Report*, illustrates the contrasting attitudes between Aboriginal men and women about women's right to seek protection from the general law.

> Did you tell him he was breaching a restraining order to stay away from you?

> Yes, I said that, and all he could say was, "Oh, that's a white man's law; it's not in our law. They're just keeping you away from me, that's what it is, they've brainwashed you" he said.

> Do you think that the restraining order is white man's law and not part of your culture and your life?

> Well it isn't our culture, but it's a law that we can all go for. I mean we're all the same people, you know, and we all live by the same laws and rules.[29]

Chapter 7

The "promise":
customary law marriage

> Certain customary practices and some aspects of tradition are often
> the cause of violence against women ... a whole host of practices
> violate female dignity ... early marriage ... Blind adherence to
> these practices and State inaction with regard to these customs and
> traditions have made possible large scale violence against women
> ... the area of women's rights change is slow to be accepted.[1]

Customary law marriage was an integral part of classical Aboriginal
society, but it can be viewed as being quite inimical to women's
rights, although it has been argued that its suppression would be
equally inimical to the continuation of Aboriginal culture. Sexual
union with very young girls and polygyny rewarded those males
who went through initiation, a ceremony that safeguarded the
transmission of the law. Men could not marry until initiation was
completed, often when they were aged about 25 years or even older.
As men could have many wives, young girls, often betrothed shortly
after birth,[2] could be faced with bridegrooms who were old men. In
extremity women were not divorced from family support; however,
the consensus among female anthropologists is that women were
not, and are not, dominant in these arrangements.[3]

There were disparate obligations for men and women in
marriage. Obedience to the law in marriage relations was enjoined
upon both sexes through the ancestral legends that defined the roles
and responsibilities of both sexes. Neither sex could indulge in
marriage or sexual relations between tribal brothers or sisters upon
pain of death, but otherwise the prohibitions upon behaviour and
duties imposed upon women regarding men were rigorous. Men
did not face corresponding obligations to women. Traditional stories
recount the violent deaths met by women who failed in their
obligations of marrying older husbands without complaint, who

broke the law by daring to hunt meat, who did not provide a sufficient variety of vegetable food for their husbands or even sons (when matricide occurred), who did not provide enough food, or did not prepare it carefully enough, who did not feed their husbands while resenting the time men spent on ceremonies, or who showed jealousy of the husband's other wives, or even gossiped. Men, by comparison, had to be studious about avoidance of mothers-in-law, careful of indiscriminate promiscuity and were prohibited from cannibalism.[4]

The Gordon Inquiry heard evidence that the sexual attitudes, which were embodied in the ancient tradition of customary law marriage, have continued into present post-classical Aboriginal society. The Inquiry reported that, "Considerable anecdotal emphasis has been placed on *'promised marriages'* as providing sanction to men to be able to have sexual relations with young girls".[5] The Inquiry rejected this evidence. They referred to anthropological evidence that *"promise marriage"* could entail the betrothal of mere infants but made several qualifications which were represented as ameliorating the brunt of marriage arrangements.

> These marriages are not to be simply read as the "simple domestic arrangements between two people, but involve the character of male accomplishment, and negotiation between a man and his prospective wife's relatives".

Further, "Young girls were not expected to take up all their duties upon being handed over" and "Full sexual intercourse, according to Kaberry, was not allowed until after puberty".

These facts are not disputed. Indeed in the 2003 Northern Territory case of *Hales v Jamilmira*, which concerned a customary law marriage consummated between a man approaching 50 years and a 15-year-old girl, the Court of Appeal found that:

> The arrangement does not portend a future relationship but established a relationship between the parties from the time the arrangement is made. Mutual obligations were created and have been met over the years.

Nonetheless, when the meaning of the words in the Gordon Report are analysed, none of the claimed ameliorating circumstances such as, "They [the young girls] initially entered a phase of preparation", obviate the fact that customary law marriage can be seen, in today's contexts, as an abuse of girl-child's rights.

The sexual use of young girls by older men, indeed often much older men, was an intrinsic part of Aboriginal culture, a heritage that cannot be easily denied. Indeed as *Jamilmira's* case shows, in western Arnhem Land customary law marriage is part of living culture. Nonetheless, in general law terms the promise entails carnal knowledge of girls below the age of consent. Hence the submissions made to the Gordon Inquiry by Aborigines, who are observing child sexual abuse in their communities, that this accepted culture still influences present behaviour, should be regarded very seriously.

Kaberry said of behaviour entailed by the promise that in the Kimberley mimicry of intercourse began at about four years of age, and actual experimentation by girls at eight or nine years.[6] The Berndts describe this as "a survival of … indigenous culture rather than a modern innovation. Quite often this takes place with older men or youths".[7] Kaberry regards these practices as preparation of young girls for marriage to much older men, to challenge that would be "part of the whole question of altering the status of women in Aboriginal society".[8] Evidence was given in *Jamilmira's* case that intercourse within customary law marriage with very young girls was "entirely appropriate-indeed morally correct".

That these beliefs could affect general behaviour is evident from the 1974 Northern Territory case of *Lazarus Mangukala* (or *Mungurala*). The 18-year-old defendant pleaded guilty to having unlawful carnal knowledge of a ten-year-old girl, with her willing consent. She was already post menarche, the stage at which a promise could be consummated. The victim had been the promised wife of the defendant's grandfather, whose death then caused her to become the promised wife of the defendant, although at the time of the offence the defendant was unaware that this was so. Both the victim and the defendant were living at Oenpelli, a remote traditional community in Arnhem Land. Evidence was given on his behalf that although customary law had been transgressed the behaviour would not be regarded seriously, and the defendant would only be sent for a while to an outstation. Justice Forster took a culturally relativist position, that is he took account of traditional culture rather than taking account of the child's position, and in sentencing said:

> I do not regard this offence as seriously as if both participants were white. This is of course not to say that the virtue of Aboriginal girls is any less value than that of white girls, but simply that social customs appear to be different.

Mangukala, who had been in custody for three weeks, was sentenced to 12 months' imprisonment with a minimum of eight months fully suspended upon entering a two-year good behaviour bond. Yet this behaviour would have would have been regarded as serious child abuse and aberrant in non-Aboriginal society, and it would have incurred a heavy sentence.

The Gordon Report's conclusions, quoted above, establish that young girls were the property of their community, the arrangement for the promise was made without their consent, they were "handed over", and they were the reward for "male accomplishment". It is a matter of little grace that actual marital sexual relations did not start until after puberty when this could occur at ten years. In the 1959 Northern Territory case of *Dumaia*, in which a three-week-old baby girl had been killed by a blow to the head with a shield, Justice Kriewaldt several times referred to the mother of the child (who was not the alleged killer) as a "little girl". In *Jamilmira's* case genealogical evidence covering the mid to late 1970s was cited being that:

> [A]mong the twenty mothers who were born after 1950, the average age at the birth of the first child was 15.6 years, 16 of the 20 bore their first child when under 16 years.

Matrimonial residence usually was patrilocal so that depending on particular customs, between the ages of about ten to 12 years according to Kaberry and McCarthy,[9] or eight to 15 years according to Kenneth Maddock,[10] a girl left her family and clan to live with her husband in his territorial clan to which her children then belonged.[11] Social organisation differed between areas, but Ngabidj related a Kimberley practice, the prelude to which, in his account, was of a child bride being taken crying from her parents, who then go far away. The child then had to bear sexual initiation by many men before being taken over by her husband.[12]

The Berndts recount various practices, some of which are similar to those recounted by Ngabidj, but not all of which were as inimical.[13] In Jamilmira's case evidence was given that among the Burarra people the young girl was not handed over until her grandmother had ascertained that she was sexually mature. The evidence also established that there was a transition period before actual consummation, during which the girl's family were still available to her, and that this was so in other areas. On the other hand, raids on other tribes to steal women were part of patrilocal structure. Successful raiding parties abducted small girls and women.[14] For instance, this was one of the causes of the continual warfare between the Arrente and the Matujarra from 1875 to 1891.[15]

Traditional marriage was the foundation of an economic unit. As a man aged, he had a succession of wives to provide for him and the children. When the wives aged in their turn, younger women became available to provide services to the family group, including sexual services to the husband. In the 1830s in the Monaro, Lingard referred to "an old man ... who had five wives; these were given to him in order to maintain him".[16] In Warrabri in the 1960s the same considerations ruled. Old men looked upon young wives "as their pension ticket"; it was also a matter of prestige to have a young wife. The wives' parents also benefited. In the 1970s when a young girl from Yirrkala was badly beaten for refusing to marry, a journalist observed that with the conversion to money economy bride prices to be paid to the parents were from $500 to $1,000.[17] In *Jamilmira's* case evidence was given that traditionally a man hunted or fished for the parents but now "money is the way".

Hence customary law marriage was integral to maintaining traditional economies, so in one sense young girls were the foundation of society, in another sense they were on the lowest rung of that society. Alie Wurraputiwai of the Tiwi, whose father Milawerri had 20 wives, explained this power structure in which young girls were subordinate to the wishes of all others, including the older wives.

> Because his father had shown great promise as a leader, a number of fathers had betrothed their daughters to him, so that when Milawerri became a big man (leader of power and prestige), those who had betrothed their daughters to him could depend upon him to support them in all their enterprises. He would be under this obligation to them all his life ... The more wives a man had the more prestige – and the more food gatherers he had, which enabled the family to raise itself well above the bare subsistence level.[18]

The missionary activity of men like Taplin[19] at Point Macleay, South Australia, and Father Gsell[20] at Bathurst Island, in promoting Christian marriages of young men and women outside traditional law struck at the very foundations of Aboriginal culture.[21] The social organisation of the clan and the authority of the old men were destroyed. In 1870, Taramindjeri, a powerful medicine man of the Narrinyeri (Ngarrindjeri) in South Australia, shouted his anger at this defiance of the law.[22]

> What do they want of us, arah! Defying the old men? ...
> Defying and laughing at us? ...
> What do they want to do that for? ...
> Get them! Bring them here, so that with the clubs we may flog
> them.

Within the strict confines of "right line" marriages clan groups consolidated rights to shared territories through exchanging women.

> Man from there [Cook Reef]...
> Women from here [Cape Lavery].
> They get that woman.
> Man from here get woman from there.
> They change women ... swap.
> Man live here [Cape Lavery]
> And man live there [Cook Reef] ...

In the 1973 report on Aboriginal Land Rights, Justice Woodward noted that in the Northern Territory – while the family group will spend much of its time in the land held by the clan – the head of the clan would expect to freely visit the country of his mother's clan and of his wife's clan. The wife or wives come from, and will belong to a different clan, their clan. Wives might not necessarily, although they usually do, come from the one clan. Anthropological evidence in *Jamilmira's* case was that "the Burrarra marriage system is intimately bound up with complex considerations of estate tenure and religion".[23]

As women aged they could attain considerable prestige in traditional society. In some areas women possibly participated in making betrothals, although Annette Hamilton provides evidence that in reality this did not occur frequently.[24] If an older woman was widowed she might have some choice in a subsequent marriage. Although among the Tiwi:

> men who were perceived to be no worth in the community had difficulty finding wives and would usually only have access to old widows whom they usually married immediately after the Pukamani ceremony of the widow's husband. Most married men had an old wife before receiving a young one.[25]

Generally women widowed for a second time could choose whether or not to make another marriage.[26] Some women had a degree of autonomy within marriage as in some areas of the central desert women could retreat to the *jilimi* (the single women's camp and a protected refuge) if they did not wish to have sexual relations.[27] This could be, for instance, if a woman did not agree with her husband's choice of a subsequent wife or wives. A 1984 Northern Territory case, *Charlie Limbiari Jagamara*, illustrates both how inviolate the *jilimi* was for women, and how disturbing their retreat to it could be for men. Jagamara, a 75-year-old traditional Warlpiri man, speared a man who later died because Jagamara believed he was having sexual relations with his traditionally married wife. In addition to other grounds, Jagamara's suspicions were aroused because his wife had withdrawn to the *jilimi*. It was accepted by the court that Jagamara was behaving in accordance with traditional law, that he had been severely beaten, speared and cut, and he was sentenced to the rising of the court.

Both Kaberry and Hamilton noted that young girls sometimes rebelled against arranged marriages, and strongly disliked the promised husband,[28] but customary law sanctions were strictly enforced by a beating or death if they did so. This was recorded in the times of first contact in the Monaro[29] and was recalled by a Djimbawu elder from Queensland in 1994.[30] However, the prospect of the union could be a terrible ordeal. Alice Nannup, who was born in the Pilbara in 1911, recounts the horror she felt when as a young girl of nine years her promised husband, who was about 60 years old, would come to visit her. She was then living with her mother on a station.

> (H)e'd say "When you're ready to come with me, you're coming, whether you like it or not. ... You my woman, you feed me." I said to him, "Mirda, nyinda buga", That means, "no! you buga, you stink." "Never mind about the buga," he said. "You my manga (woman)."[31]

Her widowed mother, who was herself facing pressure to re-marry, left the station rather than force her daughter into this marriage.[32] Hamilton notes that often the only supportive group available to Aboriginal women was the mother-daughter bond, the relationship of the matrilineally related females, not merely the actual biological relationship of western society. This is one of the reasons that Hamilton doubts that mothers were involved in arranging marriages, or if they were so they would not admit to it, because of girls' resentment.

Cowlishaw considers that infanticides were prompted by young girls' motives of resentment and revenge for being forced into a child-bearing role, "by committing infanticide she denies her brother a niece to bestow, or her husband a son to follow him in his cult rituals".[33] However, there could be mortal danger for the young mother, in circumstances of other than prescribed infanticide, if her babies did not live. In the 1967 Northern Territory case of *Garlbuma*, a young woman of 20 years was ritually executed because her two babies died.

As the force of traditional law has weakened, young girls have openly rebelled against customary law marriage. Oodgeroo Noonuccal's poem *The Child Wife* is a contemporary expression of girls' rebellion against and repugnance to these promised marriages.[34] At Warrabri in the 1960s young girls were prepared "to take the tribe on" rather than marry. On occasion they rushed into the houses in the "white" settlement to escape "the promised". Young girls wanted to, and did, form relationships with young men of their choice. Many of the girls were badly beaten up, and by their mothers also. Maddock noted similar reluctance at Mornington Island in Queensland in the 1960s and found that by the 1970s even in the Western Desert fewer young girls would accept their promised husbands. In 1982 Aboriginal elders inflicted bashings and pack rape, "sacred rape", upon young Gurindji women in the Northern Territory in order to force them to enter promised marriages.[35] In *Jamilmira's* case an Aboriginal man from Maningrida gave evidence that while the custom was breaking down and men would decide to marry for love, "if the promised wife does not want to go to the man there is 'big trouble'".[36]

Until *Jamilmira's* case, the judiciary and government had been reluctant to support women's rights as victims when customary law came into conflict with the general law. There appeared to be acceptance that Indigenous defendants had *a de facto* claim of right to commit serious assaults on young girls when enforcing "the promise". These assaults would otherwise have been regarded as criminal offences. In at least three cases in the late 1960s and early 1970s, Anglo-Australian law found that young girls' individual rights were subordinate to obligations imposed on them by traditional law.

In 1969 a 13-year-old girl, Rita Galkama, of the Yirrkala people, was widowed. She was then sent to the household of her deceased husband's brother, Jack Milirrpum Marika, aged 42 years. On her fourteenth birthday Marika attempted to take Rita as his third wife. When she refused, Marika "belted her", tore off her clothes and tried to break her right leg. He was charged with aggravated assault. At the Magistrate's Court at Gove, his defence was that "unless Yirrkala

Aborigines were given immunity from European law, the 'heart would be torn from their society'". The court accepted this argument, which is reminiscent of Taramindjeri's 1870 cries about enforcing traditional marriage in South Australia. It is incredible that the magistrate described the situation "as a storm in a teacup", and said he would not record a conviction against Marika for aggravated assault. Indeed he ignored the assault completely. Marika was merely fined $5 for resisting arrest. It was Rita Galkama who suffered for her defiance. She continued her education at Kormilda Aboriginal College in Darwin but she knew that possibly she would be permanently ostracised from her people at Yirrkala.[37]

In 1973 "the promise" arose in relation to the rights of a child and her natural family, but the significance of this case is that it illustrates the federal government's ambivalence about safeguarding young girls' rights when by doing so Indigenous rights would be contravened. Nola Gneda Garrli had been fostered in a non-Aboriginal home in Darwin from shortly after birth. But at birth she had been promised to a 14-year-old youth at Maningrida, her family home. When she was seven years old the Department of Aboriginal Affairs returned Nola to her mother. Her father said he would not force Nola to fulfil the promise.[38] On 20 September 1973, Senator Cavanagh, in response to a question in the Senate, said that the issue was the return of Nola to her natural parents, but he added a rider of general significance in relation to rights, "The Government's policy in regard to the law in Aboriginal culture that a girl should go to her promised husband has not been decided".[39]

Opposing submissions were made to the ALRC in relation to its 1986 report on customary law. It was contended that restriction of customary law marriage practices would contribute to the breakdown of traditional law; conversely it was said that traditional marriage was inimical to human rights. Cases were cited of young girls being abducted or beaten to enforce customary law marriages and that when this violence occurred there was community opposition to the girls having access to the police. Some communities agreed there should be a degree of choice as long as the marriage was a "right skin" marriage. Anthropologists' evidence was that there were some changes, girls might finish school, the age gap had narrowed, and the practice was becoming less frequent.[40]

The Northern Territory government's theoretical position was that customary law marriage amounted "to slavery" and that women should have freedom of choice. However, in practice the government refused to interfere with traditional law practices. It stated that if women were coerced they could use the resources of the police, the Aboriginal Legal Service (ALS) and the Department of Community Development, "which were readily available in most areas".[41] In view of the even now existing restrictions on women who are the victims of violence in gaining access to help when they are living in isolated semi-traditional communities, and the attitude of ALS in defending men's rights in the courts in cases of violence, the then government's views appear to be a pious hope. Its optimism about legal safeguards for women was not consistent with the realities of their situation.

The ALRC 1986 report followed this *laissez faire* approach to women's rights. It found that allowing the continuance of customary law marriage meant that the Australian government could be refusing to honour seven international rights conventions all of which had been ratified by 1986. But the Commission preferred to endorse Indigenous autonomy.

> A new law ... (about customary law marriage) ... would in its own way involve additional intrusions of the legal system into Aboriginal society. ... Any conflicts that arise within Aboriginal society should be resolved internally.[42]

In 1969, in reporting *Galkama*, the press raised the issue of internationally recognised women's rights by paraphrasing the 1967 Declaration on the Elimination of Discrimination against Women; namely a woman should have the right to refuse a marriage in which she is promised or given by her parents for a consideration, and a woman should not be "inherited" on her husband's death.[43] Earlier and later international conventions also affirmed these rights, namely Article 16 of the Universal Declaration of Human Rights by which men and women are "entitled to equal rights as to marriage, during marriage and its dissolution",[44] and in 1981, the Convention on the Elimination of all Forms of Discrimination against Women (CEDAW). Hence, given the imbalance of gender power which is entailed in customary law marriage, the ALRC's position in its 1986 report could be viewed as affirming Indigenous rights in derogation of a duty under international conventions to promote a rule of law which would protect girl-childs' rights. However, as will be discussed subsequently, there has been a significant shift by judges in acknowledging these rights. Despite this, and despite mounting concern about child abuse in the Indigenous community, in 2002 in

Jamilmira's case in the Northern Territory Supreme Court, Justice Gallop affirmed the Indigenous right of customary law marriage.[45]

This significant case has a tortuous history. In April 2002 Jackie Pascoe Jamilmira, a fully-initiated Aborigine, who had been educated in Darwin, was convicted in the Court of Summary Jurisdiction at Maningrida of having unlawful sexual intercourse with a female under the age of 16 years and that he unlawfully discharged a firearm. The facts were undisputed. Jamilmira was born in May 1951. In 1979 he entered a "culturally arranged" marriage in which there was binge drinking and violence. In 1986, a girl was born to another family and shortly after her birth a promise was arranged. In 1994 Jamilmira killed his wife, he was convicted of manslaughter and he was sentenced to seven years' imprisonment with a non-parole period of three-and-a-half years.

Jamilmira overcame his binge drinking and throughout the years continued paying off the girl's family in accordance with traditional custom. Normally there would have been a meeting between the two family groups to decide when she would be given to him. However, in 2001 there was supposedly concern that the girl was not attending school properly; she was "prowling" at night and using "gunga". Her grandmother said that she was sexually mature, and according to Jamilmira's evidence, although there was no correct family meeting, they were anxious that cohabitation should commence. Sexual intercourse occurred against the girl's will after she was brought to Jamilmira's outstation at Gamurru-Gayurra 120 kilometres east of Maningrida, her family home. The following day Jamilmira prevented the girl's attempt to return home in the company of friends by firing a 12 gauge shot gun into the air. The next day he was arrested. Jamilmira said to the police that he knew that he had committed an act of carnal knowledge, "but it's Aboriginal custom – my culture. She is my promised wife".[46] A magistrate sentenced Jamilmira to concurrent sentences of 13 months' imprisonment to be suspended after serving four months on the first count and to 18 months' imprisonment to be suspended after serving two months on the second count.

In October 2002 Jamilmira appealed to the Supreme Court of the Northern Territory. The principal lawyer from the North Australian Aboriginal Legal Aid Service (NAALAS) relied on expert anthropological evidence to argue that promised marriages were common and morally correct under Aboriginal law. Jamilmira acknowledged that he had deliberately chosen to follow traditional law. He was confident that the offence against general law would not be disclosed as matters between a husband and wife were considered private business. Further, he thought that his actions were correct and that traditional Aboriginal law and culture should be accommodated in the general law. Justice Gallop apparently accepted this view. His Honour reportedly said, "She knew what was expected of her". Jamilmira's sentences were reduced from 13 months to 24 hours for the carnal knowledge and from two months to 14 days for the discharge of the firearm.[47]

There was widespread public censure of Justice Gallop's decision. However, one letter from a non-Aborigine living in the Northern Territory spelled out the cultural importance to Aborigines of "right line" marriages. The girl's "playing up" would be seen as wrong, relations with her promised husband would be seen as right. "Wrong line" associations are tantamount to incest (children born of these liaisons are unable to participate properly in ceremonial life, and to a lesser extent social life) and parents and elders are concerned of about maintaining the integrity of the kinship system.[48]

The Director of Public Prosecutions appealed the decision. In April 2003 the Northern Territory Court of Appeal allowed that appeal in a majority decision. Chief Justice Martin was satisfied that Jamilmira was truthful about his perceptions of his rights according to Aboriginal culture and that he knew he was breaking the law of the Northern Territory but he did so "because he wanted to observe the traditions of his culture". However, his Honour said that:

> Notwithstanding the cultural circumstances surrounding this particular event, the protection given by the law to girls under the age of 16 from sexual intercourse is a value of the wider community, which prevails over that of this section of the Aboriginal community. To hold otherwise would trivialise the law and send the wrong message not only to Aboriginal men but others in Aboriginal society who may remain supportive of the system which leads to the commission of the offence.

Justice Riley said of the 24 hours' sentence that:

> It is a penalty which... fails to recognise the seriousness of the offending. It pays no account to either general or specific deterrence. Whilst proper recognition of claims to mitigation of sentence must be accorded, and such claims will include relevant aspects of customary law, the court must be influenced by the need to protect members of the community, including women and children from behaviour which the wider community consider inappropriate.[49]

NAALAS supported Jamilmira's application to the High Court to seek special leave to appeal against sentence. In February 2004 Queen's Counsel argued on behalf of Jamilmira that sentencing should be in the context of Aboriginal culture. Jamilmira had complied with customary law and the protection of the girl was only an issue "if it is perceived that she needs protection from her customary law environment". He said that effectively the Northern Territory Court of Appeal had "disapproved of the cultural reality of the Burarra people's marriage customs". The High Court did not accept the argument that cultural imperatives overrode rights protected by the criminal law. The court held that, "it is not shown to be in the interests of justice or more generally, that special leave be granted".[50] It may be difficult now for any Aboriginal man to enforce customary law marriage with girls below the age of consent.

Cultural relativism is always a difficult issue, but this debate should be settled in favour of women's rights, when culture not only contravenes international rights, but also those who must bear the practices of that culture express extreme revulsion. The victim impact statement in *Jamilmira's* case largely reflects those of many victims of common sexual assault:

> I am angry for what he done. I was sad and upset. I think about it all the time. I always get angry with everyone. This makes me upset.[51]

Further, as *Mangukala's* case established, and as the evidence before the Gordon Inquiry also attests, where culture endorses practices of sexual use of young girls, then it is hard to constrain these practices which are regarded as a norm and not abhorrent. Indeed, the inquest into the death of 15-year-old Aboriginal girl, Susan Taylor, who hanged herself on 12 February 1999, directly led to the Western Australian government's establishment of the Gordon Inquiry. At that inquest the coroner heard allegations that a possible cause of Susan's death was sexual abuse by much older men.[52]

Chapter 8

Rape

A young girl was gang-raped by youths. Their families were feuding. She ran to my sister-in-law's house followed by the gang who beat in the door.[1]

When the same Community reports three men raping a three-year-old child, who was raped by another offender ten days later, there is a crisis of huge proportions.[2]

The crucial element in the offence of rape is a woman's lack of consent to the sexual use of her person. At common law, rape is held not to have occurred if the accused can establish an honest, but not necessarily reasonable, belief that the woman was consenting to sexual relations. Mistake about consent nullifies intent, the state of mind, which the prosecution must prove the defendant had at the time of committing the act of penetration, if a conviction is to be secured.[3] Whether the belief was reasonable or not is relevant only to whether it was in fact held.[4] In the Code States, the mistaken belief must be reasonable as well as honest.[5] The burden of proof of intent is on the Crown. The central concept of rape in general law is the violation of individual rights.

Conversely, in traditional Aboriginal society the primary focus was on communal rights rather than individual rights. In many areas the society was polygynous and women were sexually available to other men at the behest of their husbands in hospitality, for ceremonial use in religious celebrations and through the punishment of "sacred rape". These mores beg the general law question of determining the perpetrator's intent. Further, women may have truly consented to some of these acts, for instance religious ceremonies, yet to other acts, within the confines of traditional society; there was probably no other practical option than consent.[6] Therefore, a human rights analysis could view the women as sexual and economic property, and these acts of multiple sexual penetration, particularly when inflicted as punishment, could be considered as rape.

Do these traditional law practices then constitute a cultural norm whereby the sexual penetration of a woman is acceptable, either irrespective of her consent or because the concept of a woman exercising her will in these circumstances is inconceivable? How far did these practices affect general attitudes? It is now difficult to say. In the 1790s, Governor Phillip[7] and Captain Watkin Tench[8] speak of Aboriginal women being beaten when sexual intercourse was refused, or of "ravishment" and "violent gratification of lust". In 1825 De Bougainville, who was sympathetic to the plight of Aborigines, noted "that young girls are brutally kidnapped from their families, violently dragged to isolated spots and are ravished after being subjected to a good deal of cruelty".[9] This may be a reference to customary law marriage, and these of course are external observations of another culture.

Nonetheless, at what point does the authority of traditional law for "rape" cease? That is, irrespective of human rights, when does a public act become a private wrong? For example a 19-year-old Gurindji woman claimed in 1982 that bashings and pack rape were instigated by tribal elders to ensure that girls married traditionally.[10] Given that senior males were, and are, the dominant authority and that they were attempting to enforce customary law marriage can this be regarded as "authorised rape" sanctified by traditional law? Even within the context of traditional society, these rapes hover on the edge of private wrongs. In absolute terms they clearly are a violation of women's human rights.

Behaviour that moves even further from the core of rapes sanctified by customary law is when a woman "might be punished for 'too much running around' by forcing her to have sexual intercourse with a number of men one after another".[11] The opinion of Melissa Lucashenko, an Aborigine, is that indiscriminate violence was unlikely even in terms of sheer survival and "that indigenous violence before the invasion of Europeans was neither random nor individualistic but sanctioned by law".[12] For cultural relativists, the permitted sexual use of Aboriginal women might now be a grey area as in traditional society it was in a different context from rape *per se*.

Many Aborigines have said that "white law" is more lenient towards sexual offenders than traditional Aboriginal law under which sexual violence was punishable by death'.[13] The difficulty now is whether this punishment can be linked to rape *per se*. Rape possibly needs to be seen in the wider context of unsanctioned sexual relations that threatened customary law marriage and which were serious offences against social structure. Further, sexual relations outside the right "skin" were abhorrent and tantamount to incest.[14] These offences were punishable by death or crippling,[15] although punishment at times could fall more heavily on women.[16]

Tench observed cases of what would now be called "pay-back" for rapes in which severe punishment, although short of death, was inflicted upon the offender.[17] In the courts there has been contradictory evidence from male elders and anthropologists about traditional attitudes towards rape. Several factors contribute to this disagreement: traditional law is not uniform, the control exerted by male elders within the communities, their monopoly of giving evidence before the courts, and the procedural difficulty of having this material introduced into evidence because of the social prohibitions which prevent young Aboriginal women from speaking of sexual matters.[18] There is now confusion about how rape was perceived traditionally. This confusion has not been assisted by conflicting evidence in the courts and in some instances by judicial observations based on the acceptance of cultural defences that the violation of Aboriginal women was within accepted social usages.

These complex issues arose in two leading Northern Territory cases in May and August 1980: primarily in *Lane, Hunt and Smith* but also in *Gus Forbes.* These cases originated in the one drunken pack rape by five Aboriginal men of an Aboriginal woman. Lane, Hunt and Smith pleaded guilty. Forbes, who subsequently murdered the victim, pleaded not guilty to murder and rape, but was convicted on both counts. The sad circumstances of the events reflect on the general plight of many Aborigines. The rapes and murder occurred in the dry bed of the Todd River at Alice Springs. Defence counsel described this as "an area of complete anarchy and lawlessness".

The victim had been discharged from hospital that day, and in the evening she unfortunately approached these men, who had been drinking flagons of port and great quantities of beer and asked them for a cigarette. Defence counsel submitted in mitigation of penalty, with some hesitation because it approached being an outrageous submission, the victim's action in making an approach to the men in these circumstances. Counsel then referred to the context of the crime, "the situation of life in the Todd River for Aboriginal people".

However, the most significant outcome of *Lane, Hunt and Smith* is Justice Gallop's conclusions about traditional attitudes to rape.

He said it was an issue that both perplexed and concerned him because:

> The punishment which I impose must be seen to be a well-deserved punishment according to white man's community standards and also according to Aboriginal standards ... There is evidence before me, which I accept, that rape is not considered as seriously in Aboriginal communities as it is in the white community, except in certain circumstances which do not apply here, and indeed the chastity of women is not as importantly regarded as in white communities. Apparently the violation of an Aboriginal women's integrity is not nearly as significant as it is in a white community. Rather on the evidence it is regarded as a matter of dishonour so far as the woman's husband and family are concerned and hence we have the integration of those factors of inevitable and certain pay-back by the woman's family and the disgrace of the wrong-doer's family.[19]

In fact, possibly because it is from a gender perspective, the expert evidence about the impact of rape in traditional culture in this case is somewhat contradictory, or at the least ambiguous. Defence counsel adduced evidence from Diane Bell who said that it was "very hard to discuss *women's* (italics added) attitudes to rape". But although reluctant to disclose her private conversations with Aboriginal women Bell did say that when "a man rapes a woman it is regarded as a transgression, as an assault on her sexual character and there is no doubt that punishment against a person who does commit this crime is carried out and it is usually very severe". The punishment was a beating particularly around the genitals, which would be inflicted by the use of sticks and bars. Defence counsel relied on Bell's statement that drunkenness affected responsibility in that a person would be "outside of that [Aboriginal] society. He submitted that "the crime of rape in Aboriginal society ... is ... definitely regarded as being different from the way that European people regard rape". Yet Bell had said that women did regard rape seriously and that there was severe punishment.

The Crown also introduced evidence from Noel Wallace from the Australian National University, who for over 12 years had been working with the people of the Western Desert to record their mythologies. Lane, Hunt and Smith were all from the Western Desert. Wallace said that rape was not considered "the cardinal sin" in Aboriginal society that it is in European society, except when it involved incest. Then the man "would certainly be put to death, as is the child ensuing from that union". There were some ceremonies where ceremonial sexual intercourse "takes a very prominent role". In the Western Desert mythology, "that apparently flows through most of the mythology, the male spirit ancestor is continually chasing the female spirit ancestor with the intent to rape-sometimes he catches her sometimes he does not".

The judge here raised the important issue of whether women had consented to ceremonial intercourse. Apparently Bell had not committed herself on this point in her evidence. Counsel said, "It's a difficult area for Europeans to get this type of information". Wallace did apparently indicate that "it was looked upon as an enjoyable experience and not as against anyone's will". Nonetheless, whatever the men's traditional perspective, the uncontested evidence was that victim had to be held down by several men in turn during the rape. In fact, Forbes eventually killed her to stop her cries.

The ambiguous evidence about rape has caused comment from both the ALRC and John McCorquodale, a lawyer who has exhaustively examined many criminal cases involving Aborigines.[20] The latter noted that Bell's evidence was inconsistent with her contemporary work. In *Law: The Old and the New*, published in 1980, Bell and Ditton state, "women said that under the old law, sexual violence was punishable by death". McCorquodale examined the reasons for this internal contradiction in Bell's views and the contradiction of her evidence with Wallace's in the trial. Bell's evidence in the book about death for rape came from Aborigines living on Murray Downs a European managed cattle station. Hence Bell's contradictory opinions might be because of differences in traditional societies, or some confusion among her informants, in the circumstances of the breakdown of customary law, about which acts of illicit sexuality, for example, incest, "relations outside the right skin", actually merited death. McCorquodale contrasted Bell and Ditton's report with Wallace's evidence about Western Desert society, and stressed "the cultural diversity and vibrancy of Aboriginal acculturation, such that the view of rape might be regarded as falling within some part of a continuum accommodating such acculturation".

In sentencing Forbes for rape and murder, Justice Gallop referred to the legislation that provided that when Aborigines were convicted of murder account must be "taken of native law and custom and its application to the facts of the offence and any evidence which may be tendered in mitigation of penalty".[21] His Honour again took account that pay-back would occur, although here apparently rather for the killing than the rape.[22] Justice Gallop noted the seriousness with which the community regarded this "horrible callous, brutal crime warranting heavy punishment", and took account of these views but also that, "[a]pparently the violation of an Aboriginal woman's integrity is not nearly as significant as it is in a white community".[23] These conclusions have been reached in other jurisdictions; even in the 1991 Western Australian case of *Mungkilli, Martin and Mintuma*, Justice Millhouse accepted evidence that:

> Forcing women to have sexual intercourse is not socially acceptable, but it is not regarded with the seriousness that it is by white people.[24]

Nonetheless, cases do support Bell's view that the traditional punishment for rape was a severe physical beating and hence it must have been a serious offence, even if not a capital one. Women carried out genital beatings of alleged rapists with digging sticks in two recorded cases in 1977 and 1989.[25] Bell and Nelson noted by 1989 that women's power to inflict punishment was being restricted. For fear of women's revenge either local policemen, or Aboriginal male police aides, were placing accused rapists in protective custody.[26] In the 1997 case of *Maynard Daniel*, the payback for three rapes was a severe kicking by the male relatives of the complainant. Daniel was left with cracked ribs but he was only caused discomfort for two weeks.

In considering the alleged tolerance of rape, a difficulty is that "sacred rape" has been pleaded to obfuscate rape *per se*. For instance, in 1969 an alleged occurrence of rape being inflicted as punishment on women at Yuendumu was raised in the Senate by Senator Cavanagh (later to become Minister of Aboriginal Affairs in the Whitlam Government) and also in the House of Representatives. The circumstances in which the rape had allegedly occurred were denied by the government of the day in both Chambers, but it can be inferred from the particularly detailed allegations that indeed three young women at Yuendumu were taken into the bush by six men (one of whom carried a rifle) to be "repeatedly raped" as punishment for an offence.[27]

Whether the incident at Yuendumu could be classified as "sacred rape" is a moot point. The events occurred on a welfare reserve where non-Aborigines were employed. They were aware of the incident, but did not intervene. In one sense their passivity supports the argument that this was traditional behaviour with which non-Aborigines felt they should not interfere (although it was alleged that they did not do so because they were frightened of losing their employment). In another sense the whole situation (welfare reserve and European employment) negates the concept that this was traditional behaviour in the true sense, and indeed it could be seen as another example of men using so-called customary law to their advantage.

Sacred rape was the basis of an unsuccessful customary law defence in the 1980 Northern Territory case of *Bango Anglitchi*. The seven male defendants, all of whom lived traditionally, pleaded guilty to a charge of conspiracy to rape two girls aged 13 and 14 years. Two of the accused were tribal elders, and one was the father of one of the girls. A plea based on customary law was raised with particular reference to the two elders. Defence counsel relied on Professor Stanner's work on mass rape in traditional society, the evidence being "that an Aboriginal woman who offended, may in the past, traditionally have been required to repay by sacred coitus". Justice Muirhead was not convinced that the girls had committed a traditional offence. He found that the father was not under duress from possible tribal retribution, and that "none acted under cultural impulse or fear". Indeed the motivation of one elder was "lust and liquor" not "tribal lore", references to which was a convenient form of self-justification. Justice Muirhead's observations illustrate his perception of the dilemma consideration of traditional law posed for judges.

> In its work involving Aborigines, this court has sought to understand and respect not only the difficulties, but the true traditions and laws of the Aboriginal ... This court makes allowance for ... tribal law, but the law we apply must be careful to ensure that such old customs or laws are not falsely applied or utilised in the exploitation of other people. ... In this case, there has been ... an effort to justify the inexcusable by reference to tribal lore.

Confusion about customary law in relation to sexual use of women has left an inimical heritage for Aboriginal women who are victims of rape *per se*. In 1990 Sharon Payne, an Aboriginal woman, blamed defence counsel for abusing customary law when Aboriginal accused have asserted the "traditional right to rape".[28] She describes this as another example of "bullshit" law.[29]

> As an Aboriginal woman, I find the implications of increasingly common findings based on so-called cultural norms frightening. Apart from the fact that these types of defences set a dangerous precedent, they also denigrate Aboriginal men and Aboriginal culture.

Payne's observations are from a contemporary and revisionist view-point of ancient cultural practices such as "sacred rape" which, whatever their place in traditional society, have adversely affected women's present rights. Judicial findings on the evidence of community standards, relied upon in support of a customary law "defence", have influenced judges to give lighter sentences in the interests of reconciling each society's idea of justice. Yet it can be argued that by doing so, a grave wrong was done to Aboriginal women. Because traditional society was breaking down, concepts of traditional society as it was seen to be, but without the legalistic principles of that society which had existed, militated against Aboriginal women being given the protection of deterrent sentencing. Traditional concepts of sacred rape or group rape under any name, or on any pretext, should not mean that Aboriginal women are subjected to rapes, an assault from which every other Australian woman is protected. Perhaps as traditional practices come to be less frequently observed, "the right to rape" will be less frequently claimed and the concept of rape *per se* will become paramount.

Bango Anglitchi's case is evidence that from at least 1980 some judges have been more wary of accepting these "cultural defences". In the 1988 case of *Dennis Narjic*, where the accused pleaded guilty to four counts of rape, Justice Maurice refused to accept a plea in mitigation that it was "normative behaviour". A more ambiguous judicial comment was made in the 1990 Western Australian case of *Andrew Leering*. Leering, a "tribal" Aborigine aged 19 years, who was in regular employment as a station hand, held down a 16-year-old girl whom his co-offender had hit over the head with rocks in order that he, the co-offender, could rape her five times. While doing so Leering made his intention known of also committing rape. He was very drunk at the time. Leering pleaded guilty and a Commissioner sentenced him. The Commissioner commented on the accused's callous attitude and drew from that the inference that "rape is not entirely abnormal in his (the accused's) peer group". He possibly did not mean to imply that the community condoned rape, but rather that this was the reality which Aboriginal women endured. The Crown appealed against a sentence of six months' imprisonment for deprivation of liberty and 18 months for five other counts, all to be served concurrently. The Court of Appeal found that the Commissioner had erred in considering the circumstances of the Aboriginal community, which could lead to drink and despair, and in not giving enough consideration to general deterrence. The sentence was increased to 12 months imprisonment in relation to the deprivation of liberty and two years and nine months' imprisonment for each of the five offences of aggravated sexual assault. All sentences were to be served concurrently and the respondent was eligible for parole in respect of each of the sentences. In *Hagan*, a 1990 case which involved the multiple rape of a 14-year-old girl, heard in the Northern Territory Supreme Court, Justice Kearney did not accept as correct evidence from the father of one accused that it was his son's right under customary law to have intercourse with the victim. His Honour said:

> Aboriginal women have a right as all other women do to be protected by the law ... Rape ... in circumstances such as this case where there are no elements of tradition involved, are crimes of violence in their essence.

Another defence to charges of raping an Aboriginal woman has been alleged perceptions of their sexual identity. The distortion of cultural values about communal use of women, which were once part of a total morality and law, together with colonial abuse, and the impact of alcohol are an inimical triumvirate for Aboriginal women when a belief about consent is at issue. Within some Aboriginal societies there apparently can be a link between accepting alcohol and implied consent to sexual relations. Burbank noted that in Arnhem Land, sharing alcohol with a member of the opposite sex was one of the reasons for punishing (by stabbing or cutting) a spouse as this behaviour implied possible infidelity. Venbrux said that among the Tiwis this behaviour by a spouse would be regarded as "serious" provocation. Tiwi males hand beer, often give "take away" cans, to their lovers when they want to make an assignation.[30]

The supposed "availability" of Aboriginal women in return for alcohol was unsuccessfully relied on as to belief in consent to sexual intercourse in the 1987 case of *Verdon*. Lesley Verdon, a non-Aborigine, had lived in the Kimberley area for 20 years. He claimed to know many Aborigines and said he had recently ended a de facto relationship with an Aboriginal woman. He stated that "the custom in the area was that any Aboriginal girl would exchange sex for two cans of beer". The translation of Indigenous social mores that are present in some communities into asserting the existence of a general belief that Aboriginal women in accepting alcohol are consenting to sexual intercourse is quite unwarranted, and it was not accepted as a defence. These misconceptions about Aboriginal behaviour possibly arise from imprecise understandings of Aboriginal male and female interaction, and the place of Aboriginal culture in governing these relationships.

In Aboriginal society itself, despite men's "alcohol culture", "there is little sympathy for an Aboriginal woman who is raped when drunk".[31] For instance, in the 1981 case of *Philip Holden and Trevor Boxer* the victim, who had been drinking, joined two men who were drinking amongst a group of men near the Aboriginal camp at Katherine. She drank a can of beer with them. She was later forcibly raped. The accused and the victim were all heavily intoxicated. The sentence for each accused was imprisonment for four years and ten months' with a non-parole period of 16 months. In sentencing, Justice Muirhead remarked that there is some evidence that:

> Aboriginal women who join men to drink under this type of situation may be courting the risk of forcible sexual attack ... Nevertheless, the law must endeavour to protect all sections of the community.

This closely approaches the situation of blaming the victim. There seems to be a grudging concession that, despite the victim's actions, the law must endeavour to give her some protection. On the other hand, the sentence was relatively heavy and it is possible that Justice Muirhead was attempting cultural empathy with the supposed perspective of some Aboriginal men.

Possibly because male elders have controlled cultural evidence male judges have had more difficulty in comprehending, and thus taking into account how particular traditional culture may aggravate a sexual assault on an Aboriginal woman. In 1996, the Australian Institute of Judicial Administration found it was "recognised that the judiciary have exhibited both gender bias ... in individual actions (and) also in cultural traditions and institutional practices of the law".[32] Aboriginal women can be permanently devalued within their communities after a "wrong skin" rape. The prohibited relationship makes the act one of incest in customary law. For instance, a young girl was raped by her "wrong skin" step-father and as a result bore a child. Three months after the birth, when she was aged 16 years, her two uncles incestuously raped her. She said that, "Since the rape I am scared that other wrong skin men will rape me. Under Aboriginal Law my uncles should respect me".[33]

In a Northern Territory case of indecent assault in 1980, in which the victim and the four accused were intoxicated, Justice

Gallop refused the application on behalf of the victim to prohibit publication of her name on the grounds of wrong skin for any (agreed) sexual relations with one of the accused. With what may be regarded as either remarkable insensitivity to the position of the victim, indifference to cultural traditions, or gender bias, his Honour remarked on the desirability of sitting locally (in this case Oenpelli rather than in Darwin or Alice Springs) "to show the people of those localities how interested the Court is in administering justice and bringing justice to the people". It may be said that his Honour did not observe these principles of deterrence in sentencing. The four youths aged between 18 to 20 years were released on recognisance of $500 for 12 months.[34] The victim was humiliated and disgraced before her own community. Hopefully, these judicial attitudes have gone. For instance in the 1997 case of *Maynard Daniel*, where a man raped a woman three times in quick succession, the court noted that the gravity of the offences was increased because of the prohibition on any sexual intercourse between them, their customary law relationship being that of uncle and niece.

As traditional law disintegrates, actual rape has become more prevalent. Perhaps because of this distinction Memmott reported that "certain types of violence appear to have been occurring only comparatively recently over the last five to 10 years in many communities (eg group rape)".[35] The Gordon Report repeats this observation.[36] These comments are surprising in the context of cultural traditions of sacred rape and group sexual use of women and in the context of the following cases, some of which are group rapes occurring from the 1980s onwards.

Rapes of Aboriginal women by Aboriginal men can occur in the most violent and brutal of circumstances which preclude arguing consent, the common defence in non-Aboriginal rape cases. For example, a 16-year-old girl was beaten around the head with a rock when she refused to perform fellatio, upon which the accused made five attempts to penetrate her vaginally, while she was being punched in the face and restrained by a co-accused who was urging the first offender to hurry in order that he could also rape her.[37] A seven-year-old girl, a niece of the accused, was raped after being taken from playing near her grandmother's house.[38] A former *de facto* wife was beaten, her nose was broken, her head was pushed down a men's lavatory pan and then she was subjected to seven rapes in the course of a few hours.[39] A 16-year-old girl was so badly

beaten while she was unconscious and being raped, that she suffered, amongst other horrific injuries, a:

> blow-out fracture of the left orbital flooring causing a condition
> known in lay terms as "sinking of the eye". That condition is
> almost certainly permanent.[40]

Brutal pack rapes by up to 11 offenders at one time are not uncom-
mon, some of these men committing repeated rapes.[41] The plight of
women in a violent society is apparent when it is understood that
the extent of violence in these cases is not unusual.[42] Aboriginal
women are not subjected to "simple" rape; in nearly every case it is
of the most brutal and violent kind.[43]

The changing attitudes, both cultural and judicial discussed
above are perhaps slight indications for some optimism for
Aboriginal women's treatment as victims of sexual assault. However, a more wide-reaching indication is the 2000 case of *Harrison
Green*[44] in which the Northern Territory Court of Criminal Appeal
and the offender's community sent a strong message that violent
sexual assaults would not be tolerated. The Court refused Green
leave to appeal against an indefinite sentence imposed by the trial
judge who concluded that the Green was a serious danger to the
community. Green, 38 years old at the trial, had 12 previous convictions for assault since 1978, and since 1980 "had committed four
serious sexual offences, the last three on young children". He
showed no remorse, he had refused parole several times because he
would not accept "vigilant supervision" and his community at Ali-
Curung did not want him to return. These attitudes, if replicated in
the courts and the communities, will strike at the high rate of rape
and sexual abuse that presently exists in Aboriginal society.

Chapter 9

Different cosmologies

We can't go back. The old law was for the old problems. Now we got this new law – this whiteman's way. And we got these new problems. This law does not fix them either. It's no good. What we got to do is put them both together – the old and the new. Mix them up. And they'll be hard and strong like cement.[1]

[W]hat is meant by "crime"? A white lawyer, a white judge, a white jury may easily answer that question by reference to a whole host of factors, influences, criteria, all of them reflecting the cultural bias and experiences of the respondent. But what of those actions, criminal in a white or Caucasoid milieu, but part of traditional Aboriginal society, ritual or custom or sanctioned as such?[2]

The interaction of two laws, which originate as if from different universes, has created an inimical environment for Aboriginal women. Black males have inflicted violence upon women under the aegis of traditional law, and until about 30 years ago, because of judicial cultural relativism, which entailed acceptance of customary law "defences", lawyers and judges effectively condoned this violence. Other factors in this abuse were that non-Aboriginal contaminated Aboriginal society through alcohol, which both accelerated the rate of cultural violence against women and destroyed much of its traditional context.

However, while the Gordon Report referred to, it did not accept, the evidence of Aboriginal communities that Aboriginal men accused of violence against women have relied on customary law to sanction assaults on, and killings of, Aboriginal women. It found that:

During community consultations the Inquiry was advised that men charged with family violence and child abuse had argued that customary law sanctioned their actions. While no criminal cases were identified that supports this claim in WA during an appeal in the NT, it was argued that customary law sanctioned the assault. (*Ashley v Materna* 1997).[3]

This finding belies both the many cases where customary law "defences" have been pleaded in extenuation of violence and the obligations on sentencing judges to take account of a prisoner's environmental, ethnic and cultural background.

It is correct that there is no formal customary law defence as such. The colonial powers very soon interfered in disputes between Aborigines. In 1836, the New South Wales Supreme Court held in *Murrell* that it had jurisdiction to try an Aborigine accused of murdering another Aborigine. Murrell's defence counsel unsuccessfully queried the doctrine of *terra nullius* as the basis for the assertion of British sovereignty and the subsequent ousting of customary law; he argued further that where the law afforded no protection it could not command observance; and finally contended that this was a revenge killing and Murrell was put in double jeopardy as he was also subject to customary law. The court threw out all these arguments. Notwithstanding this decision, in many future cases in both civil and criminal jurisdictions these arguments were to be variously pleaded on behalf of Aborigines. They were never successful.

Then in 1992 in *Mabo [No 2]* the High Court held that *terra nullius* was a legal fiction in the Australian situation. Indigenous entitlement to land was recognised, although the court found that an Australian court could not itself challenge the Crown's sovereignty over Australia. There was immediate speculation among lawyers that, in the words of Professor Stanley Yeo, "native laws governing other spheres of Aboriginal life could have likewise survived settlement and remain unextinguished by subsequent legislation or executive acts".[4]

Aborigines took up the challenge; however, in each area of law they were again unsuccessful. In the 1994 criminal appeal case of *Walker*, the High Court ruled that Aboriginal customary law no longer existed as a criminal law defence. Chief Justice Mason held that:

> Even if it be assumed that the customary criminal law of Aboriginal people survived British settlement, it was extinguished by the passage of criminal statutes of general application. In *Mabo [No 2]*, the Court held that there was no inconsistency between native title being held by people of Aboriginal descent and the underlying radical title being vested in the Crown. There is no analogy with the criminal law. English law did not, and Australian criminal law does not, accommodate an alternative body of law operating alongside it.[5]

His Honour also relied on the Commonwealth *Racial Discrimination Act* 1975 to find "that all people should stand equal before the law. A construction which results in different criminal sanctions applying to different persons for the same conduct offends that basic principle".

A different reality exists for judges and magistrates in those areas of Australia where many Aborigines are living traditionally or semi-traditionally. Cases from the 1950s establish that Aborigines charged with performing acts, which were criminal under general law, have appealed to customary law to justify their actions. In recognising that Aborigines are burdened by the reframing of their law and social customs, judges have taken these claims into account, not as formal defences that exonerate violence, but in mitigation of sentence.

Justice Murphy took judicial notice of this disjunctive legal system in the 1980 High Court case of *Ngatayi*. He remarked on the difficulties of reconciling two parallel systems of law "with their very different attitudes to guilt and responsibility" and of deciding the extent to which each should have a bearing on the other.[6] Judicial cultural relativism was an attempt to accommodate this dichotomy. By 1977 concern over the problems arising from this conflict of laws, including the "need to ensure that every Aborigine enjoys basic human rights" caused the then federal government to act. It established the Law Reform Commission's inquiry into whether the courts and Aboriginal communities should deal with, or apply, customary law and traditional punishments. The ALRC Report 1986 did recommend recognition of customary law in some specific areas of law (although not where acts of violence were involved) but these recommendations have not implemented. The failure to do so has caused frustration and disillusionment among Aborigines.

Nonetheless, lawyers practising across Northern Australia say that there is *de facto* recognition of some aspects of customary law particularly in the Northern Territory and Western Australia. This is so because Aboriginal defendants can still be faced with severe difficulties in alien legal proceedings. Conflicts arise when the mental elements of, and the defences that apply to, crimes under the general law do not accord with the patterns, or standards of behaviour, of Aborigines acting in accordance with customary law. Hence issues arise about how Aborigines should plead to criminal charges, how to give evidence and of understanding Aboriginal "criminal" culpability in relation to sentencing.

For instance, in the 1985 Northern Territory case of *Jacky Jagamarra*,[7] which involved the unlawful killing of one male by another, "committed in an entirely traditional setting", there was difficulty in "interpreting meaningfully the plea of not guilty into the Pintubi language". As traditional punishment had been carried out, the judge decided the legal system should not interfere, and sentenced the accused to the rising of the court. In a case that occurred in about the mid-1970s an Aborigine was charged with aggravated assault on his wife after she was found in the street with a head wound. After it was explained to him that it was unlawful to hit his wife, the accused said he had hit her with a stick and pleaded guilty. He *then* said he had done so after she had pulled her pants up; he had actually caught his wife in adultery. This of course changed the law that would apply. The man had a viable common law defence. A plea of not guilty was then entered and the case went to trial. The accused was acquitted on the grounds of provocation.[8]

At present customary law is considered without consistency in an *ad hoc* fashion, on a case by case basis, outside the actual principles of legal precedent and possibly outside relevant legislation. An example of these inconsistent applications of customary law are apparent in the judiciary's contradictory attitudes to "payback", often raised by the defence on the issue of sentencing. There are Aboriginal communities in both the Northern Territory and in Western Australia to whom customary law is of equal importance[9] and these communities can be across State boundaries. Payback is still formally rejected in Western Australia. In the Northern Territory payback is formally recognised in the mitigation of sentence[10] even when it is only symbolic as in the 1992 case of *Minor*[11] or surrogate as in the 1981 case, *Pat Edwards*.[12] Pat Edward's wife died after a beating. In traditional law if the culprit cannot be found one of his kin can be punished instead. Justice Muirhead in sentencing Edwards took into account that "your sister ... having been speared, and a brother ... also having been speared with the result that his thigh has been broken ... [so] ... that by virtue of tribal payback, community indignation no longer exists". By comparison, symbolic or surrogate retribution is alien to Anglo-Australian law that is based on deterrence and sanctions against the individual.

The Aboriginal concept of communal guilt is also alien to Anglo-Australian law. This includes not only payback upon a family member in lieu of the offender, but the visitation of responsibility on individuals who, in the eyes of non-Aborigines, would be entirely removed from any chain of causation. The Aboriginal Legal Service in Western Australia successfully submitted to the Director of Public Prosecutions that assault charges against six men and a woman should be dropped on the grounds that the assaults on a woman and girl were tribal punishment. The seven accused were amongst a crowd of 20 people who beat the two females with timber, sticks, crow bars and nulla nullas and inflicted very severe injuries upon them. The tribal crime committed by the two victims of the assault was:

> *that with other passengers* they had alighted from a community vehicle and a fellow member of the community was killed by a passing truck. *If no one had alighted the death would not have occurred.*[13]

Other problems occur. Because customary law is forced into the mould of general law it is distorted and taken out of its true context (which can occur simply because the legal system necessarily adopts a version of customary law). Moreover, there are different Indigenous cultural traditions. There is not necessarily a universal truth about a particular traditional law on which courts can rely in attempting to interpret that law in relation to any particular set of facts.[14] There can be conflicting assertions of what the law is, or was, and indeed questions of whether it can be defined as "law" in the western sense at all.

> [T]raditional law is much more than simply matters of crime and punishment. The term "law" is quite inadequate in fact, and does not accurately translate the various language terms used. Rather it is a religion – a way of life completely governed by a system of beliefs ... the Dreaming is the ever-present ground of being – of existence – which appears symbolically and becomes operative sacramentally in ritual.[15]

Aborigines appreciate that it could be very difficult for magistrates or the judiciary to understand traditional law.[16] It is hard for non-Aborigines to comprehend the extent of the differences in culture and in worldview that creates conflict between the two laws. In contrast to the general law with its heritage of written definitions, whether of precedent or legislation, the basis of customary law is one of myth and sacred concepts.[17] In non-Aboriginal society the actions of an individual, if criminal, incur punishment. Aboriginal customary law is rather a general belief system for regulating the balance of society as a whole, through "dispute, discussion and reconciliation".[18] In short, the gulf between the two forms of imposing or restoring social order is immense.

Justice Kriewaldt regretted his lack of anthropological training.[19] In 1956 when charging the jury in the murder trial of *Nelson* he said:

> Native trials are always difficult. Some of you gentlemen ... have had a good deal of experience with natives ... Some of you have had little experience ... I have only had ... five years of such experience. At the end of my fifth year I feel less qualified to express an opinion about natives than at the end of my first year. The older I get the less I know about them. However nothing can be done about that – you must decide this case as best you can.[20]

Lawyers and judges in attempting a just reconciliation of these values have determined that an accused Aborigine's culture should be examined in order to determine intent, which in criminal law is relevant to fault.[21] In the 1959 case of *Balir Balir*, Justice Kriewaldt observed, "I think one can draw a distinction between Aboriginals and whites, not by a different law, but by a different application of the same law".[22] So where an Aborigine might be technically guilty under Anglo-Australian law for an act proper in Aboriginal society, there would not be complete exoneration but Aboriginal law or custom would be taken into account. In 1975 Justice Muirhead, sitting in the Northern Territory Supreme Court in the case of *Bobby Iginiwuni*, said:

> Both aboriginal and white people are generally speaking subject to the same laws. For years, however, the Judges of this Court in dealing with aborigines have endeavored (sic) to make allowance for ethnic, environmental and cultural matters.

A difficulty in doing so is that there can be conflicting evidence about customary law, one example being the conflict previously discussed in relation to rape. Nonetheless, the judicial discretion to take account of evidence given by Aboriginal male elders and anthropologists is well established. Hence the ALRC 1986 report found that a formal customary law defence would be redundant because:

> In criminal cases, the courts have been prepared to take customary laws into account in determining a defendant's intent, in relation to the 'defences' of provocation, duress and claim of right, and especially in sentencing.[23]

Cases involving Aborigines in which these defences have been raised are discussed below, but first there is a brief recapitulation of the relevant criminal law. Murder is committed if one person kills another person with the intent to kill or to cause grievous bodily harm, or if they foresee the probability of death or grievous bodily harm. The two partial defences to murder are first, provocation, which consists of an act or series of acts done by the deceased to the accused, which would cause an ordinary person in the position of the accused, and actually does cause the accused, a sudden and temporary loss of self-control. Second, diminished responsibility, which is an abnormality of the mind that substantially impairs the mental responsibility of an accused for acts or omissions that caused the death of a person, arising from a condition of arrested or retarded development of the mind or any other inherent cause, or induced by disease or injury. These defences are partial as they do not completely exonerate criminal responsibility but they reduce a charge of murder to voluntary manslaughter. Involuntary manslaughter is committed where the unlawful death of one person is caused by the act of another person who did not intend to cause the death but performed an unlawful and dangerous act or was criminally negligent in performing an act. In the circumstances of chaotic violence in many Aboriginal communities it is the lack of intention, rather than criminal negligence, which usually applies to this kind of violence. Duress is a defence of necessity in that it is claimed that criminal actions were performed because of threats (express or implied) of death or really serious injury to the person, or to family members, being threats of such a nature that a person of ordinary firmness and strength of will would have yielded to them. Duress is generally not available as a defence to murder and in some jurisdictions is not available for any offences of violence to the person, but it has been raised in Aboriginal killings because of the imperatives of acting in accordance with customary law.

In 1960 Justice Kriewaldt made several observations that are relevant to the question of how the interaction of the two laws affected these defences of duress and provocation. He said that the issue of subjection to, and protection by, the law was a basic principle. Justice Kriewaldt thought the problem of white offenders against Aborigines was mainly solved but a more intractable problem for the future was the "protection of an aborigine against crimes by other aborigines".[24] Justice Kriewaldt considered further that in every case that came before him, save one, the accused even if acting according to the dictates of customary law knew that his act was against "white law". Nonetheless, Aboriginal men charged with violence to women have claimed justification under customary law for acts that are criminal in the general law. As the strict legalism of classical Aboriginal society has increasingly broken down the context in which customary law defences have been argued, and judicial attitudes towards them, have changed during the last 50 years of the past century and in the early years of this century.

There are no definite chronological markers for these changes, which segued into each another. The first period is roughly between the 1950s and 1960s when customary law killings occurred. Justice Kriewaldt was concerned by the idea of a "purely tribal defence". He questioned, "Is lust, or anger, or the desire for revenge to be regarded as 'tribal' or not?" Nonetheless, he did hear cases that were argued in tribal contexts.

Muddarubba in 1956 and *Sydney Williams* in 1976 are two Pitjant-jatjara "customary law" cases that illustrate how the different application of the law of provocation benefited Aboriginal men. In criminal law prior to the 1997 case of *Moffa*, offensive words were not accepted as provocation for homicide. In *Muddarubba* Justice Kriewaldt acknowledged that he applied the partial defence of provocation creatively, and sympathetically, to Aborigines charged with murder:

> [T]he same rules apply in the trial of a white person as in a trial of a native. The rules relating to provocation have given me some worry in native trials. After much thought I have when summing up to a jury in a case where a native is on trial perhaps departed somewhat from the strict rule applied in trials of white persons.[25]

Muddarubba speared a woman who taunted him with a word that was offensive in a tribal context and was charged with murder. Justice Kriewaldt, in charging the jury, said that customary law did not amount to a defence, but while mere words could not be provocation for "white persons", the test was "the state of mind and the condition of the average Pitjantjatjara man" for whom words could be provocation. He took particular account of the accused's culture, "if the Aboriginal word 'karlu' was used by the woman I have no doubt you will regard the use of this word as a serious insult". He finished with a strong judicial comment favourable to the accused, "I repeat this is a matter for you to decide, but I have given you my recommendations". The verdict was manslaughter. The sentence was nine months' imprisonment with hard labour.

In *Williams* the victim and Williams had been drinking together near Yalata in far western South Australia. The defence case was that the woman taunted Williams, a fully-initiated man, about male tribal religious secrets, causing him to lose self-control. He beat her to death. Justice Wells took the issue of male secret culture seriously. He found that there was sufficient evidence of provocation to reduce the charge from murder to manslaughter, and with the Crown's consent accepted a plea of guilty to manslaughter. His Honour invoked the authority of the tribal elders in sentencing Williams. They were directed to assume responsibility for training Williams, and controlling his drinking for one year. Williams was sentenced to imprisonment with hard labour for two years suspended upon payment of a $10 bond to be of good behaviour for two years. The elders did not assume control of Williams. He was subjected to a token spearing which he thought was "a bit of a joke" and he went on to commit a series of assaults on other women. Williams was later imprisoned in 1978 and 1980, and it appears that the community had tired of him, because the Yalata elders refused to act as sureties for his release on bail pending trial in 1978.

Any other killing of a woman in Australia at the time of these two cases for these reasons, that is, provocation by words, would have been treated as murder. However, it was correct that within Aboriginal society these killings were not culturally unprecedented. In *Muddarubba* the meaning of the offending word, *karlu* is not explained. From the lack of any reference to "secret men's business" it can be inferred that *karlu* was probably an obscenity. Langton explains the importance that swearing and the utterance of obscenities have in Aboriginal society, culminating in "obscene references to the pudenda that constitute the grossest insults in the language".[26] The Aboriginal women in Burbank's "Mangrove" women study were aware of these gradations in their relations with men:

> "Big penis", this is bad word. If you say it that man might strike you. "Big vagina", this is really bad. If you say it there will be fighting.[27]

There are other instances of women being killed in traditional society when they uttered words which men found offensive. For example at Jay Creek in the early 1960s a woman was killed for "bad mouthing men". She was suffocated by sand being thrust into her mouth, her eyes and her ears.[28]

In *Muddarubba* and *Williams*, although in the former case to a greater extent because it was within a more traditional cultural context, the general law virtually accepted Aboriginal men's cultural rights to kill Aboriginal women. In both these cases women were seen as offenders against cultural mores or traditional law and hence, when killed in punishment, their behaviour became grounds for founding a defence of provocation under common law (within a cultural relativist or pluralist construct). This denial of the general laws' protection to Aboriginal women is emphasised by their lack of reciprocal customary law rights to kill men. However, a coda to contextualising *Williams* within the general law is that outrage about this sentence partly led to the 1986 Law Reform Commission's inquiry into Aboriginal customary law.

Duress raises other customary law issues. Aborigines have pleaded duress when executions or other violent acts have been committed under the imperatives of inflicting customary law punishments. In the 1967 Northern Territory Supreme Court case of *Garlbuma*, the defence of duress was pleaded to a charge of murder of a woman.[29] Ildimbu was 20 years old, her two children had died at birth, her husband subsequently died. Traditional Aborigines believe that untimely deaths are caused by sorcery.[30] Although Ildimbu may not have physically caused these deaths, under customary law she was held to be accountable and she was sentenced to death. A male Aborigine Gannanggu gave evidence that at a tribal ceremony at Oenpelli, Garlbuma had been selected to kill Ildimbu. Gannanggu refused to name those who had ordered the execution because this was "blackfellow customs". Garlbuma speared Ildimbu and clubbed her six-year-old nephew, who survived. He was found guilty of murder and of assault causing actual bodily harm. Justice Blackburn said that Garlbuma would not be sentenced to death. At that time capital punishment was mandatory for non-Aborigines convicted of murder but judges had discretion to impose sentences other than death on Aborigines. Contemporary newspaper accounts, the sources for this case, do not say what was the actual sentence.[31]

However, the 1953 Northern Territory "tribal" case of *Charlie (Mulparinga)* does gives some idea of judicial attitudes to the defence of duress. A young male, Selly, had been killed at the direction of male elders during a corroboree for an allegedly wilful breach of sacred law. He was accused of twice revealing men's sacred law to women. Justice Kriewaldt found that Aborigines were subject to Anglo-Australian law and even if the accused had acted "in accordance with his customary law ... which he regarded as binding on him ... which, if he broke it, might mean his own death, that is no excuse in this Court for his act", but that it would go to sentence. He found it likely that Aborigines would consider only the actual killer guilty of "breaking the law of the white people" and, if there were no punishment, all the tribes who met at this corroboree ground would think the killing was condoned. He considered the assimilation policy was irrelevant to sentencing unless the legislature directed otherwise. Justice Kriewaldt balanced the deterrence with the jury's strong recommendation of mercy; he sentenced Charlie to imprisonment with hard labour for 18 months. After Charlie's trial, Tiger and Captain, the elders who allegedly had ordered Selly's killing, were tried. Both were acquitted, possibly because of Justice Kriewaldt's direction to the jury about the evidence and also undoubtedly juries at this time were reluctant to interfere in cases between Aborigines. So both judge and jury did pay regard to the cultural context of these killings.

The second period of interaction between customary law and general law dates from the mid-1960s, a time when classical Aboriginal society was being increasingly disrupted. As alcohol took hold, pure tribal cases gradually disappeared. Men's customary law rights to inflict abuse under the guise of moral violence and sacred rape were still argued, but the violence that was inflicted was in the changed circumstances of a once legalistic society, the structure of which was breaking down. A "right" which was once sanctioned within a traditional cultural context was being distorted by alcohol, in itself also an accelerant to violence. In the 1958 case of *Namatjira v Raabe* Justice Kriewaldt had already noted that the majority of violent cases involved alcohol. By the 1970s nearly every case of moral violence also involved alcohol. These cases show a sad conformity; intoxicated beatings of women leading to their deaths and a claimed customary law "defence" of righteous justified violence because the women had been misbehaving. For example, in the 1974 Northern Territory Supreme Court case of *Benny Lee*, the accused was intoxicated when he injured his tribal wife who later died. He believed he was entitled to do so because "Ruby had been misbehaving herself in some way" and pleaded guilty to attempted murder and causing grievous bodily harm. Justice Forster found that "the customs of most of the Top End tribes is that a husband in those circumstances [of suspected adultery] ... is not only encouraged, he is almost required to punish", but nevertheless he was not satisfied beyond reasonable doubt that the injuries caused death. Lee had no prior convictions and was on bail, although he had already spent three months in custody. He was sentenced to 12 months' imprisonment suspended upon entering a two-year good behaviour bond.

The customary law "defence" of the right to inflict physical violence under the guise of moral violence was often loosely based on both duress and provocation without clear distinctions being made by either judges or defence counsel. Provocation has been argued in addition to, or as an alternative to, duress, on the basis that the woman's disobedient behaviour provoked the man's attack, but also because she was disobedient according to customary law she had to be punished.

Until the early 1980s, "moral violence" was construed with great liberality for the benefit of the accused as justification for frightful assaults on women. For instance, in the 1978 Northern Territory Supreme Court case of *Barney Jungala*, which was a brutal killing, Justice Muirhead said, "There is no suggestion that the [defendant] intended to cause the death of this young woman, and I accept the fact that he acted as he believed the law which he respected compelled him to do". The accused was convicted of manslaughter on grounds of lack of intent to kill, not duress. But non-Aboriginal juries had difficulty in assessing whether customary law obligations were still community imperatives and whether the accused's belief was genuine and reasonable. The rub was not caused by acts performed according to elders' specific dictates such as in *Garlbuma* and *Mulparinga* but arose within the more amorphous concept of, as the ALRC 1986 noted, "a person [being] 'forced' by his adherence to customary laws to commit an offence".[32]

The third period dates from about the late 1970s when the prosecution and judges became increasingly concerned about the extreme violence of these attacks on Aboriginal women. In the 1977 South Australian case of *Young*, the jury retired for only 34 minutes before acquitting a Pitjantjatjara man from Yalata of murder. He and his wife were both drunk, and Young beat her over the head when she refused to go to bed. She died from inhaling her own vomit while unconscious. Doubt arose whether the beating actually caused her death. Immediately after the acquittal the Crown prosecutor filed an information charging Young with having assaulted his wife occasioning her actual bodily harm, "because [the Crown] felt it must take a stand against Young's violent behaviour to protect members of the community". Young pleaded guilty to the assault.

He was sentenced to nine months' imprisonment, but as he had been in custody for three months, the sentence was suspended upon Young entering into a $50, 12 months' good behaviour bond.

Similar issues arose in the 1978 Western Australian case of *Larry Colley*. The accused, a fully-initiated man, suspected his traditional wife of infidelity. While both were intoxicated he beat her to death. His defence was he felt compelled to punish her because of customary law. He was charged with murder and convicted of manslaughter. Again the Crown raised the issue of deterrence "[otherwise] the respect for our law as such ... that our law does punish offenders appropriately would be lost". As Colley had already spent six-and-a-half months in custody, his sentence was three years' imprisonment with a minimum term of three months.

The remarkably lenient sentences in *Young* and *Colley* illustrate that in the late 1970s judicial concern about violence was yet a matter of form than rather than substance. Young's assault was only regarded as "reasonably serious". In *Colley* it was accepted that under customary law he "would have been expected ... to have inflicted some punishment on her – but certainly not under their law or ours, the punishment which was in fact inflicted". Sentencing in both cases was on the basis that there might be some form of traditional punishment. The specific deterrent effect on men's violence of sentences such as were imposed in *Williams*, *Young* and *Colley* must have been minimal, and in *Williams* actually proved to be nil. The $10 and $50 good behaviour bonds imposed in the two former cases are abhorrent in the context of the value put on the lives of Aboriginal women. These drunken killings were cloaked by cultural traditions. As for general deterrence, what did the women at Yalata feel when within eight months of each other, after killing women, Williams and Young were both free to return to the community? Their freedom must have demonstrated to other men that violence to women would be virtually unpunished by the general law.

The first intimations of the fourth, and present, period (which may be said to have become established in the early 1980s) dates from the last years of the 1970s, when judicial attitudes moved rapidly from forbearance of, to condemnation of, cultural "defences. In the 1974 case of *Benny Lee* Northern Territory Chief Justice Forster had been reluctant to accept Aboriginal men's right to inflict moral violence. By 1979 in *Stott* His Honour refused to do so. In sentencing Stott he observed:

> According to the old ways you were entitled if not required to give your de facto wife a beating [but] women whether black or white and whether virtuous or not must be protected from this potentially fatal sort of violence. You and people like you must be discouraged from acting in this way.[33]

From the mid-1980s a series of cases in the authoritative Courts of Appeal in Queensland, Western Australian and Northern Territory, establish that judges will no longer either countenance customary law "defences", or other violence to Aboriginal women. In *Bulmer* and *Watson* in 1986, the Queensland Court of Appeal rejected claimed customary justification for stabbing or cutting as a traditional right to punish for infidelity or other misbehaviour. In *Bulmer*, the court said, "far from calling for leniency in sentencing, it represents an attitude which the courts must be vigilant to discourage".[34] Watson, who had caused the death of a woman by "cutting" her in an effort to make her return to him, stated his belief in his right to do so in the police interrogation. "She has to be taught a lesson. She was my woman. She had to do what I say". Watson was convicted of murder, rather than manslaughter, and the verdict was upheld on appeal.[35] The Court of Appeal condemned the use of cultural rights of provocation to excuse violence. Similar issues arose in 1993 in the Northern Territory Supreme Court case of *Najpurki v Luker*,[36] an appeal against sentence, in which a man knifed his wife, leaving a deep wound in her face, because she had committed adultery with his brother. Chief Justice Martin upheld the sentence of 18 months' imprisonment with a non-parole period of eight months. In doing so he emphasised the importance of deterrence, and said that there are offences in which the deterrent purpose of punishment must take priority over mitigating factors.

An ancillary argument which has been advanced to support that of the traditional right to punish non-submissive women, is that the victim consented to the appropriate and recognised punishment. As discussed earlier, Sansom described a victim's passivity during an episode of moral violence. But although consent can be a defence to a charge of assault, provided the degree of force is within the limits of the victim's consent, it cannot be a defence to such serious offences as grievous bodily harm or unlawful wounding. In *Watson* the issue of consent to violence was explicitly raised by the defence on the basis that "cutting" was a traditional punishment. The court found that:

[E]ven if in some unexplained fashion it [community acceptance] could be construed as constituting the giving in advance, by each and every woman in the Palm Island community, of her consent to physical cutting as a form of legal discipline, it would afford no lawful justification or exculpation for the infliction of such an injury.[37]

In the 1999 case of *Iness Wurramara*, moral violence was not involved. A young man stabbed his wife and attacked another young man with machetes within the space of one month. He caused life-threatening injuries to both. There were no directly explicable reasons for either attack, other than smouldering rage. Wurramara's wife continued to support him, and the sentence of the trial judge was comparatively lenient. The Crown appealed against sentence on the basis that the sentencing discretion exercised in a case of severe violence was unsound. The Northern Territory Court of Criminal Appeal increased the sentence and, in reviewing cases of Aboriginal violence dating from 1992, spelled out three sentencing principles all of which emphasised deterrence.

First, the courts have been concerned to send the "correct message" that Aboriginal women, and children and the weak will be protected against personal violence. Second, Aboriginal offenders are not to be treated differently from other offenders in the wider community but rather the usual matters considered in relation to the imposition of sentences will apply, which includes the proposition that offences of serious violence call for condign punishment. Third, whilst proper recognition of claims to mitigation of sentence must be accorded due weight the court must be influenced by the need to protect the weaker members of the community, particularly women and children from excessive violence.[38]

The previously mentioned 1997 Northern Territory Supreme Court appeal case of *Ashley v Materna* might be a straw in the wind, but it possibly indicates the impact in the Aboriginal community of deterrence on some traditional violence on women. The customary law defence in this case for a man's violent assault on his sister, was that he was offended by her husband's abuse of her, which should not have occurred in the presence of himself, her brother. The prisoner unsuccessfully appealed against sentence on the ground that the magistrate did not properly account for the cultural context of the case. Evidence had been given on his behalf by a male elder of the Ngukurr that established that the brother's attack on his sister was correct in customary law. However, he effectively said that because of the deterrence of criminal sanctions traditional violence now rarely occurred unless people were drunk.

> That's what's happening, yeah. In the old ... (inaudible) ... from the 50s to the 60s and now we don't use that sort of thing because of (inaudible) when European system came and didn't give us a chance to let our culture go ... And that's why ... You can't do it these days now because that man gets up and hit that man (sic.) then you got ... your laws there ... You got coppers. They come and pick it up – pick them up – you know.[39]

However, even if some strictly traditional forms of violence against women are disappearing two cases involving the Mungatopi families in the Tiwi Islands illustrate the persistence of the strength of men's status and their traditional right to inflict violence. In the 1991 case of *Mungatopi*,[40] discussed earlier, the provocation offered by the slain wife was claimed to be a suspicion that she had committed adultery, that he was insulted by her refusal in front of other women, with whom she was drinking and playing cards, to accompany him home, and that she had not properly looked after the children, who had been left with babysitters.

In the 2002 case of *Cook*, the 37-year-old Jennifer Cook killed her husband David Mungatopi who for 18 years had flogged her daily. Cook had been promised to a very old Tiwi man who bequeathed her to his grandson, Mungatopi, who was a "big man" in Milikapiti. In May 2000 the drunken Mungatopi had continued drinking after his arrival home. When Cook refused to continue drinking with him he beat her remorselessly and said, "I'm not finished with you yet. You need more hiding". Cook finally lost control, she stabbed her husband and killed him. The Crown Prosecutor said Cook had "lived a life of helplessness and brutality", and only sought a suspended sentence. Justice Riley agreed saying that "after years of black eyes, and coughing blood ... he did not think that she ought to 'serve an actual sentence'".[41]

Cook's sentence was just only in the eyes of non-Aborigines. Within the Aboriginal community at Milikapiti she faces remorseless hostility for killing her abuser. Her horrific and sad case typifies the isolation of a promised wife in a "foreign" community and the terrible retribution from the community if a woman acts against moral violence. Cook had no refuge from the daily beatings. Mungatopi's relatives dominated the community, they ran the women's shelter, she was prevented from seeking medical attention and the police station was 75 kilometres away down a dirt track. After she killed Mungatopi her life was in danger, and it is said that she will never be able to return to the community. Mungatopi's relatives have taken control of her six children and she is rarely allowed to see them. Meanwhile Mungatopi's memory is honoured and revered; the Snake Bay beach has remained closed as a mark of respect even two years after his death.

Chapter 10

Yolgnu and Balanda

[B]ecause we got Law, white fella law coming up we are facing two laws now, we facing Balanda [white] law and our own Yolgnu Law, and that's I think deeply we are asking questions you know.

Banambi, Yirrkala[1]

Gender bias (in the judiciary) can ... arise out of myths and misconceptions about the social and economic realities encountered by both sexes. It exists when issues are viewed only from the male perspective, when problems of women are trivialised or oversimplified, when women are not taken seriously or given the same credibility as men.[2]

Widely separated Aboriginal communities have expressed concern about how customary law is manipulated within the criminal law to exonerate men from culpability for their violence. However, while their concerns about the final outcome were identical, they identified different causes. In Western Australia, Aborigines submitted to the Gordon Inquiry that although men used customary law to sanction violence, the responsibility lay with Aboriginal men. Aboriginal women in Queensland submitted to the Task Force Report that the legal system "used" customary law to exonerate men from culpability for violence, and the responsibility lay with the legal system.

[T]hey were aware that some judges and police used cultural distortions of rape to legitimise men's behaviour. There have been many accounts in recent times where members of the judiciary, in their summation of sexual offences against Aboriginal women, legitimised and excused the offence as a cultural right of men.[3]

The idea that customary law is being distorted underlies many explanations for the apparent judicial disregard for women's rights and the empathy for men's rights that has existed in so many cases of Indigenous intra-cultural violence. Atkinson's view is that the fault lies with the Aboriginal Legal Service and white defence counsel who justify violent assaults on Aboriginal women by wrongly claiming acceptability for this behaviour under traditional law.[4] Sharon Payne considers Aboriginal men have fabricated a third law, labelled by some Aboriginal women as "bullshit law",[5] in order to justify present violence, a violence which John Upton, a non-Aboriginal lawyer, has asserted never existed in traditional society. Some lawyers, Upton included, and anthropologists have expanded this argument by attributing apparent judicial disregard for Aboriginal women's rights to the "invisibility" of Aboriginal women in the legal system. They refer not to the actual constraints which traditional law placed upon women, but rather refer to non-Aborigines' ignorance of women's areas of autonomy in traditional society.[6]

Several fairly basic facts are relevant to these explanations. First, in the preparation of a case and during the hearing neither the police nor defence counsel, judges or magistrates can simply fabricate evidence about customary law. They must rely on evidence which is usually either that of Aboriginal male elders or expert evidence from anthropologists. However, customary law is presented to the courts in isolation that is out of its true context, a context that now can never be re-established because traditional society has been so damaged. Secondly, in non-Aboriginal society gender inequality and women's lack of power (which are gradually being redressed) have not meant that judges sanctioned indiscriminate violence to women. Insofar as the criminal law is concerned, Aboriginal women's "invisibility" originates in the constraints, discussed later in this chapter, which traditional culture places upon women rather than in any anthropological ignorance of their social role. Thirdly, from Kaberry's work in 1939 onwards, there has been recognition of, and continuing evaluation by women anthropologists of, the areas of autonomy which Aboriginal women undoubtedly had in traditional society. Aboriginal women increasingly have not been "invisible" to non-Aborigines but the violence has not abated. This supports the general conclusion of many female anthropologists, discussed earlier, that there was an imbalance of gender power in traditional society and men held sway by force. Fourthly, the weight of evidence is that there was considerable violence to women in traditional society from men. Even in 2001, Balgo women said of men's violence that after the traditional initiation ceremony "once they're men, they think that they can do whatever they like – because they are the men".[7]

Nonetheless, as discussed in the previous chapter, an analysis of cases establishes that on the basis of customary law "defences" prior to the 1980s Aboriginal women's rights as victims in general law were subjugated to men's cultural rights. Further, although judges will no longer countenance customary law "defences", the situation for Aboriginal women has not improved and the communities' concern is warranted. The ALRC in its 1994 report, *Equality Before the Law: Justice for Women*, commented that the "law provides [Aboriginal] women with little or no protection".[8] It found that men who commit violent assaults are not made accountable for their actions and that the reason is largely due to the policy of Aboriginal and Torres Strait Islanders legal services which protects male interests. It also commented that many cases of assault go unreported. Why is this so?

A combination of Atkinson's and Payne's explanations possibly provides some answers. It is not that judges have "used" the law but rather that a fundamental difficulty has been the cultural relativism of judges in understanding customary law violence to women upon the evidence presented by Aboriginal men. Aboriginal women are under pressure from the male members of their own community. Their disadvantage commences with violent assaults, and then continues with male imperatives about male rights in Aboriginal culture. Traditional views, other than customary law "defences", disadvantage Aboriginal women's general law rights to be protected from violence.

This was apparent from talks held in 1995 at Yirrkala and Millingimbi in north-east Arnhem Land between the Yolgnu and Justice Sally Thomas and two women anthropologists. The talks were part of a program to increase cross-cultural awareness between Northern Territory Supreme Court judges and Aborigines.[9] The Yolgnu's views are perhaps a microcosm of those of many northern Indigenous communities where traditional law still commands substantial observance. The Yolgnu discussed three main difficulties with Anglo-Australian law. First, the problems of offences which are serious in customary law, and which should receive severe traditional punishment, but which are not necessarily regarded as serious under the general law. Secondly, they wished to avoid or minimise the need for outside intervention against domestic violence through their own strategies. Thirdly, they wished to participate to a greater extent in the court process.

The Yolgnu *rom* is the law, culture, right way, which includes *madayin*, sacred law and sacred things; *makaratta* is a ritual of retribution destined to restore the balance. The Yolgnu said the suppression of traditional sanctions, such as death or wounding by spearing and *makaratta* rituals had diminished the ability of the leaders to restore the *rom*. The Yolgnu said that for offences regarded as serious in both laws, such as murder or manslaughter, the *balanda* (white) general law system should now prevail. However, family life and religious beliefs and ceremonies were, and are, the strengths of customary law. They have retained control of these areas and they thought that this control should continue.

The Yolgnu instanced blasphemous behaviour, such as misuse of sacred objects, grossly offensive behaviour through swearing by obscene references to the genitalia or excrement, and any reference to reproductive functions in mixed company, as behaviour that once would have incurred death, exile, or other serious sanctions, but now comes before the courts as comparatively trivial offences. It was emphasised that young girls were taught to avoid giving offence in these matters. The Yolgnu wished to have the opportunity to explain to the courts the gravity of such offences so that appropriate punishment could be imposed. If the community leaders imposed customary law sanctions, they would become liable in general law because of the necessary severity of traditional punishment.

The Yolgnu were divided about the management of domestic or sexual violence. It is not clear if this was a division on gender lines. Some resented domestic violence legislation and intervention orders, and saw the removal of women and children as disrupting the community and preventing dispute management. They felt that it should be a community matter to restore the *rom*. Others felt that protection was necessary. At Yirrkala the community women had set up *Ngali ngali mittji* ("peaceful family") to provide kin-based intermediaries with non-Aboriginal family violence counsellors, crisis accommodation and legal and other support services.

Although Yolgnu women in this group saw themselves as supporting traditional family values, some admitted difficulties arising from acting within a closed community. Significant obstacles to women's interests could arise if offending men were important in the community or were significant relatives of those trying to mediate. Further, if the women were from other Yolgnu communities, or other clans altogether, the women were then divorced from kinship support, while men were bolstered by it.

The Yolgnu's discussion about their lore illustrates how, from the viewpoint of non-Aboriginal society and law, Aboriginal women can be circumscribed by their culture. Male elders have the power to confine women in violent situations within communities. A man's status controls the level of support an abused woman might receive. Amongst the Yolgnu, if a woman is outside the immediate clan, she is very vulnerable because there is no support in the community. Women must not give offence in sexual matters and they must not refer to these matters in mixed company. This, of course, makes it very difficult for a traditional woman to give evidence about sexual assault in court, so Aboriginal men can control the presentation of evidence. Other matters signify the imbalance of gender rights; sexual assault is regarded as a community matter, a man's right to beat his wife, "morally justified violence", is something between the two of them. They are isolated from Anglo-Australian law under which these offences would be regarded as serious. Many of these issues are apparent in the 2002 Tiwi Islands case of *Cook* already mentioned.

Despite areas of autonomy in traditional society, Aboriginal women have not enjoyed either in traditional, colonial or post-colonial societies the kind of ascendancy which would enable them to superimpose their rights on men in cases of violent assaults upon them. The cultural inhibitions, which prevent Aboriginal women from giving evidence about sexual matters in a predominantly male court, or from speaking of sexual matters in front of particular relatives who may be in court, are at a severe disadvantage in cases of sexual assault. In 1957 women's inhibitions were an issue in the Northern Territory Supreme Court case of *Kunoth* which concerned sexual abuse of a girl by her father. In the mid-1960s Eggleston noted a case where a young girl, who had been raped, was reluctant to give evidence in her mother's presence in court but "had less hesitation when her mother was absent. This was interpreted by some observers as being due to the fact that she was still largely tribally oriented".[10]

Effectively, two male cultures spoke to each other when male elders gave evidence in the often predominantly male environment of the courts. In 1988 Justice Maurice queried Aboriginal women's silence before the courts. In the Northern Territory Supreme Court case of *Narjic*, the accused pleaded guilty to four counts of rape of one woman and to two counts in relation to another woman. Both women were his wife's younger sisters. Justice Maurice was sceptical of the defence arguments that this was normal tribal behaviour. The elders indicated there was little chance of payback. Justice Maurice recognised that the elders would be influenced in their evidence by the importance of the accused so he asked:

> Why should we only hear from the men? If we're going into this question of what's culturally acceptable behaviour, why shouldn't we hear from some female, some female leaders of the community at Port Keats? Why should it be men who are arbiters of what's acceptable conduct according to the social and cultural values of Port Keats?[11]

Upon the defence answering that it would be difficult to get the women to speak, Justice Maurice replied: "It's just that historically no one ever asks them". In reality it is unacceptable in traditional society for women to do so.

The predominance of Aboriginal male evidence has been inimical to Aboriginal women. The ALRC 1986 report found that the most significant obstacle in considering the merits of a "customary law defence" is that there are no general absolute standards on which the courts can rely in attempting to interpret that law in relation to any particular set of facts.[12] So males have had freedom to present a fabricated law (Payne's "bullshit" law) to the courts in order to exonerate other males from culpability in a foreign law.

The other issue that was identified by Atkinson and the ALRC is the bias of the Aboriginal Legal Aid Services. Two male lawyers have recounted how as barristers they successfully defended Aboriginal men within this male culture. In the 1970s John Coldrey, now a judge of the Victorian Supreme Court, appeared for a Central Australian Aboriginal Legal Aid Service (CAALAS) client in Alice Springs. The point of his anecdote is the importance for the defence of a close liaison with male elders in order to ascertain customary law.

> The accused, a traditional Aboriginal man, had inflicted 201 separate injuries on his deceased wife who had thereafter bled to death. He was drunk at the time. His instructions were that he had wanted to punish her for being with other men earlier in the day but had not wished to kill her, or cause her serious injury.
>
> Consultation with a tribal elder confirmed my suspicion that these (that is the wounds) were traditional sites for the infliction of punishment. I had initially been unable to grasp this fact and elicit this information from the accused. He had not been able to volunteer it. Fortuitously it had emerged for consideration by the jury. They acquitted of murder, convicting the accused of the appropriate offence of manslaughter.[13]

The facts of the case are consistent with Sansom's anthropological evidence of men's traditional right to inflict moral violence on women. The victim was passive, there were no defensive wounds, the wounds on her back indicate she was crouched down, the wounds on her legs were in traditional "punishment places". Justice Coldrey does not mention the court's sentence for this homicide.

In 1993 Frank Brennan recalled his 1981 success as junior counsel in the trial of Alwyn Peter for killing his *de facto* wife. "Like many defence counsel, I was proud of our win in reducing the charge (of murder) to manslaughter and obtaining a sentence which guaranteed Alwyn almost immediate parole". In Peter's case the defence concentrated on the circumstances of dispossession, which went to diminished responsibility. A panel of experts gave evidence about loss of culture, community dysfunction, alcoholism, and trauma caused by repeated violence in the disjointed life suffered by the accused and his community at the Aboriginal reserve in Weipa South.

After his win a female anthropologist said to Brennan that in reserves like Weipa customary law sanctions against violence did not exist and that "all you will succeed in doing is removing the limited sanction applicable by whitefella law. There will be nothing left to protect the black woman". Brennan said "her words came back to haunt me" after he read Langton's 1990 report to RCIADIC about alcohol and violence and "the daily parade of women with bandaged heads and broken arms, especially where there is access to alcohol".[14] However, Mr Edmund Ware, a senior man at Yalata, South Australia, had said almost identical words after the customary law exculpation of Sidney Williams for his killing, "There is going to be continual killings if they are going to be let off like this".

In the 1970s, CAALAS lawyers met with tribal elders to ascertain customary law, but do so no longer. Indeed in 1989, one CAALAS lawyer objected to the recognition of Aboriginal customary law at all because "the lack of impartiality and other principles in Aboriginal Law were in direct contradiction to the spirit of European law".[15] These opposing cultural attitudes to facts do create inordinate difficulties in achieving just resolutions in cases involving Aborigines because general law can only properly be applied when the true facts have apparently been determined.

Chapter 11

"What is truth?"

Proof of customary law is difficult because of its variability between different groups, their differing application in the circumstances of each case, the court's incapacity to direct or control them, need for flexibility, and the fact that they are generally not recorded in writing.[1]

We didn't have any history according to the white man. We're one of the poor old races that didn't have anything in writing so it's only hearsay, if you put it in writing it's history.[2]

In considering the affect of the interaction between the two laws and cultures on Aboriginal family violence, it is necessary to understand that each has a very different understanding of the concept of true facts. This affects interpretations of how events occurred in the past and hence how Aboriginal evidence is given in, and comprehended by, the courts. The ALRC 1986 reported that for Aborigines "community opinion" might determine the presentation of evidence. In these cases leaders may speak on behalf of all, either for or against an offender, despite possible conflicts of opinion or interests.[3] This attitude is neither a deliberate distortion of the perceived legal "truths" of non-Aborigines nor is it necessarily perjury, it is simply a different perception of truth. There can also be other influences on Aborigines when giving evidence; their attempts to still retain control of their law (the Yolgnu *rom*), their experiences of white treachery and their well-founded distrust of non-Aboriginal institutions.

Two of the most important issues for Aboriginal women as victims of male violence are the alterations in the "story" for the courts under the pressures of "community opinion" and the cultural difficulties for women in giving evidence about sexual acts.[4] Both these issues arose in the 1957 Northern Territory case of *Allan Kunoth* briefly referred to previously. Kunoth was aged 40 years, and engaged in regular sexual conduct with his daughter, aged 20 years, for over three months. He was found guilty of indecent assault, but not of rape. Justice Kriewaldt, the trial judge commented:

> [T]he decrease in the nature of evidence on successive repetition has been a common experience of mine where Aboriginal witnesses are concerned. I cannot readily call to mind any case where the evidence given by an Aboriginal witness in the Supreme Court has been anything like as full as the evidence recorded in the depositions, or the statement taken by a police officer, and I have had many cases where I have had access to all three.[5]

The ALRC 1986 report found that:

> [P]roof of customary law is difficult because of its variability between different groups, their differing application in the circumstances of each case, the court's incapacity to direct or control them, need for flexibility and the fact that they are generally not recorded in writing.[6]

In European thought there is an "assumption that there is a critical disjunction between the past and the present, that the past is unchangeable".[7] This is a view of the past where time is pinned by the written record. Interpretations may change, and bias or deliberate distortions can contaminate evidence, yet often there are recorded facts through which the past may be revisited. Henry Reynolds' scrutiny of Colonial Office records was one such revisitation of colonial policy. His research into the historical context of grants of pastoral leases arguably positively influenced judicial interpretations of the substantive land rights of Aborigines in the 1996 High Court case of *Wik Peoples v Queensland*.[8] *Wik* also illustrates how in the Anglo-Australian legal system courts can only apply the law after they have determined the perceived "true facts".

For many Aborigines, on the contrary, reshaping facts is valid in the context of oral tradition. This is a paradox in that in one sense Aboriginal law, as sacred law, is more immutable than the written general law, which develops, and changes. Aborigines have commented on the gulf that exists between these two understandings of law. Ginger Nganawilla of the Walmatjari said of "paper law", "Paper is nothing. Paper can be washed away. Our Law, Aboriginal Law, will last forever".[9] Bill Neidjie of the Bunitj in Kakadu explained the Aboriginal view of their law as:

> Law never change, always the same. Maybe it hard, but proper for all people. Not like European law, always changing. If you don't

like it you can change. Aboriginal law never change. Old people tell us, 'You got to keep it'. It always stays.

Yet despite Aborigines' views of an unchanging law, Sutton has commented on Aborigines' "culturally conditioned preparedness to reinvent the past for one's own convenience".[10] His conclusion is supported by the 1981 papers of the Working Party of Aboriginal Historians who said that the very essence of Aboriginal history or transmission of past events is not objectivity in the western sense, but a "world view", an experience, a transmutation of the past into living tradition. This has its own validity but is one that is different from western empiricism. Langton wrote of being "ultimately responsible to 'our own mob', and not to the discipline of history nor the white concept of knowledge".[11] Hence the many interpretations of the "Captain Cook" legend which all signify the historical reality of invasion and dispossession by whites. It is irrelevant for Aborigines that Cook appears in many guises and localities: the reality is dispossession.[12]

Oral history is also innately fragile because it depends on living humans for transmission. In Aboriginal society the past is interpreted through myth and legend. The "rights" to a story are owned by succeeding generations.[13] These rights are centred in place rather than in the time of European historiography, and when the connection with place is disrupted tradition is distorted or lost.[14] Archaeologist Ian Crawford worked with Aborigines in the north west Kimberley and observed that:

> In traditional Aboriginal cultures, there is a certain amount of deliberate putting away of the past. The names of people recently dead are strictly not mentioned, and thus their songs are not sung and events in which they played a central role are not narrated. After a period of years, the restrictions are dropped, but by then some of the details are lost. … [V]ery old narratives … are brief, whereas narratives of more recent events are relatively long.[15]

Tim Flannery found that the pre-colonial Tasmanian Aboriginal population fell below sustainable levels for transmitting knowledge.[16] But mainland Aborigines were able to guard against loss of knowledge by reshaping individual understanding of facts in at least two ways. First, by incorporation, which entailed radically shifting an individual's world perspective.

> In Southern Arnhem Land … when a group that is custodian for important ceremonial knowledge appears in danger of dying out,

new members are recruited from larger groups. For an adult so recruited, the transfer of spiritual ties from his own original group is a severe psychological wrench.[17]

In *Milirrpum v Nabalco Pty Ltd* the anthropological evidence of Professors Stanner and Berndt was that when a whole clan was incorporated or absorbed into other clans there would be a "dropping out of a clan linkage from aboriginal memory ... [which] would take not less than three generations".[18] The evidence of Aboriginal witnesses caused Justice Blackburn to accept that this view was correct.

Secondly, as Sutton has observed, facts also can be transmuted into myth or reinvented to suit the convenience of those doing so. When facts are reshaped individual and community rights in both customary and general law can be affected. Sutton dissects this process, at which he was present, in relation to translation of land rights. The myth-making enabled a "politically and ceremonially dominant" group to establish land rights that prevailed over the interests of three other groups who had actually been established in the area.

> [A] new, territorially expanded version of the key relevant myth was floated at a meeting of senior men who, after some debate, settled on "one story" and ratified the correct version. ... [Sutton concludes] One of the roles of mythology in that region (north Australia) is to provide an idiom, a legislative code in the third person, in which relationships between known people, ... [and rights] ... must not only be ratified but negotiated.

These practices affect judicial hearings and outcomes. Sutton recounts how:

> One such debate (about mythology) took place, briefly, before the Aboriginal Land Commissioner in the early 1980s, in the middle of evidence during a land claim. This was not a disagreement of innocent and differing memories, nor a case of "cultural breakdown" or "decaying traditions". It was, as such a debate often is, systematically normal and, for want of a better word, traditional.[19]

Anthropologist Deborah Bird Rose has deconstructed a similar process of myth-making, which she terms "negotiation of meaning", in a case of Aboriginal men deciding how evidence about a man's killing of a woman was to be presented to the court.[20] The rights, which were affected, were initially those of the slain woman. At the conclusion of the process of transmuting facts about the killing, the men had subjugated all the women's rights to those of the male killer.

It is worth considering Rose's analysis in detail, because it illustrates so well the inner world of traditional Aboriginal communities and how little the traditional attribution of guilt and retribution fits with common law concepts of responsibility and penalty. It also illustrates how hard it would have been for the non-Aborigines involved in the trial to understand the circumstances of the killing, and hence the culpability of the killer.

In 1982 a drunken man called Smith killed his wife. Her family mourned the victim, but the wrong was seen as being done to her community of the Yarralin Lingara people. The killer's community was also involved. However, extreme care was taken to closely define that community so that retribution would not disturb wider inter-communal relations. Eleven days after the murder, when grief and anger had largely subsided, formal community "fighting" occurred. Both the deceased's brother, because he "let" his sister be killed, and the killer, had to face boomerangs. Neither was injured.

> The brief fight allayed many feelings ... In this regard the fight was gestural. It allowed the relations of the dead woman to express their right to kill Smith, but as physical punishment is controlled by the Australian judicial system, the real payback would come later, via "Traffic" [a type of sorcery], or some other extra-human agency.[21]

For the community, the proprieties had taken place, so that when the trial came, people "began to be concerned about Smith's relationship to the European authorities". Several Yarralin then decided to go to Katherine to advise the Aboriginal Legal Aid Service what the traditional law view of the case would be. Rose says they had two motives: to keep Smith out of prison because they thought he was going to die soon, and secondly to "define themselves as 'Law men' in the European context".

In order to resolve their conflict of interests as kinsmen and as spokesmen for the perpetrator, "vis-à-vis European Australians ... the whole issue was re-opened and ultimately re-defined"[22] within the community. The emphasis shifted from physical responsibility to moral responsibility and from the killer to the victim. The community thought Smith's intoxication absolved him from responsibility for the killing. But about 20 years earlier, the victim, as a very young girl, had been promised as a bride to a very old man, himself, at the time of her death, long dead. Instead of caring for him "once she was big enough" she ran off with Smith, who was by kinship sub-section her son-in-law. Therefore the victim was culpable: she had abrogated her moral obligations by failing to care for her elderly husband, and marrying within a prohibited degree of relationship. There came to be talk that her death was a punishment inflicted by *munpa* (a killing of somebody already marked to die by sorcery), and that Smith too was in danger of this retribution. The men at this stage were satisfied, as the deceased's kinsman, Nelson, one of the Law spokesmen put it, "We are all sorry for that thing [the death] but Smith's not the one". The older men all said that Smith should tell the truth, but "just trust the men who were there to back him up".

Then there was a further narrative shift: this was to satisfy the women who "were extremely dissatisfied with the proposition that women who run away from their old husbands will be killed". In this version Smith is removed as an agent of death altogether; the deceased's death is attributed to an act of direct sorcery: somebody ate her kidney fat during the night. The last word was from an old man who in alluding to the men's final version said, "that sort of *munpa* had not been practised for decades and that the story was 'bullshit' when dealing with Europeans ... but it was useful bullshit".

Rose's anthropological interpretation of these events is that the Yarralin people developed the *munpa* version of events partly because they believed it to be accurate, and partly because it resolved difficult relations between the respective communities of the deceased and her killer. "At the same time there was also a sensitive reading of European concepts of Aboriginal people." The *munpa* version was probably of vital importance to the community:

> [B]ut given that the context of murder also included Australian law and justice, the *munpa* version was probably the only one which would have had much impact in Australian courts of law. In the Northern Territory many European Australians have an attitude towards what they term "tribal" that is a mixture of awe, arrogance, and avoidance. Their concept of "tribal" includes sorcery, punishment of women, and any other customs which they firmly believe are not present in their own culture. So in defining the event as *munpa*, Yarralin people proposed the one story which their experience of Europeans had led them to believe would go unquestioned. My understanding of European Australians in the area is not that they necessarily believe these stories but that they treat such cases with avoidance. If anything could convince the judge that this case was best handled by Aborigines, the *munpa* story would do it.[23]

If this narrative is re-examined from the point of view of Aboriginal women, it appears that they are experiencing "multiple oppressions simultaneously". Although payback was staged according to traditional law, the fight was "gestural" because "physical punishment is controlled by the Australian judicial system". The male elders, despite being the victim's kin, then colluded to present an alternative theory *munpa* with which apparently to raise the spectre of tribal law in an attempt to dazzle the judiciary. The elders' motives were to ensure that in fact Smith would not have to bear punishment under the Australian legal system. Rose accepts that there was a valid belief in the *munpa* theory, but if so it was achieved through the kind of debate about mythology referred to by Sutton above. There was discussion until the "correct version" in the interest of the dominant group, the men, was achieved. One of the old men asserted that he knew quite well the *munpa* theory was "bullshit". However, it is the men who go to court to give evidence, not the women.

Rose's claim that Aborigines believed that the judiciary were gullible about this kind of theory, and her slightly different version, that it was not so much gullibility as "avoidance" perhaps explain the judicial attitudes of apparent acceptance of customary law practices which patently derogated from the position of women as victims. Rose does not allude to the beliefs of the Aboriginal women as to whether the *munpa* theory was "bullshit". Aboriginal women have publicly claimed, as discussed, that males do use "bullshit" defences and it may well be that they were cynical about this theory. Certainly they were not prepared to let it continue as a useful male construct to enforce the marital subservience of young girls to old men. They raised the issue of a more serious and traditional belief, death through an enemy eating kidney fat. This death can occur through the machinations of a generally aggrieved enemy.

In this case Aboriginal women's rights were subordinated completely to those of Aboriginal males: a woman is killed, her killer faces token traditional punishment, he is supported by the victims' kin, and male elders with a representation of traditional law which they know may be fallacious, but which is intended to mislead the court. This construction of the truth both made the victim culpable and acted as a moral injunction upon the women. Further, the court imposed a remarkably light sentence. Possibly the verdict was manslaughter. When the elders gave evidence for the accused of *munpa*, their interpretation of customary law, the judge may have complied with that "moral" imperative which the elders had shrewdly anticipated when constructing their myth.

The *munpa* story provided an acceptable customary law cloak in which to dress the views of the male community for presentation to the court. Aborigines living in traditional society or semi traditional society understandably do not want to surrender their members to an alien, and imposed, law. However when members of a society do not have equal status, if society's mores shift blame to women, then women are vulnerable when representations of community attitudes by men are taken into account in sentencing.

Rose did not know "precisely what the verdict was on Smith, but he was given the unusually short sentence of approximately two years in prison". Upon release Smith stayed with an associated community for about a year. By 1985 he had returned home and remarried. The postscript was that several years later Rose was asked by the Solicitor-General's office in Darwin to interpret at a murder trial. Rose had to disqualify herself because Smith was the accused, charged with murdering his new wife.

Justice Kriewaldt and other judges faced with trials of Aboriginal accused have commented on the difficulty of achieving justice because of the conflicting cultural traditions about interpreting the circumstances in which the criminal act has been committed. Justice Kearney in *Jabarula v Poore*, when considering "the ordinary standards of the community" in relation to the issue of provocation in "the special context of Aboriginal communities (in the Northern Territory)" found that:

> [T]he question is particularly difficult when the fact-finder is not a member of the "community" in question, and that community consists of persons whose background and cultural values are different to his and are recognised by the law as relevant matters.[24]

Another difficulty in criminal trials is that male elders' ideas of customary law appear to depend on their view of particular circumstances at any one time. For instance, in two Northern Territory cases, both of the accused were from the same culture at Elcho Island, but quite contradictory evidence was given about attitudes to rape in customary law. In the 1975 case of *Iginiwuni*, the elders took a lenient attitude about a very serious offence. A heavily intoxicated 30 year old man raped a two-and-a-half year old girl. She suffered serious injury. Evidence was given that the Council at Miligimbi decided that if the accused returned to the community the probable, and only, punishment would be that the defendant would be "sent bush" for some time. In the light of this evidence, Justice Muirhead was remarkably lenient. Iginiwuni was sentenced to imprisonment for five years and eight months with a non-parole period of two years. After five months' imprisonment he was to be released on a three-year good behaviour bond to live at either Miligimbi (where he had been living) or Elcho Island.

In the 1980 case of *Gunambarr* the facts were very similar but because of the evidence of male elders the outcome was very different. Gunambarr, aged 22 years and also heavily intoxicated, attempted the rape of a six-year-old girl. This offence and the effect on the victim were actually less serious than the offence of Iginiwuni five years' before. But the completely contrary evidence given by male elders about customary law influenced the judge to sentence Gunambarr more severely. The elders said that death or serious injury would be inflicted upon a man in customary law. In sentencing the accused to six years' imprisonment with hard labour and a fixed non-parole period for three years and six months, Justice Gallop said: "The community would be revolted by this crime". On the evidence of male elders in the case of *Iginiwuni* which occurred five years earlier this was patently not so.

The real difference between these cases seems to be not customary law but the attitude of the male community elders to the accused. Gunambarr had a bad record for violence and dishonesty. At 22 he had already spent the past six years in prison. Evidence was given that the tribal elders refused to have him back to Elcho Island. Iginiwuni had no previous record of violence and the male elders were prepared to accept him. Perhaps the elders were acting in accordance with usual sentencing principles, a first offender of previous good character is treated differently from a repeat offender. However, to achieve this end they were prepared to manipulate their evidence about customary law. The actual crimes and the consequences for the victims seem to be treated as irrelevant.

Judges have taken the views of the community, that is the men's views, seriously in sentencing,[25] so the men have had real power to influence the outcomes of trials. For instance in *Andy Mamarika*, a Groote Eylandt case, Mamarika had, in an apparently unprovoked attack, killed another man by spearing him in the chest with a shovel spear. He successfully pleaded not guilty to murder but guilty to manslaughter on the basis that he did not intend to kill or to cause grievous bodily harm. In mitigation of sentence, defence counsel called as witnesses members of both Aboriginal communities on Groote Eylandt. They gave evidence that the defendant's family had been speared without serious injury while the defendant was in custody. As a member of the victim's clan said, "we settled this business". Justice Gallop sentenced the defendant to three years' imprisonment with hard labour, with a 12 month non-parole period that was suspended on the defendant entering into a recognisance in the sum of $500 to be of good behaviour for a period of three years. Justice Gallop said that "A very significant matter for a sentencing power is the attitude of the community, particularly the community in which the accused lives and works ... the fact that the trial by spears has already been carried out, imprisonment is not expected by the community in relation to this offence".

In the 1959 Northern Territory case of *Dumaia*, in which a woman was charged with the killing of another's child, Justice Kriewaldt, who perhaps suspected community condemnation, twice cautioned the jury about the difficulties of Aboriginal evidence. He said that the concept of hearsay evidence was one that was alien to Aborigines, "if an Aboriginal believes a story he will say that he personally saw the events". Further, that gratuitous concurrence is frequent (that is responding with "yes" to every question) and "that question and answer in my experience have greater value if the Aboriginal makes a positive statement in answer to a question".

The wariness with which judges treated evidence about customary law is also apparent in the 1995 Northern Territory case of *Wilson*. Wilson found his mentally disabled son acting indecently in bed with his own mother, Wilson's wife. Wilson then shot his wife. Everybody concerned was drunk. Wilson was charged with murder, but his plea of guilty of manslaughter, on the grounds of provocation was accepted. The prosecutor then agreed that the three witnesses called to give evidence about traditional punishment should do so together. The trial judge, Justice Kearney observed, "When it comes to considering traditional matters of law and custom it's preferable indeed that the evidence come from a representative group than a single person".

Courts have also relied on anthropologists in order to determine how customary law might be applicable. Langton considers this evidence appropriate in establishing customary law.[26] Eggleston concluded that expert evidence should always be used to establish traditional law, and Kathleen Strehlow said that one ground of criticism of the *Sydney Williams* case was that expert evidence had not been called about traditional law. The case of *Milirrpum v Nabalco Pty Ltd* established that anthropologists' evidence was not excluded by the hearsay rule and should properly be treated as expert evidence in order to ascertain traditional law. Although this evidence was accepted in *Milirrpum* there are difficulties, which sometimes are insoluble, in equating concepts of Aboriginal and European law.[27] Further, at times anthropologists can be mistaken about whole areas of customary law. For instance, in land claims in the Northern Territory in the 1970s, such mistaken views were so to the detriment of women that their role in land care, and thus their entitlement to land, was not appreciated.[28] In *Putti v Simpson*, Justice Muirhead was critical of "half-baked notions where language or cultural differences jeopardise understanding".

The ALRC 1986 report noted that the courts "are increasingly insisting upon proof of Aboriginal customary laws or traditions ... rather than relying upon statements of counsel which may be vague, unsubstantiated or poorly informed".[29] It referred to three cases between 1982 to 1983: *Joe Murphy*, *Moses Mamarika* and *Jacky Anzac Jadurin*. Jadurin had beaten his wife to death. On appeal the Federal Court considered, and rejected, the explanation that an Aboriginal man was entitled to beat a woman for disobedience. The court said that "it should approach the matter on the basis that the appellant beat his wife in anger when they were drunk, and that this brought about her death".[30] That is, the usual common law standards applied, without customary law being a mitigating factor.

These cases should theoretically be a precedent for later decisions where customary law is advanced as a defence. But in a case of child sexual abuse, alleged to have occurred in Broome in the late 1990s, the defendant's version of Bardi customary law was accepted in exoneration of a charge of sexually molesting his step-grand daughter – a ten-year-old girl. He admitted doing so, but claimed it was "to warn her of the dangers out there ... What he did was part of his culture, his right and duty". The prosecution had called two male elders whose evidence would have been "that it was not Aboriginal custom for grandfathers to teach their grandchildren about sexual matters". But the Aboriginal Legal Service barrister managed to have this evidence excluded "on the grounds that what was and wasn't custom was not relevant for the jury; the crucial thing was what was in the [accused's] mind". The accused was acquitted. Afterwards the barrister commented, "We would have been sunk if those two had testified". Ironically, evidence of customary law would probably have secured a conviction.[31]

The case also illustrates how difficult it is to bridge the gulf between the two laws. While the jury were considering their verdict, the accused's relations angrily gathered outside the court: "There [was] a railing against white justice, of the inability of whites to understand Aboriginal law". It is not clear whether they meant that the accused should not have been charged at all, or that the whole matter should have remained in the small Bardi community centred on One Arm Point. But during the case it was noted that, "It is clear how serious and painful the whole thing is for the child". The child's evidence was that her step-grandfather said to her, "Now if you get a boyfriend you'll be good enough for him". An elderly Aboriginal woman said outside the court, "It's been going on for three years. But then it came out in the open". What has been done to this child as a result of the admitted abuse for which there was allegedly no punishment at all?

If this case and its whole context has been correctly reported, it illustrates the dangers for Aboriginal females of allowing any evidence of customary law to be introduced at all as justification for violence or sexual assault. These crimes should be treated as a criminal violation of women's human rights. Of course if this approach is taken, the difficulty arises of denying claimed Indigenous rights, which have also been recognised in international law. This rights dilemma is considered in a subsequent chapter.

Chapter 12

Cultural disintegration and violence

> The most profound form of violence violates the spirit and soul, tearing at individual and collective identity. Colonisation and post-colonial interactions have made many Indigenous people feel disempowered and dispirited, as they face an isolating and brutalising life.[1]

Culture stress and the attendant alcohol problems caused by the disintegration of classical Aboriginal society have meant that while customary law "defences" are becoming less appropriate, for many Aborigines diminished responsibility, intoxication and involuntary manslaughter are increasingly relevant as general law criminal defences. These defences present a lethal combination for Aboriginal women as victims of violence and are perhaps almost as inimical as were customary law "defences". In essence, although the judiciary has now rejected the claimed traditional right to inflict violence, culture stress and intoxication can found substantive general law defences. Further, in sentencing, judges have taken account of the "circumstances of Aboriginality" – legal shorthand for the effects of deprivation, drink and despair. So the traumatic lives suffered by many Aboriginal women and their abusers, while not exonerating perpetrators of violence, do go to legal defences and sentencing.

John Cawte, a psychiatrist and anthropologist, found that "culture stress" among Aboriginal communities supported an argument for the existence of internalised stress that so affected some community members that their condition was tantamount to an "inherent abnormality". When a culture collapses without replacement "individuals express their loss and bewilderment in emotional and behavioural disorder".[2] Gross stress or culture stress is a post-traumatic disorder first described in the 1940s as a result of work with combat troops and concentration camp survivors. The comparison between Aboriginal society and concentration camp survivors, which has also been drawn by the criminologist Paul Wilson,[3] indicates a severely traumatised society. This is a recognised psychiatric syndrome for the purposes of the diminished responsibility defence.[4]

The Aboriginal Legal Service of Western Australia (ALSWA) identified a community affect of lethargy and despair arising from the policy of taking Aboriginal children from their families as "culture stress". It found that in successive generations this attempt at assimilation had caused social and cultural problems including lack of education, identity crises, lack of access to culture and heritage, involvement in the criminal justice system, mental trauma, emotional distress and alcoholism. ALSWA described Aborigines as living in a society where "the change has been sudden and all-pervading, going right to the roots of their religious and mental adjustment".[5]

By the late 1930s or early 1940s, many Aborigines, historians and anthropologists agreed that traditional knowledge lay in waste, leaving communities with fragments of sacred knowledge and traditional law. Porteous, Strehlow and Elkin write of the irrevocable loss of men's sacred knowledge.[6] Elkin recounts the scorn with which younger men treated elders and the refusal of the male elders to pass on knowledge to those they considered unworthy of the trust "with the result that sacred knowledge has been lost for ever and social disintegration and depopulation follow".[7]

For numerous Aboriginal men their traditional status has gone and the meaning of life has disappeared.

> When I was young my father was a warrior and I grew up thinking that I was going to be a warrior and when I got older all I saw was the grog, men sitting looking into space with no jobs and no future.[8]

The RCIADIC found that Europeans offered no replacement culture to Aborigines who were condemned to "dispossession and subordination within an often hostile society".[9] Both RCIADIC and the Mental Illness Inquiry of the Human Rights Commission identified particularly high levels of stress in the Aboriginal community resulting in depression, substance abuse, self-destructive behaviour, high levels of domestic violence and anti-social behaviour.[10]

Alcohol became an early instrument of destruction. Legislation to prohibit Aborigines from having access to, or being supplied with, liquor alcohol was largely ineffective,[11] further there was an argument that this policy was another denial of Aboriginal autonomy.[12] However, Justice Kriewaldt, who was sympathetic to Aborigines, strongly supported prohibition because alcohol caused so much violence. Prohibition ceased from the late 1950s as the States progressively repealed Aborigines' Acts. Unfortunately this access to alcohol had disastrous effects because of events in the next decade.

Aborigines' strikes for equal pay and land rights in the mid-1960s were well merited. Aboriginal stockmen's work and knowledge of "country" contributed enormously to the establishment of the cattle industry but their skills were often abused because their reward was commonly merely rations for themselves and their families. Their stance for equal rights rebounded disastrously. In 1967 the introduction of equal pay meant that from being the mainstay of the cattle industry, Aborigines became unemployed. Cultural connections were broken, because the stockmen were ousted from their traditional lands on which they had been able to remain as employees with their families. Misha Peters, once a stockman "on rations" in the Kimberley, said "Equal wages meant no more jobs for us". Many families were relegated to the status of itinerant fringe dwellers. In 1975 Patrick Dodson, then a Catholic priest, observed:

> With little employment opportunity they are left with nothing to do. Many appear to resort to drink as a way of relieving their frustration.[13]

The efforts of elders to avoid this problem in their communities were often circumvented by non-Aboriginal profiteers. The results were disastrous. Chief Justice Forster remarked in 1979 that in the eight years he had sat in the Northern Territory Supreme Court there was only one trial where an Aborigine was sober when he committed a serious offence.[14] Cawte observed that the demoralisation and the submission necessary for survival led to a philosophy of instant gratification, whether through sex or alcohol.[15] This behaviour is common to people who do not see long-term solutions. In 1990 the National Committee on Violence found that alcohol:

> remains a source of violence and misery in many Aboriginal communities because of its appeal to those whose relative

powerlessness is manifest. It follows, therefore, that the only long-term solution to the problems associated with alcohol in Aboriginal communities is the regaining of real economic and social independence from white Australia. Many Aborigines presently lack viable alternatives to the services upon which they have been encouraged to depend.[16]

Possibly some Aborigines are becoming habitualised to alcoholic violence as a means of surviving in a devastated society which continues to face inimical pressures. Both the ALRC in 1986 and the Model Criminal Code Officers Committee of the Standing Committee of Attorneys-General (MCCOC) in 1998 found that customary law is still continually evolving, and that to attempt codification would destroy the verity of that law.[17] Aboriginal society, like any other society, is not static and there is now a debate about whether – if drinking rituals are becoming formalised behaviour – this is cultural evolution or replacement for traditional culture.

In 2001 Sutton defined evolving culture in anthropological terms when he analysed Noel Pearson's refutation that alcohol was part of traditional culture.

> [Pearson] contests the way modern drinking patterns are sometimes identified with Aboriginal culture. He refers to the deformation, corruption and manipulation of notions of cultural tradition by the drinkers themselves. Such distortions are, in his words, "not culture, not tradition, not identity"… In an anthropological sense, rather than in the sense used by Pearson, such ingrained and widely repeated patterns of practice and value do form part of a society's culture, or at least that of a subset of its members, as it is at the moment of observation. In this technical sense culture is not merely a consciously assumed personal attitude that may be donned or doffed at will.[18]

Wilson's view is that "alcohol culture" which promotes drinking and fighting as positive virtues has replaced traditional culture. He attributes its growth not only to the easy availability of alcohol and to displacement, but also to a racial psychological scarring. Wilson quotes Becket's observations that because Aborigines' connection with the distant and continuous past has been disrupted, value is placed on the immediate present in which alcohol enables people to "feel better", to "get on top of things".[19] Aboriginal men drink and fight "to establish manliness". The men are aware of the consequences, "police reprisals, personal injury, family and community violence", but Wilson considers the sense of male ritual associated with drinking has replaced that of sacred male rituals and it is too important to Aboriginal men to be relinquished. The cause of the violence is not alcohol, but the powerlessness and despair which can particularly afflict Aboriginal men, and for which alcohol becomes the disinhibitor.

Wilson's "replacement" view has virtually achieved the status of being an orthodox pronouncement. It has possibly contributed to the formulation of explanations, for instance that of Payne, that violence in Aboriginal communities is caused by non-Aboriginal factors. Therefore it is worth quoting the anthropologist Venbrux' criticisms of this theory at length. Venbrux takes account of the detrimental effects of colonisation upon Aboriginal society, but concludes that traditional values still affect present behaviour.

> The view that Aboriginal violence is primarily related to anomie resulting from colonisation (including missionisation) and excessive state intervention, however, is problematic in a number of respects. First it denies Aboriginal people a commitment to their own deeds and strips them of dignity. Second, it ignores the possibility that Aboriginal people might perceive their acts of violence differently. In many contexts, conflict and fighting generate meaning; despite our moral judgments these are meaningful activities for Aboriginal people. Finally the enforcement of state law and the "pacification" of Aboriginal societies have also been part of the history of colonisation. The ethnographic literature shows that before colonisation Aboriginal societies had high rates of violence and homicide. Might the increase in violence which has been observed not also be related to the disappearance of the so-called Aboriginal reserves as "total institutions"... tightly controlled by white government or mission superintendents?[20]

When the misery which existed on the reserves is considered, Venbrux' "pacification" theory is controversial. However, others including Langton and Burbank agree in part, viewing present violence as the continuation of traditional conflict patterns, "a society where anger has always been expressed by aggression".[21] The radical change, which Langton has identified, and which Memmott notes, is that, through alcohol, structured violence has evolved into uncontrolled violence.[22] Hunter found that "The 'drunken comportment' of many Aboriginal drinkers includes an expectation of violent behaviour which facilitates displacement and frustration from the inter-cultural to the inter-sexual domain".[23] Perhaps because it feeds into these cultural attitudes alcoholic violence is difficult to eradicate.

> [T]here appears to be a substantial cultural elaboration of ex-
> pressed anger in an Aboriginal context, and ... these cultural forms
> are intertwined with "being drunk", in a state which fosters the
> recollection of past wrongs, the expression of anger, and the
> seeking of redress (with relative impunity).[24]

As mentioned earlier, culture stress and drunkenness support
defences of lack of intent, intoxication and diminished responsibility. For Aborigines the defence of diminished responsibility goes
particularly to the circumstances of deprivation. The technical
elements of the defence are an abnormal state of mind at the time of
the killing arising from mental disease or illness including brain
damage and a psychopathic disorder. These matters go beyond out-
bursts of "normal" emotions such as rage, jealousy or anger or lack
of control. Even if the abnormality is the result of external stress and
trauma it must be internalised[25] so that it is effectively inherent, but
not necessarily permanent.

For instance, the 1990 case of *Juli*, the 25-year-old Kimberley
rapist, already discussed, illustrates both a court's attitude to some
of these issues and the terrible circumstances of many ravaged
Aboriginal lives. Juli successfully sought leave to appeal against a
sentence of ten years' imprisonment for raping a woman on two
separate occasions when he was very drunk. He had pleaded guilty,
expressed remorse and had no significant prior convictions for
personal violence. Two factors influenced the grant of his application; the crushing effect of such a prison term on a Kimberley
Aborigine and the tragic, but not atypical, circumstances of his life.

The Court of Appeal found that drunkenness does not normally
constitute an excuse, but the general problems of Aboriginal society,
which lead to alcohol consumption, can be grounds for mitigation.
Juli was depressed at the time of the rapes and had displaced
suicidal symptoms; he was indifferent as to whether he lived or
died. His alcoholism exacerbated an underlying paranoid psychosis.
To describe Juli's background as dysfunctional is accurate, but it is
also glosses over the trauma and lack of purpose in his life. Juli's
father, who had little connection with him, died when Juli was about
15 years old. Juli had not done well either at school or in his sporadic
employment; his real occupation from the age of 16 years was to
drink heavily. He never had a steady girl friend and when sober was
shy and withdrawn. The psychiatrist's report said:

> His mother still lives in Turkey Creek, but she drinks heavily at
> times and has shown signs of chronic mental disorder for many

years. (His brother) … has had at least 2 psychotic breakdowns due to alcohol (he is now quite well and working) and one sister drinks extremely heavily. There is a lot of violence in the family, with poor marital records and prison records for drinking and fighting.[26]

The Chief Judge found that "while the applicant knew what he was doing, and that it was wrong, and consequently remained criminally responsible, his responsibility was diminished because his concern for the significance of his actions had been suspended".

The traumatised circumstances of his victim, and by extension her young child, are also horrifying. Raped twice at 18 years old by a man who had a violent reputation in her community, she was already the single mother of a 16-month-old child. They lived in a camp with her grandparents. She was intoxicated at the time of the first rape, and had been drinking during the night prior to the second rape.

At common law, intoxication can be held to negate the formation of intent or *mens rea*.[27] The three States with the largest Aboriginal populations, the Northern Territory, Western Australia and Queensland, have Criminal Codes in force that alter the application of the common law concerning the defence of intoxication. The thrust of the Codes is to limit the defence of intoxication to involuntary intoxication. In none of these jurisdictions can the accused's wilfully induced state of intoxication be sufficient for a successful defence, but it can be an advantage in that because inhibitions are lowered in this state, an argument as to lack of intent can be established. However, in the Northern Territory, Queensland and Western Australia, intoxication can be relevant to the defence "(1) as a basis for negating a mental element such as intention; (2) as a basis for negating voluntariness; (3) as relevant to some matter of justification or excuse".[28]

The relationship of assault to alcohol is apparent when even a small sample of cases is reviewed. The ALRC 1986 inquiry into customary law reviewed 47 cases of murder, rape and assault in all jurisdictions between 1974 and 1980.[29] Of these cases 26 involved a female victim; in only one was there a female offender.[30] Alcohol was a factor in 23 out of the 26 cases, which mainly involved violent assaults on women. Between 1989 and 1994, of unreported court cases, 13 involved assaults on Aboriginal women and in 12 of those cases the accused (and sometimes the victim) had consumed alcohol. In neither group of cases was intoxication pleaded as a formal defence for negating intent or voluntariness nor was it adduced as justification, but it was frequently pleaded in mitigation in the circumstances of the violent environment which Aboriginal people can experience on the reserves, and was taken into account in sentencing.[31]

A subjective standard operates when considering the gravity of the offence because intoxication is known to induce relaxation of normal controls. That the degree of deliberation with which the accused became intoxicated can aggravate the circumstances of the crime is illustrated in the 1991 New South Wales case of *Jerrard*,[32] in which the respondent, having drunk three flagons of alcohol, was "real drunk" and could not remember beating his female victim around the head with a rock. Justice Finlay found that his drunken state aggravated the circumstances of the crime "because of the recklessness with which the offender became intoxicated", particularly in the context of the respondent's past record of four violent assaults on different women and four breaches of restraining orders when under the influence of alcohol.

According to general sentencing principles, the judiciary have taken into account mitigating factors arising from the Aboriginal environment. Although intoxication is not normally a mitigating factor, judges have applied the subjective standard sympathetically to young male Aboriginal offenders, recognising that there is an environment peculiar to them of deprivation and violence. Generally when intoxication has been an unusual circumstance of the accused's behaviour, and out of character, judges have been treated this singular behaviour as an extenuating factor even when the offence is very serious.[33] In the 1989 case of *Rogers and Murray*, the respondent Rogers appealed against a sentence of six years imprisonment for raping his seven-year-old niece. Rogers, aged 18 years, had come from an isolated and "dry" community to visit town. Throughout the day he had been drinking. He was very drunk when he raped the child. By a majority the court reduced the sentence of imprisonment to three years. Factors taken into account were Rogers' previous good record and that he was unaccustomed to drinking. Chief Justice Malcolm commented "the general circumstances which have led to problems associated with the consumption of alcohol may themselves provide circumstances of mitigation".[34]

Many cases where alcohol and a deprived environment have been factors in the accused's behaviour are reviewed in the 1990 case of *Juli* and in the 1997 case of *Daniel*. Daniel, a drunken rapist with a criminal record, argued in his appeal against sentence that he and his victim lived in a dysfunctional community in which alcohol abuse and violent crime were more "prevalent and tolerated than in the general community". President Fitzgerald noted that in many cases the court had taken account of the tragic lives of both victim and offender, and the traumas caused by dispossession. However, in *Daniel*, heard in 1997, His Honour held that Aboriginal women and children "are entitled to equality of treatment in the law's responses to offences against them, not some lesser response because of their race and living conditions".[35]

As discussed earlier involuntary manslaughter is committed where the unlawful death of a human being is caused by the act of another human being who did not intend to cause the death but performed an unlawful and dangerous act or was criminally negligent in performing an act. In the circumstances of chaotic violence in many Aboriginal communities it is the lack of intention rather than criminal negligence that usually applies to this kind of violence. Frequently when Aboriginal women die through the violent assaults of Aboriginal men, the perpetrator may lack the intent to kill, and may not even contemplate the probability of death or grievous bodily harm. The perpetrator of the attack can be surprised that death has occurred.

The 1980 case of *William Davey* illustrates an environment of endemic violence in which people can be fatally injured without the incident being taken seriously. The male victim had intervened in a violent drunken argument between the accused and the accused's wife who was the victim's niece. Davey struck the victim, Roberts, on the head, first with a jerrycan and then with a six-foot length of four-inch by two-inch dressed timber. Roberts fell from his seat, unconscious. Surprisingly this caused no alarm and nobody paid attention. He was assumed to be drunk or merely stunned. Roberts later died of a subdural haemorrhage to the left side of the brain. Davey was found guilty of manslaughter. A community adviser gave evidence that Roberts' behaviour was provocative in Aboriginal culture in his initial interference between a man and his wife when a beating was being inflicted.

The violence has not abated. In 1994 in *Alh*, the New South Wales Supreme Court accepted the defence of lack of intent on the basis that perceptions of physical mortality can be distorted by exposure to constant violence. In this case a young male Aborigine charged with murder pleaded guilty to the manslaughter of another young man. The Crown accepted the plea and the court said:

> [T]hat you had no intention to kill or inflict grievous bodily harm, but were engaged in an unlawful and dangerous act. You told ... (the psychologist) ... that you had seen people bashed before but they had recovered, and you expected McGowan to do the same.

Men who have habitually violently abused their women for years become immune to the reality of their violence. There are "altercations, [where] an extra punch or kick in a long chain of punches or kicks can be one too many. Serious injury or death occurs, much to the amazement of the perpetrator who, after years of seeing the person he or she attacks get up and carry on, is amazed to see the victim dead".[36] For those who have not experienced this horrific environment of violence, two incidents recounted by Atkinson, and Women's Task Force on Violence are incredible. In each incident, men violently attacked their partners, the culmination of years of habitual violence. Later the attackers picked up the women, and in one case bathed her, and put them into the bed in which they slept also. The following morning they were astounded to discover that their victims were dead.[37]

Lack of intent was one of the defences raised in the 1986 Queensland case of *Watson*.[38] The defence argued that cutting was a common practice, that the accused had himself survived many knife and bottle wounds and did not consider these to be serious or a danger to life and finally that severe injuries were considered "differently" in the Palm Island community. At the trial supporting evidence was excluded because it was non-expert evidence. Hence "cutting" in this case became an issue between public knowledge of an existing culture and the judge's disbelief. Justice McPherson said the defence argument was tantamount to a "racist slur"[39] in that it implied that Aborigines were incapable of appreciating the dangers of knife attacks. But the accused's "sang froid", of which his Honour spoke, could perhaps be seen not as a matter of intellectual incomprehension but rather as an accurate response to his environment. Culturally, cutting is both an accepted form of punishment and a common manifestation of Aboriginal despair. Wilson reports that an Aboriginal welfare worker said many survive cutting, a form of self-mutilation that can be a release for frustration, anger and latent hostility to oppression.[40]

Judges have been frustrated by government and public indifference to the circumstances of this violence. In 1985 Justice Muirhead, sitting in a Northern Territory manslaughter case, in which alcohol had been a factor, said that for ten years he had done everything he could to draw attention to the necessity of reforming the laws, controlling alcohol supply and of establishing detoxification centres and that:

> I have not been alone in this exercise but it's been entirely fruitless ... The courts can achieve little if nothing ... the fundamental reasons for alcohol abuse and consequential violence go much deeper. It is Australia's problem: it won't go away ... and it cannot be dealt with. I have not been alone in these matters and it cannot be dealt with by the Aboriginals themselves without a lot of support and action.[41]

Recommendations 52 and 53 of the National Committee on Violence were expressed in similar terms.[42] Yet nothing has changed. The comments of some Brisbane Aboriginal women at a meeting in 1998 illustrate their despair. They claimed that the circumstances of males convicted of violence were better in prison "(three meals a day, exercise, medical services, etc) than those of abused women who remain in remote communities without adequate medical care and various basic needs".[43]

The belief in the non-Indigenous population that Aborigines live in an environment of uncontrolled violence as a result of heavy drinking will possibly be self-fulfilling. In attitudes, which parallel judicial consideration of "Aboriginality", juries in homicide trials are likely to find the accused not guilty of either murder or manslaughter because of these circumstances. In one sense this is akin to the concept of non-voluntary manslaughter. In an environment of chaotic violence the accused does not realise the effect of his drunken behaviour but where murder, or manslaughter can be strongly argued the jury's verdict is still likely to be not guilty of murder. A recent Western Australian case illustrates these attitudes, which abort the rule of law and promote anarchy.

In October 2000 at Derby in the Kimberley Jeffrey Qualla killed his sister-in-law, Merrilee Mulligan, the mother of two children. The Crown case was that Mulligan had threatened to tell a seven-year-old girl's family that Qualla was molesting her. That night when Mulligan was sleeping, Qualla bashed her over the head and dragged her into a vacant block where he attacked her with a file. He was charged with wilful murder, but the judge ruled that a video confession was not admissible because the tribal man had not understood his right to silence. The prosecutor believed that it would be hard to prove that Qualla deliberately killed Mulligan without the "graphic confession". The Director of Public Prosecutions (DPP), Robert Cock QC, agreed to accept a plea of guilty of manslaughter. Qualla will serve less than two years in prison. The DPP considered appealing the sentence that was at the lower end of the scale. Associates of Mulligan at Fitzroy Crossing, where she "was a respected worker for her people" said that the manslaughter verdict was an insult. The family of Sarah Johnston, an Aboriginal woman stabbed to death in Darwin in 2002, bitterly commented that "the death of an Aboriginal woman is never treated as murder, it is always manslaughter". In commenting on *Qualla's* case, Cock confirmed that this is so:

> Juries believe alcohol-fuelled violence in Aboriginal communities is so common they are more likely to convict Aborigines of manslaughter than murder. Unless a gun or knife was used in the killing it was difficult to prove intent to kill (the prerequisite for wilful murder) as opposed to the everyday violence in some Aboriginal communities. We are lucky to get manslaughter because of the type of tolerance of alcohol, juries have not accepted our submissions that the only inference available is the intention to commit wilful murder.[44]

Chapter 13

Reconciling rights in sentencing

> The human rights of Black women, not the arguable role of Black men in inflicting that violence, should take precedence in the debate.[1]

The Gordon Inquiry found concern in Aboriginal communities about the way that the Australian legal system was dealing with violence. It reported that:

> Family violence and child abuse, as breaches of customary law, destroy the harmony in communities and there needs to be a mechanism to restore that harmony. This has implications for the use of the non-Aboriginal justice systems. Many communities spoke of the need to follow customary law in dealings with the problems of family violence and child abuse.[2]

This statement raises issues of injustice and oppression. Aboriginal family violence is rampant, and it has not been contained by general law that has subverted traditional law and robbed Aborigines of autonomy. Reconciling traditional rights with the Australian legal system in criminal law sentencing involves considering the inter-active role of several laws: the causes of general law's failure to control violence, the place of customary law in Australian society, and the possible conflicts in domestic law arising from competing human rights in International law.

International law recognises both women's rights and Indigenous rights, but the exercise of one set of rights may be inconsistent with another set of rights. In Australia increased appreciation of Indigenous rights has led to calls for the recognition of customary law. Proposals for recognition have come from, or are associated with, the establishment of Aboriginal courts, Indigenous community justice projects, Aboriginal Justice Agreements, the Council for Aboriginal Reconciliation, the New South Wales Law Reform Commission and the Northern Territory and Western

Australian government inquiries which were commenced independently of each other in 2002. However the almost universal subordination of women[3] and the realisation that men's rights do not necessarily embrace women's rights[4] has also become an issue for international law.[5] Hence the difficulty for both Aborigines and the state is whether the recognition of Indigenous human rights, which are properly owed to Aborigines, will subsume concerns about the role of customary law in Aboriginal family violence?

Family violence is not, as its name implies, private violence. As an abrogation of women's human rights, this violence should concern the whole community. Justice Elizabeth Odio said at the Vienna Declaration of Violence against Women that "we need to ... make the international community understand that men and women must work toward the elimination of the absurd discrepancies between public and private rights".[6] But in considering the ratification of customary law, Aboriginal activists generally are concerned with international law in relation to establishing Indigenous autonomy, rather than with that law in relation to intra-cultural violence that affects women's rights.[7] They rely on international declarations that espouse Indigenous rights when examining, and arguing for, Australia's obligations under international law to Aborigines and Torres Strait Islanders.[8] However, they have not taken up those international declarations that affect women's status in the Aboriginal community.[9]

State recognition of traditional law would be complex because neither Aboriginal communities nor their laws are heterogeneous, and because of the increasing urbanisation of many Aborigines. Nonetheless, recognition would be a significant assertion of "internal self determination", a human right for Indigenous peoples affirmed in both the International Covenant on Civil and Political Rights (ICCPR) and the International Covenant on Economic, Social and Cultural Rights (ICESCR). Larissa Behrendt, an Aboriginal academic lawyer, sees this right in the Australian context as "increased Indigenous autonomy within the structures of the ... state. The challenge to Australia is to alter our institutions to incorporate that vision".[10] However, recognition of customary law also cannot be separated from the issue of Aboriginal intra-cultural violence to women, because this violence itself is partly a reflection of the traditional gender roles in a highly legalistic society.

These concerns are not new. In 1851 in South Australia they were debated with great fervour in circumstances akin to, and with some similar arguments to, those of the 1836 New South Wales case of *Murrell*. In two cases of intra-Aboriginal killings, the grand jury in its presentment said it was "morally incumbent" on the colonists "to confine their interference to the mutual protection of both races in their intercourse with each other" because:

> prior to the occupation of this country by the colonists, all these native tribes, as distinct communities ... would have been held by all jurists to be in a situation to make laws and adopt usages for their own protection and government.

As in Murrell's case this view was not accepted. The Executive retained the right to grant clemency and did so in this instance. However, many had agreed, as did the majority of newspapers, that Aborigines should be free to exercise their own laws. The *South Australian* put a dissenting argument phrased in the language then thought appropriate. It said that Aborigines should be liable in the criminal law to protect Aboriginal women, "who are regarded by the brutal males as property over whom they have the power of life and death".[11]

A fundamental problem in the present debate is that many Aborigines and non-Aborigines possibly have competing views about which set of human rights should prevail. Broadly, the international declarations which are in potential conflict and the dates on which they were entered into force for Australia are: the International Convention on the Elimination of All Forms of Racial Discrimination (CERD), 1975, the ICCPR, 1976, the ICESCR, 1976, and the Convention on the Elimination of all Forms of Discrimination against Women (CEDAW) 1979.

It is ironic that the general law has failed Aboriginal women in part because both lawyers and judges were concerned about respecting claimed customary law rights of Aboriginal men. Sentences for Aborigines convicted of serious crimes, including violence against Aboriginal women, have been mitigated either initially because of judicial cultural relativism in relation to customary law "defences" or later because of a proper application of general sentencing principles arising from the particular situation of Aborigines. In their particular contexts these are not attitudes to be decried. Yet probably the outcome has been effectively to send a message to Aborigines that in general law women's rights to protection and dignity are subordinate to those of male offenders.

In the late 1960s Eggleston conducted a survey of Aborigines within the justice system from a very sympathetic perspective of the injustices Aborigines have suffered. Nonetheless, it led her to believe that taking tribal law into account, particularly in circumstances of alleged provocation, was a problematic concept: "sentimentality should not permit Aborigines to escape with over-lenient sentences". Eggleston's observations are interesting as she was able to observe both tribal cases of violence and those cases where the right to inflict moral violence was argued. In the context of the 1960s, Eggleston concluded that there should be recognition of tribal law but that this should go to mitigating punishment. Contemporary judges took this approach. However, in her debate about competing rights Eggleston redressed the balance in favour of other rights as she considered the educative deterrent value of criminal law and the "interests of the community as a whole, including the Aboriginal community" were important. She notes that imprisonment even if not "the ideal method" do change customs that might be regarded as inimical to general human values.[12] Implicit in Eggleston's views is the conflict between customary law and other human rights.

In general law deterrence is that sentencing factor which acts as a warning that the law will not tolerate a particular form of behaviour. General deterrence is a judicial warning to the community against committing particular criminal acts; specific deterrence is a warning to the prisoner against repeating criminal behaviour. Effectively in many cases concerning Aboriginal men's violence to women sentences have not constituted either a specific (to the prisoner) or a general deterrence (to other men) against committing such acts.

In 1991 evidence was presented to the National Inquiry into Racist Violence that courts are viewed as treating Aborigines more severely than non-Aborigines, which leads to a "strong perception of institutionalised injustice in relation to the court system".[13] Aborigines have incurred discrimination in courts of summary jurisdiction, the Magistrates' or Local Courts, where minor offences, such as nuisance against public order, are heard.[14] Separate from these offences is Aboriginal men's violence to women, and its claimed justifications, whether of traditional law or moral violence. These do meet Eggleston's human rights test, because these acts do abrogate Aboriginal women's human rights. Yet because of the intensity of the violence, Aboriginal men frequently commit indictable, that is serious, offences that are heard by a judge and jury in District,

County or Supreme Courts. Paradoxically it is in these courts that judges have dealt with Aborigines more leniently than non-Aborigines, although men's violence might be seen as behaviour where deterrence should be particularly important.

These are long-established judicial attitudes. In 1954 in a case of attempted rape Justice Kriewaldt held "an Aboriginal should never receive a more severe sentence than would be awarded a white person for a similar crime".[15] In 1986 the ALRC considered that over the preceding 20 years discriminatory practices against Aborigines in sentencing were not apparent.[16] This finding was supported by a 1993 survey that analysed sentence length (in days) by offence group, sex and race. It established that "for males and females alike median sentences for Aborigines are substantially lower than for non-Aborigines". The difference is substantial for "against person offences" which included property offences. For indictable offences, Aborigines are "about one-quarter" more likely to receive a custodial sentence, but then will receive shorter than usual sentences.[17]

Judges have long been aware that there is a separate sentencing tariff for Aborigines.[18] Chief Judge Heenan of the Western Australian District Court (now Justice Heenan of the Western Australian Supreme Court) estimated that this tariff was about half, and said that although the sentencing principles are the same, "the application of those principles to a particular Aboriginal offender will frequently lead to a disposition which is different from that which it would have been in the case of a non-Aboriginal offender".[19] Judges acknowledge that they have "endeavoured to make allowance for ethnic, environmental and cultural matters".[20] As well as particular disadvantage, such as the severe deprivation and tragic circumstances which marks the lives of some offenders, judges take into account in mitigation the particular stress a tribal Aborigine would suffer in serving a sentence in a southern prison, payback when it "transcends vengeance and is of value in restoring community relations"[21] and banishment from "the land with which he [a prisoner] identifies himself".[22] This is simply an application of the sentencing principle that a judge should take into account, and give such weight as is appropriate, to the relevant particular circumstances of an offender. These guidelines in relation to sentencing Aborigines were set out in the High Court cases of *Neal* in 1982 and *Lowe* in 1984 and were reviewed by Chief Justice Malcolm in the 1989 Western Australian Criminal Appeal case of *Rogers and Murray*:

the relevant mitigating factor is not the mere fact that the offenders concerned are Aboriginal but their personal circumstances, which are related to their membership of the Aboriginal race and the particular circumstances under which they live.

In sentencing these are matters that are favourable to the prisoner, but sentencing is always a synthesis of all the factors, including deterrence, which should be taken into account.

Consideration of the often traumatised circumstances of the accused can be viewed by some Aborigines as pitting the rights of the accused against the rights of the victim to have the law's protection from violence. The victim and the community also have suffered. Sharon Payne, when she was Aboriginal Assistant Manager of the Law and Justice Section of ATSIC, commented with some acerbity on "Aboriginality" as a mitigating factor in a case in Canberra in 1991:

> [T]he defence of a particularly hideous attack on a young Aboriginal woman was based on the loss of lands and culture on the part of the young males involved. Apparently the young woman had no such defence although she too had lost her heritage.[23]

Payne remarked on the light sentences, "five and eight months respectively", the lack of general deterrence and failure in "the judgment to mention something of the real situation. It was the combination of being young, male and drunk which led to the assault". The sentence of the main offender was later extended after an appeal. But Payne considers the present system provides little incentive for the rehabilitation of violent men, it would have been preferable that the judgment mentioned something of the real situation.

Mitigation of sentence arising from circumstances is a perilous concept if it overwhelms deterrence. As discussed already many attacks presented by the defence as exercising cultural rights were complicated by intoxication of the perpetrator and sometimes the victim. Judges may have felt powerless when faced with alcohol-induced violence. In the 1987 Western Australian case of *Charlie, Uhl and Nagamarra* three heavily intoxicated men who had long records for offences relating to alcohol confined one woman in a motor vehicle against her will and then pack-raped another woman. Chief Justice Burt found that their prison experience had been "negative" and therefore to effect rehabilitation, they were to be returned to their "identifiable tribal" communities in which they were "to serve a significant proportion of their sentence" and to be under supervision, and to abstain from alcohol for the parole period. To this end a minimum term of seven months was fixed of a total four years imprisonment. This seems to be a manifestly inadequate sentence and the community's views were apparently ignored. They might well not have welcomed either these violent alcoholic rapists being returned to their midst or the supposed responsibility of supervising their abstinence from alcohol.

Because of the extreme violence that now exists, it is doubtful if those judges who did so were right to resile from the principles of deterrence. The ALRC 1986 report observed that a "sentencing judge or magistrate acts on behalf of the [wider general] community", and that the community's views should be taken into account. As discussed earlier, when judges are outside the culture and law of a society there are inordinate difficulties in sentencing on behalf of the general community, particularly when doing so from the perspective of a dominant culture. Nonetheless, judges have endeavoured to take account of the local Aboriginal community attitudes, usually presented to the court by male elders, in relation to the standing of the offender in that community,[24] the culpability of certain actions in Indigenous culture and tribal punishment. However, in sentencing, judges must also take account of wider community attitudes.

Probably Indigenous intra-cultural gender violence now has reached intolerable levels for both Aborigines and non-Aborigines. This of course is particularly so for those who suffer it, but also for others who see silence as assent to the perpetuation of abuse. The growing debate about this violence has been influenced by social and legal developments. First, renewed understandings of Aboriginal identity and entitlement to equal rights has meant some Aborigines have condemned judicial leniency, which in one context could be considered to be patronising, and which is, in many instances, in contrast with the severity of traditional law. As Lucashenko has observed, judicial leniency based on consideration of customary law, or of the disadvantaged situation of Aborigines, might well be unacceptable to those living the reality of community life.[25] Aboriginal concerns about lenient sentences for serious crimes have been voiced in the ALRC 1986 Report, by Langton in her 1990 report to RCIADIC and in other recorded comments of elders:

> Many elders because of the stringency of their traditional Law ... feel that "humanitarian" European laws provide no deterrent to

Aboriginal offending. Indeed Aboriginal law seems to have worked to prevent breaches by the threat, if not the actuality in most instances, of severe corporal punishment and even death.[26]

The lore is tough if someone makes a problem. They are punished in the bush and the elders talk to them to educate them in right behaviour. With European law a fellow goes to jail. Nobody talks to him. What comes of it? When he comes out he might do the same thing again.[27]

Yet paradoxically it is the evidence of male elders which has supported those customary law defences which have gone to lenient sentencing. Has their stance been an expression of a refusal to surrender autonomy to an alien law?

Secondly, judicial attitudes have also been affected by shifts in social perspective about these issues. As discussed earlier, judges have moved from an initial perception of Aboriginal women as legitimate (in traditional cultural terms) targets of violence to an increased regard for women's rights. Arguably this change occurred because a relatively homogenous and patriarchal society was segueing into one where diverse rights were respected. Domestic equal opportunity and anti-discrimination legislation acknowledged gender and human rights, all developments partly influenced by feminism and the international declarations against discrimination on the basis of race or gender, namely CERD and CEDAW.

CERD has influenced the 1975 Commonwealth *Racial Discrimination Act* (RDA) and in turn the effect of this legislation goes to the heart of the competing rights being discussed here. Because of the RDA, Aboriginal claims for formal recognition of customary law have been dismissed, but Aboriginal women's rights have been affirmed, because the customary law "defence" of Aboriginal men's right to inflict violence has also been dismissed. In the 1994 High Court criminal appeal case of *Walker*, discussed earlier, the RDA was one ground for Chief Justice Mason's ruling that Aboriginal customary law no longer existed as a criminal law defence because "all people should stand equal before the law". In the 1987 Queensland case of *Watson* Justice McPherson applied the same principles. His Honour held that condoning customary law justification for violence would disadvantage Aboriginal women in relation to other Australian women and also contravene State and federal law (being s 245 of the Queensland Criminal Code and s 9 of the RDA). The latter section incorporates a reference to Art 5 of CERD being "The right to security of person and protection by the State against violence or bodily harm whether inflicted ... by an individual, group or institution".[28] However, in other instances exemptions to the RDA have been granted affirming Aborigines' claims for recognition of their particular rights as Indigenes. Thus the question of the reintroduction of customary law is still open.

In the 1980s two federal governments considered the interaction of customary and general law. The first inquiry led to the ALRC 1986 report. Subsequently, following *Mabo [No 2]*, the Model Criminal Code Officers Committee of the Standing Committee of Attorneys-General (MCCOC), was set up to consider Aboriginal social justice. Each report concluded that Aborigines do have unique entitlements to cultural recognition in Australian society but this does not amount to justification under customary law for murder or other serious violence. The ALRC 1986 report recommended functional recognition of customary law where it impinged on Aborigines standing in general law, and that there should be government legislation to ensure that judges took customary law into account. The decision not to do so has caused frustration and disillusion in the Aboriginal community.[29] Alan Rose, then President of the Australian Law Reform Commission, says that one of the impediments to implementing the recommendations of ALRC Report No 31 was the position of women under some customary laws.[30]

The MCCOC was also concerned about the position of Aboriginal women. They disagreed with the proposal of the ALRC 1986 that a partial customary law defence should be established. The Committee found two parallel legal systems could well mean that interpretations of customary law by Aboriginal men, giving evidence in the general law courts, could make Aboriginal women more vulnerable to violence. They recognised that this would probably be the reality if the defence were introduced: "The defence may reduce itself to no more than a means of partially condoning pay-back killings and legitimising the correction of wives".[31] This would have been a return to the practices of the 1970s and earlier, the era of judicial cultural relativism.

But, as discussed earlier, the impetus for the recognition of customary law is gaining momentum. In 2002 the Northern Territory and Western Australian governments commenced further inquiries into the recognition of customary law. Each has the hope that, by doing so, dignity and autonomy will be restored to Aborigines. Cheri Yavu-Kama-Harathunian, the Indigenous Project manager for the extensive Western Australian Inquiry, criticised the ALRC

1986 evaluation of customary law as one that was constrained by the "20th century notions of recognition and cultural acceptance by the dominant culture".[32] She hailed:

> [This] quintessential moment in time when ... committed ordinary men and women and those in government look beyond themselves or their party and visualise an event that will change the landscape of a state or a nation forever, something that will potentially impact in the present and resonate in the future for decades to come.

Both the present inquiries embrace wide areas of interaction between the two laws, going beyond issues of criminal law. Aborigines are more directly involved in the conduct and management of the Western Australian Inquiry but each inquiry, although differently constituted, relies on consultation with Aboriginal elders and custodians of traditional law. By October 2003 the Northern Territory report had been completed and was waiting the Attorney General's approval for release. The Western Australian Inquiry was still continuing consultations with elders and communities.

Yavu-Kama-Harathunian has acknowledged the possibility of cultural conflict, but the Aboriginal material "will be captured and handled with respect, equity and equality". Further, customary law is to be preserved and continued as a living tradition. These are very important issues, and there is no intent in the following comments, which relate solely to Aboriginal family violence, to either subvert or pre-empt the outcome of this dialogue. Indeed this violence is a central issue in the Western Australian Inquiry:

> [T]he increasing "coming to voice" of indigenous women and, linked to this, a growing awareness of extreme levels of violence (including sexual violence) in some Aboriginal communities, have prompted a number of recent and ongoing inquiries ... research into Aboriginal family violence, attest[s] both to the significant degree of suffering within Aboriginal communities and to the profound limitations of non-Aboriginal forms of intervention to deal with the problem.[33]

However, the Western Australian inquiry is focused on affirming a fundamental practice of customary law. Yavu-Kama-Harathunian envisages that urban Aborigines will be covered by customary law, because of their spiritual affinity with Aboriginality, but that only the outcome of the inquiry will decide if Aborigines will be able to choose between the two laws for judgment.[34] She sees payback as "restorative justice ... [which] has always included the story of the victim or the victim's family", swift retribution would alleviate community tension, and also circumvent custodial sentencing.

Some questions which arise in relation to these issues are: first, the worst violence against Aboriginal women occurs in the most traditional communities where by implication customary law is still a stronghold, and traditional gender power structures are intact. Secondly, drinking accelerates traditional violence. As discussed already, there is evidence that a drunkard is "outside" customary law, that is, is not responsible for his or her actions. If drinking rituals have become part of an evolving culture, will customary law sanctions be invoked against drunken "moral" violence? If not, what sanctions will be applied? Thirdly, judges already take the certain infliction of payback into account in sentencing leniently, which affects both prompt settlement of disputes and length of custodial sentences. Should the general law step aside altogether? For instance, in October 2003 a 26-year-old Aboriginal man, Aaron Butler, was speared through the legs in two serious attacks and belted around the head in retribution for the alleged murder of his pregnant 22-year-old de facto wife. The grief and anger of his community in the Great Victoria Desert was patent. One attack was after his arrest. Butler is in hospital and will be tried. If the Aboriginal community regards the matter as being settled should this be sufficient? Fourthly, the increasing urbanisation of Aborigines raises issues about to whom customary law could properly apply? In 1977 Justice Wells stated the common law position in *Wanganeen v Smith*. His Honour held that where an Aborigine lives in urban circumstances, while his background is taken into account in accordance with the ordinary principles of sentencing, he is treated "just like any other citizen who lives in a town or city, and who makes use of the various facilities provided there". Langton, like Yavu-Kama-Harathunian, refutes the idea that Aborigines living in cities are severed from cultural links[35] and as mentioned earlier Sutton found "a persistence of pan-cultural values". However, culture is more amorphous than law. The MCCOC considered urbanisation is pertinent to the extent to which an individual can be held to be under the paramount influence of traditional law because of removal from traditional lands, the intermingling of different Aboriginal people and cultures on reserves, in town camps, towns and cities, in which case different constructions of customary law might apply.[36]

Fifthly, and most importantly, would Aboriginal men's claimed customary law rights to violence be reinstated? Justice Merkel of the Federal Court, basing his argument on UN declarations and covenants,[37] has argued for an increasing recognition of "the right to difference" even if principles of equality (before the law) are undermined in affirmation of that right.[38] On this basis if Indigenous rights to practice customary law are recognised, would this affirmation of a cultural right mean dismissing what may be regarded as Aboriginal women's right to have the same protection from violence which other women in Australia have? The Northern Territory Attorney General has addressed these issues in his qualification that the recognition of customary law is to be consistent with "universally recognised human rights and fundamental freedoms", and that the Criminal Code "applies to all citizens of the Northern Territory without exception. This means that the Northern Territory does not condone any of the crimes in that Code, including but not limited to murder, manslaughter, dangerous act, rape, incest, carnal knowledge, kidnap, assault and theft".[39] This caveat protects women from all assaults whatever the customary law justification might be and also from customary law marriage.

Aboriginal women themselves have voiced conflicting views about the introduction of customary law. In 1986 the ALRC found that Aboriginal women's "attitude towards the processes of customary law are, to say the least, ambivalent".[40] In 1988 Bell found that most Aboriginal people preferred the "notion of the two laws existing side by side and taking account of each other".[41] In 1994 the (female) Western Australian Attorney General, said that proposals to take account of customary laws in redrafting sentencing laws, had led to "concern within the Aboriginal community, particularly among women who believe such a move could make them a 'second-class lot of citizens' if there were two different laws".[42] In 1996 Queensland women endorsed the idea of "payback" continuing as certain and swift means of settling violence.[43] Now it can be hoped that in the present inquiries, they have had, and will have the opportunity to speak independently.

Frank Brennan foreshadowed the difficulty of resolving these issues in 1993. Brennan, a lawyer and Jesuit priest, strongly advocated Indigenous self-determination, but commented:

> There is a need to strike a balance between the collective right of a community through its elected Council or unelected elders to determine the law including the application of the traditional law to community disputes, and the individual rights of community members demanding due process and just outcomes reviewable by courts and tribunals of the national legal system.[44]

Chapter 14

Is anybody listening?[1]

> If we deny a problem exists, we allow others to intervene and impose their solutions. And history shows, their solutions just become our future problems. By acknowledging the problem, and looking for reasons why, we are developing ownership of the solutions. Once we understand what is happening we want to find answers because we can see what it is doing to us.[2]

> There's too much mythology about Aboriginal politics in this country and it's all about blokes promoting blokes.[3]

Violence suffered by Aboriginal women and children is rooted in the brutality of colonial devastation of Aboriginal society, harsh government policies, and racist destruction of Aborigines' pride, dignity and achievements and in some elements of traditional law and culture. The violence contravenes international conventions about human rights and women' rights, but for different reasons for many people, both Indigenous and non-Indigenous, it is an uncomfortable problem.

Aboriginal women including Atkinson, Langton, O'Shane and O'Donoghue, have spoken against intra-communal violence since the 1980s but because of cultural loyalty the problem has been largely closeted within Indigenous society.[4] Further, Indigenous issues are predominantly presented to mainstream Australian society through the perspective of male Aboriginal leaders.[5] Until comparatively recently, in public debate about Aboriginal issues, the gendered distinction between public and private has been maintained. Hence, domestically and internationally, human rights for Aborigines have usually been seen as Indigenous rights – particularly in relation to land rights, calls for a treaty, claims for sovereignty or self determination and the formal re-introduction of customary law.

In 2001 in the Charles Perkins Memorial Oration, Noel Pearson pointed to the real issues of Aboriginal welfare by asking:

Why has a social breakdown accompanied this advancement in the formal rights of our people, not the least the restoration of our homelands to our people? Aboriginal families and communities now often live on their homelands, in very much flasher housing and infrastructure than decades ago – but with a much diminished quality of life ... Indeed this social breakdown afflicts with equal vehemence those Aboriginal peoples who have never been dispossessed of their lands and who retain their classical traditions, cultures and languages.[6]

Pearson said that neither Labor nor the Coalition had holistic solutions, but a barrier to addressing these issues was that "[i]nstead of real radicalism which goes to the *radix* or root of the problems ... the Australian progressivist middle class is mainly preoccupied with ... quasi-radicalism".[7]

In 2001, in the fourth *overland* lecture, Langton specifically took up many of Pearson's points. She castigated the "caffe latte" politics of those who had never met Aborigines. Langton agreed that neither the left nor the right had complete solutions and noted:

This belief in the Left's contribution to our rights is highly overstated. Indeed, until the 1990s it was right-wing federal governments that legislated for both civil and statutory land rights for Aborigines.[8]

In December 2002 when the Premier of Western Australia Dr Geoff Gallop instigated the Gordon Inquiry he observed that the issues of Indigenous family violence and child sexual abuse have, "For too long ... been swept under the carpet because of cultural sensitivities and quite frankly, political correctness".

That these observations are noted here is not part of a political polemic or partisan politics. Indeed Langton spoke of "the hatred and fear that drive the various leftist and rightist views about us". The point at issue has been reiterated by Pearson, "[T]he cost of ... policy and political failure will be disproportionately borne by the black vulnerable: the children, the women and the elderly".[9] That is, allegations about cultural denigration or of re-imaging are irrelevant to the issue of facing up to human rights responsibilities about dealing with this abhorrent violence.

The continuing public denial that violence is part of traditional culture remains a large part of the "root of the problem". As discussed, despite contradictory evidence from the Aboriginal communities and anthropologists, the Gordon Report based its findings on this hypothesis. In 2002 and 2003 Mick Dodson acknowledged

Aboriginal men's responsibility for violence publicly at both the National Indigenous Men's Issues Conference and at the National Press Club, where he reportedly admitted that Aboriginal and non-Aboriginal leaders had failed to address Indigenous violence.

> Women and girls are precious to any society, we have to value, appreciate and support our women. We have to understand their worth to us not treat them like rubbish.[10]

The Task Force Report charges that the "people who could have made a difference [in dealing with violence] have failed to intervene". This covers not only the public silence of most Aboriginal male leaders, but also the indifference of governments, and the attitudes of those non-Indigenous Australians identified by the Task Force Report as those for whom "[i]nterventions were dismissed as politically and culturally intrusive in the newly acquired autonomy of Indigenous Communities".[11]

Unfortunately, despite its generally fine work in law reform, it is probably accurate to level this last charge against the ALRC. In its 1986 report, the Commission's affirmation of customary law marriage was tantamount to Aboriginal women's rights being subordinated to community cultural rights.[12] For Aboriginal women, therefore, the Indigenous basis of their identity as Australian citizens effectively robs them of possessing equal rights with non-Indigenous Australian women.

In 1994 the ALRC (Report No 69 Part I) acknowledged the particularly serious nature of the intra-communal violence[13] suffered by Aboriginal women in male-dominated and isolated communities. The Commission recognised that Aboriginal women are the most disadvantaged of any women within the legal system, and recommended that specialist legal services be established for them.[14] But the 1994 report ignored the particular needs of Aboriginal women in Recommendation 12.2 which is:

> [T]hat a Violence Against Women Unit should be established within the human rights area of the federal Attorney-General's Department. Its role should include annual reporting on the implementation of the National Strategy on Violence Against Women, the development and promotion of minimum standards to be met by service providers and through State and Territory legislation, and the promotion of a 'best practice' model for dealing with violence against women in the home.[15]

Further, this disregard of Aboriginal women's rights contrasts to the regard that the ALRC and the High Court have paid to the situation of some women, who are at risk of domestic violence within their own communities, and who are in Australia either as migrants or asylum seekers. The ALR (Report No 69 Part I) acknowledged the rights of migrant women,[16] but it did not acknowledge the unique cultural position occupied by Aboriginal women within Australian society in respect of human rights abuses because of family violence, nor was there consideration of the possible conflicts which could arise between Aboriginal women's rights in relation to immunity from violence and Aborigines' claims to autonomy[17] or recognition of customary law.

The rights of women seeking asylum in England or Australia on the grounds of domestic violence have been affirmed in the House of Lords in 1999, and following the House of Lords' decision, the High Court of Australia in 2002. The two cases of *Islam v Home Department; R v Immigration Appeal ex parte Shah*[18] and *Minister for Immigration and Multicultural Affairs v Khawar*[19] each concerned the applications of Pakistani women for asylum on the grounds of their vulnerability to domestic violence and the failure of the authorities, the state, to intervene in that abuse. In each case the judges of the highest court in England and in Australia found that a state has the responsibility to protect an individual against persecution in the form of domestic abuse. Aboriginal women of course may not wish to exit from the culture of their Indigenous communities. But following these decisions, surely the issue is that Australian governments, federal and State, have a duty, consistent with their powers, and in consultation with Aboriginal women, to establish programs which will protect women. As discussed below, Australian governments are recognising that failure to do so would be an abrogation of human rights obligations.

Many Aboriginal male leaders have disregarded family violence. In the mid-1990s Aboriginal women raised this as an issue during a consultation process with the Council for Aboriginal Reconciliation. The Council, then chaired by male Aboriginal leader Pat Dodson, made general submissions to the Commonwealth government about the future welfare of Aboriginal people. In this submission there were 78 recommendations concerning rights of Aboriginal and Torres Strait Islanders generally. But only one paragraph and one recommendation (Number 28) was concerned with women and violence. On the other hand, two-and-a-half pages and four recommendations (Numbers 24-27 inclusive) were concerned with Aboriginal deaths in custody and men's issues. The problem of intra-cultural violence was ignored. Domestic violence was described as "an ugly and largely hidden element throughout all Australian society". This is correct, but as a reference to the real plight of Aboriginal women, it is both inadequate and misleading. The Council's solution was to propose separate funding for legal advice and representation "particularly for those women subject to domestic violence". Given that the main policy of the Aboriginal Legal Service is to prevent Aborigines from being in custody, this might address a secondary issue for Indigenous women. The response completely avoided dealing with the source of the problem, Aboriginal men's violence to women and children. An Indigenous male leader, who is a national spokesman for reconciliation, privately acknowledged that there was both traditional and drunken violence against Aboriginal women, but "when men meet it never gets on the agenda".[20]

Aboriginal women have made scathing indictments of some Aboriginal leaders' misogynist attitudes. For instance, in 1997 Lucashenko said:

> [T]he politics of victimhood ... has allowed some Black men to cling to the rhetoric of oppression in which their individual circumstances as leaders of Black communities clearly show them to be privileged over most Blacks and particularly over Black women ...[21]

and in 2001, O'Shane:

> accused all indigenous men involved in politics "without exception" of only relating to white men in power rather than trying to improve the conditions of women and children in their own communities.[22]

ATSIC, the bureaucratic face of the Aboriginal community, has generally been dominated by males and they can be seen as failing to protect Aboriginal women against abuse. In the Senate in August 1999 Senator Aden Ridgeway called for increased government commitment to both ATSIC and Indigenous self-determination. In reply Senator Ferris said that John Herron, then Minister of Aboriginal Affairs, had:

> [R]eset the priorities [of ATSIC spending], and ATSIC has also recognised that this special problem [of violence] needs special

funding. It will be reducing *its multimillion-dollar travel and information budgets* (italics added) so that $1 million can be put aside this year to fund programs to tackle indigenous family violence.[23]

In 2002, Mick Dodson queried the lack of female representatives in:

> peak bodies such as ATSIC. There are so few that we are virtually squandering half our human talent and resources. The notion that men should lead our organisations and make decisions while the womenfolk look after children ... is nonsense.

Former ATSIC commissioner Jenny Pryor said that power politics played by men ensured that it was difficult for women to be elected or re-elected. In 2003 Alison Anderson was the only female member of ATSIC but at one stage she was considering resigning because of opposition from a male regional ATSIC councillor.

The imbalance in spending priorities has not changed. On 19 June 2001 ATSIC said that it had spent $3.9 million in 2000-01 on funding the national family violence legal counselling and prevention program. This was begun in 1998 and 12 family violence units have now been established.[24] However, Sutton said that one study established that of 130 remedial programs set up in Aboriginal communities in the 1990s, only six had been reasonably formally evaluated. There has been no written discussion or tabulation of failed programs. He asked, "Was this silence some other form of negligence on the part of those who funded these programs?"[25]

In April 2003, amid increasing public concern and speculation about ATSIC's allocation of funds, possible conflicts of interests, high expenditure on overseas travel and effective delivery of service to Aboriginal communities the Coalition Federal Government anticipated a government sponsored independent review of ATSIC by announcing the creation of the Aboriginal and Torres Strait Islander Services (ATSIS), which effectively, is now a bureaucratic barrier separating policy and funding. In mid-2003 the ATSIC review panel, the members of which embraced Labor, Liberal and Indigenous perspectives, generally reported adversely on ATSIC's operations ("review report"). It found that male control led to women's roles being ignored and reluctance to discuss issues relating to women and children.

External ideological and political pressures have impinged on the shuttered cultural silence about violence. Many Aboriginal women have been justifiably wary of the false universalism that was initially part of western feminism. In 1989 Langton tackled this issue by saying:

> Cultural difference is not a justification for brutality … Without the concerted effort of feminists to raise the issue of domestic violence over the past two or more decades, Aboriginal women would face a grim future.[26]

As Coomaraswamy observed, there might be universal oppression of women but the feminist movement has realised that the forms of oppression are not universal. However, in 2000 the Task Force on Violence Report was able to say that "feminist theories provide a general understanding of the position of women".[27]

The Gordon Report is the latest in a number of Commonwealth and State inquiries into violence dating from the mid-1980s. Several of these, like that of Daylight and Johnstone have been conducted with co-operation of Aboriginal women. Nonetheless, these inquiries have not, until recently, caught the public ear. Journalists like Tony Koch and Paul Toohey have ensured that the violence has become too scandalous to ignore. Aboriginal women leaders are publicly challenging the silence. In 2001, O'Donoghue admitted that family violence is "the most difficult and sensitive issue of all … [talking] … about indigenous violence is risky business because it exposes so much vulnerability. But I believe there are times when we have to find the voice to speak out".[28] In the same year Dr Evelyn Scott, Chair of the Aboriginal and Torres Strait Islander Corporation for Women since 1994, said violence needed to be addressed publicly.

> [For] … many generations, Aboriginal women were either too frightened or too culturally constrained to speak out … Only by reporting the instances of sexual abuse to the proper authorities, for consequential action to be taken, only by encouraging terrified and sexually abused women and children to come forward will men be discouraged from this course of action: and only by this subject being on the public agenda, shining the light of truth on to what was once the secretive and hidden province of men will it ever be brought under control.[29]

Now there are signs that the state is assuming its obligations to Aboriginal women. In July 2003 Prime Minister Howard met Indigenous leaders and experts to discuss Indigenous family violence. More than half of the delegates were women. Jackie Huggins, co-chair of *Reconciliation Australia*, said that most viewed this as a "significant demonstration" of a will to tackle violence. Following the meeting the Prime Minister committed an initial "down pay-ment" of 20 million dollars to developing programs to tackle Indigenous violence and child sexual abuse. In commenting on this development Huggins also instanced the Western Australian government's commitment, following the Gordon Report, of 75 million dollars. She said, "When we see it matched and extended by governments across the country, we might be in a better position to say that Australia is truly committed to tackling this problem".[30] Huggins observed that the Prime Minister was aware, as others should be, that particular cultural issues could arise in implementing these programs, "the white, feminist approach to domestic violence is not always right in every situation for every woman".

Possibly for many Aboriginal women it would be difficult to address violence through a further destruction of identity. Their primary focus could well be on cultural rather than gender rights. O'Shane said when questions arose of "race politics versus gender politics and when push comes to shove, more often than not, the women will say this is about race politics".[31] Langton said "We Aboriginal people can only rely on each other to interpret the world around us to ourselves".[32] Huggins called for "flexibility and insight in addressing Indigenous family violence". Hence although the values of women's rights have been contrasted to cultural rights in this book, the reconciliation of these rights for Aboriginal women can be achieved first by focusing on their own right to choose.[33] This would mean better support for education about alternatives, and providing more practical access to refuges, legal aid, and legal services. All avenues to legal redress, including courts, should be culturally appropriate and sensitive. If these things happen Abori-ginal women hopefully will feel that they have actual choices and the knowledge about how to implement them and what are the consequences of such choices.

Approaching the issue by either imposing non-Indigenous bureaucratic solutions which do not take account of Aboriginal women's cultural integrity, for instance, their wish to stay in their communities, or in the alternative of leaving the situation entirely intra-community, that is within the control of Aboriginal commu-nities, is to deny women their autonomy. In either scenario non-Aboriginal (and predominantly male) government bureaucracies and legislatures, or male-dominated Aboriginal councils are making the decisions.[34] Neither of these options helps Aboriginal women to choose their own destinies, or in many of their own communities, where, as Huggins commented, there might be "poor local governance", even guarantees that they would have the power to do so. Therefore Pearson's concept of an inter-regional response by Aboriginal women can be seen as the chance for strength and independence, and it is one that Aboriginal women are attempting.

Since the late 1980s women have initiated a number of community projects to deal with sexual assault and domestic violence. Achievements have been the establishment of refuges, increased awareness of legal remedies, provision of counselling, referral services and often some kind of liaison with police.[35] The range of these Australia-wide initiatives is impressive; for example the Women Out West (WOW) in Wilcannia, the Ngaanyatjarra Pitjantjatjara Yankunytjatjara Women's Council in Central Australia, meetings of Western Australian Women at Balgo to organise night patrols and community centres.[36] Aboriginal women have created networks of successful initiatives across communities. For instance, the women at Bourke wanted to establish a centre for victims of family violence and were able to follow some of the procedures already established by the women of the Mygunyah Aboriginal Corporation at Dubbo.[37] Similarly, the idea of policing communities through night patrols has been another women's initiative which has spread by successful example[38] from the Julalikari Council's night patrol at the Aboriginal town camp organisation in Tennant Creek[39] to similar patrols by women at Yuendumu and the Tangentyere's night patrol at Alice Springs.[40]

Many Aboriginal women are reluctant to have non-Aboriginal women involved in community initiatives against violence.[41] They feel "that if Aboriginal women were to run their own centres they would be able to take into account the racist aspects of rape and with the problems of black men raping black women".[42] An interesting exception is the centre at Bourke, which is open to both Aboriginal and non-Aboriginal women, and which is run by a committee of both races.[43] However, in many instances Aboriginal women have found non-Aboriginal women's intervention to be either unhelpful or too autocratic.[44] Where legal assistance programs or refuges are to be established, Aboriginal women's autonomy is essential.[45] For instance, in 1994 there was an attempt to establish an Aboriginal Women's Legal Centre in Victoria modelled on the WOW Legal Resources Project in New South Wales. The initiative was begun by an Aboriginal woman under the auspices of the Women's Legal

Resource Group[46] in Melbourne, but it foundered on the issue of who was to control the project and the Centre. Since then the Indigenous Women's Legal Resource Group has been established in Victoria, funded by Community Legal Services, Legal Aid and Family Services, and the Attorney General's Department.

The other direction for change lies within the legal system. In 1992 and 1993 the Australian Institute of Judicial Administration (AIJA) initiated two developments in judicial education that directly address the experience of Aboriginal women who have been victims of violence. In 1992 after the release of the national *Report on Violence*,[47] a sub-committee was formed to consider international approaches to judicial education in gender awareness. A program was developed and funded by the Commonwealth Attorney-General's Department and the Office of Status of Women, and the AIJA has recommended that it be included in a proposed national judicial orientation course. From 1993 the AIJA has been concerned with an Aboriginal cultural awareness program. Recommendation 96 of the RCIADIC report was for seminars to be held to improve cross-cultural understanding between judicial officers and Aboriginal people. Through co-operation between the Commonwealth Attorney-General's Department, the AIJA and ATSIC, seminar programs have been conducted in most jurisdictions. In some jurisdictions magistrates have participated in seminars, separate seminars have been held for Northern Territory magistrates, and in some jurisdictions judges have visited Aboriginal communities.[48]

Some solutions might be founded on a combination of law and social order. The trial Aboriginal Law and Justice Programs are perhaps promising initiatives. One commenced at Lajamanu and Ali Curang in mid-1999. There is self-responsibility. Aboriginal people themselves have taken over their own justice system, through the elders, night patrols and the police. Aborigines are exercising their own authority including the application of some customary law as part of a community effort. The communities control the programs which include educational and diversionary programs. Women's shelters have been built to provide safe quarters, and reportedly domestic violence cases have decreased from about 30 incidents a month to few. The communities are more peaceful and attendance at schools rose from 48 per cent in 2001 to 60 per cent in 2002.

The Gordon Report recorded the favourable evaluation in 2002 of the Joondalup Family Violence Court (JVFC). This was established in 1999 for a two-year trial period. "The aims of the then pilot scheme were not only to improve the criminal justice response to family violence, but also to support the victims and reduce the incidence of family violence in the pilot area".[49] There was inter-agency cooperation and collaboration. On the other hand the Strong Families project which was set up in 2001 in the Midland and Great Southern Regions, whilst involving interagency organisations and aiming at holistic community solutions was not regarded as being successful. The Gordon Report heard that there was a reluctance to become involved with government agencies.

In relation to these interventions the final verdict must come from Aboriginal women but as Huggins said to them:

> Men are an integral part of our struggle too. And I guess you position yourselves in the relationships you have with men … Sisters it's a privilege to applaud each other and we should do it more often otherwise our families suffer too … It's just knowing at which point to strike and break the cycle which counts … We must be considered as people first and not just objects of affliction.[50]

Aboriginal people are "not just objects of affliction"; their culture has enriched that of non-Aborigines through legends and the arts. Every non-Aboriginal person living in Australia, even the most recent arrival, has benefited from the displacement of Aboriginal people. This is where non-Aborigines' responsibility for violence lies, because in their own country, their land, the situation of Aborigines is analogous to that of refugees. A recent UNHCR report found that:

> Refugee camp life removes women, men and children from their proper, culturally defined networks of protection, support and social discipline, thereby magnifying previously existing social patterns of abusive behaviour.[51]

In addressing these problems there is optimism in the increasing number of Aboriginal graduates in law and other disciplines. But two reports released in October 2003 – one of a Senate Inquiry and the other of the Australian National University's Centre for Aboriginal Economic Policy Research – establish that over the next decade generally there will be increasing unemployment and further social deterioration in Indigenous communities. Violence will flourish. Huggins links solutions to reconciliation, and unless this, together with Pearson's aim of strong economic outcomes, can be achieved, how can the "feelings of powerlessness and hopelessness" captured in the words of a young Queensland man be overcome?

Sometimes I wonder where I fit in, when I will be accepted and will I ever find my place in life. Right now I feel so confused and so alone and scared by what I am seeing. I don't want to be part of it anymore. I have had three friends who couldn't cope who suicided and I wish I had the courage to do it as well. I just don't know how to cope anymore. I just want to find peace in my life and to be accepted for myself.[52]

Notes

Preface

1   B Robertson (ed), *The Aboriginal and Torres Strait Islander Women's Task Force on Violence Report* (State of Queensland, 2000), p xxxii (hereafter Task Force Report).

2   R Coomaraswamy, "Broken Glass: Women, Violence and the Rule of Law", Lecture, Melbourne University Law School, October, 2001.

3   L O'Donoghue, "Indigenous violence: it's everyone's business", *Age*, 22 October, 2001, p 15.

4   G Cowlishaw, "Studying Aborigines: Changing Canons in Anthropology and History", in B Attwood and J Arnold (eds), *Power, Knowledge and Aborigines* (LaTrobe University Press, Melbourne, 1992), p 20.

5   E Eggleston, *Aborigines and the Administration of Justice* (PhD thesis, Monash University, 1970), p 432.

6   D Bell and T Nelson, "Speaking About Rape is Everyone's Business" (1989) 12(4) *Women's International Forum* 403.

7   M Langton, "Medicine Square", in I Keen (ed), *Being Black: Aboriginal Cultures in 'settled' Australia* (Aboriginal Studies Press, Canberra, 1994).

8   R Coomaraswamy, cited by H Charlesworth and C Chinkin, "Violence Against Women: A Global Issue", in J Stubbs (ed), *Women Male Violence and the Law* (AIC, Sydney, and Federation Press, Sydney, NSW, 1994), p 13.

9   I Clendinnen, "True stories" (ABC Books, Sydney, 2000), pp 8-9.

10   L Hiatt, *Arguments About Aborigines* (Cambridge University Press, Cambridge, 1996), (n 7), p 186.

11   P Sutton, "The politics of suffering: Indigenous policy in Australia since the 1970s" (2001) 11(2) *Anthropological Forum* 127.

12   J Huggins, R Huggins and J Jacobs, "Kooramindanjie: Place and the Post-Colonial" (1995) 39 *History Workshop Journal* 166.

13   Clendinnen, op cit, p 16

14   P Sutton, "Families of Polity: Post-Classical Aboriginal Society", Discussion paper published by the National Native Title Tribunal, p 6.

15   Australian Law Reform Commission, *The Recognition of Aboriginal Customary Laws: Report No 31* (AGPS, Canberra, 1986), paras 88-95, p 72. (hereafter ALRC Report No 31, 1986).

16   Sutton, op cit, p 3.

Chapter 1

1   Anonymous speaker, FTEA&R Centre (SA) Inc, *No Shame – No Violence* (Port Lincoln, 1995), p 7.

2   Task Force Report, p xi.

3   P Sutton, "The politics of suffering: Indigenous policy in Australia since the 1970s" (2001) 11(2) *Anthropological Forum* 127.

4   J Cunningham and Y Paradies, *Mortality of Aboriginal and Torres Strait Islander Australians* (Australian Bureau of Statistics, Canberra, 2000), p 29.

5   P Memmott, R Stacy, C Chambers and C Keys, *Violence in Indigenous Communities* (Attorney-General's Department, Canberra, 2001), p 22 (hereafter Memmott et al).

6   M Sumner, "Substance Abuse and Aboriginal Domestic Violence" (1995) 19(2) *Aboriginal and Islander Health Worker* 16; A Bolger *Aboriginal Women and Violence* (Australian National University, North Australian Research Unit, Darwin, 1991) Chs 1 and 2; J Atkinson, "Violence Against Aboriginal Women: Reconstitution of Community Law – the Way Forward" (1990) 2(26) *ALB* 6; *Rohan John Clinch* (1994) 72 A Crim R 301 at 309 (WACCA).

7   Office of the Director of Public Prosecutions, Queensland, *Indigenous Women within the Criminal Justice System* (Office of the Director of Public Prosecutions, Brisbane, 1996), p 15 (hereafter DPP, Qld).

8   J Atkinson, "Violence in Aboriginal Australia, Part 2" (1990) 14(3) *Aboriginal and Islander Health Worker*, p 5.

9   Aboriginal and Torres Strait Islander Social Justice Commissioner, *Second Report* (1994), pp 195-96.

10 Atkinson, "Violence in Aboriginal Australia, Part 2" op cit, p 5.

11 E Johnston, *Royal Commission into Aboriginal Deaths in Custody: National Report, Overview and Recommendations* (AGPS, Canberra, 1991), p 4 (hereafter RCIADIC Report).

12 Royal Commission Government Response Monitoring Unit, Aboriginal and Torres Strait Islander Commission, Annual Reports, 1992/1993, 1993/1994, 1994/1995, 1995/1996, 1996/1997 (Commonwealth of Australia).

13 S Gordon, K Hallahan, and D Henry, *Putting the picture together, Inquiry into the Response by Government Agencies to Complaints of Family Violence and Child Abuse in Aboriginal Communities* (Department of Premier and Cabinet, Western Australia, 2002), pp 316-17 (hereafter Gordon Report).

14 Memmot et al, p 6.

15 J Mouzos, *Femicide: The Killing of Women in Australia 1989-1998* (Australian Institute of Criminology, Canberra, 1999), pp 19-22 for all the following statistics (*Femicide*).

16 J Mouzos, *Homicidal Encounters: A Study of Homicide in Australia 1989-1999* (Australian Institute of Criminology, Canberra, 2000), pp 19-22 for all the following statistics (*Homicidal Encounters*).

17 Atkinson, *Beyond Violence: Finding the Dream* (Office of the Status of Women, Canberra, 1990), p 13.

18 Memmott et al, p 39.

19 A Ferrante, F Morgan, D Indermaur, and RW Harding, *Measuring the Extent of Domestic Violence* (Hawkins Press, Sydney pp 36-37 (hereafter Ferrante et al).

20 Memmott et al, op cit, pp 9, 39.

21   A Bolger, *Aboriginal Women and Violence* (Australian National University, North Australian Research Unit, Darwin 1991), p 23.

22   *Advertiser* (Adelaide), 15 January 1977.

23   Atkinson, "Violence Against Aboriginal Women", op cit, p 6.

24   ATSIWTFVR, op cit, p 181.

25   *Australian* 14 January, 2002 p 1.

26   P Wilson, *Black Death White Hands* (Allen & Unwin, Sydney, 1982), p 5.

27   Ferrante et al, op cit, p 36.

28   J McCorquodale, "Alcohol & Anomie: The Nature of Aboriginal Crime", in B Swanton (ed), *Aborigines and Criminal Justice* (AIC, Canberra, 1984), p 27.

29   Ferrante et al, op cit, pp 35-36.

30   M Carnegie-Smith in M Carroll, *Ordinary people, extraordinary lives* (New Holland Publishers, Sydney, 2001), p 35.

31   M Langton, L Ahmatt, B Moss, E Schaber, C MacKinolty, M Thomas, E Tilton, and L Spencer, *"Too Much Sorry Business": Report of the Royal Commission into Aboriginal Deaths in Custody: Vol 5 Appendix D I* (AGPS, Canberra, 1991), p 204 (hereafter Langton et al).

32   Ibid, p 311.

33   V Burbank, *Fighting Women* (University of California Press, Berkeley, 1994), p 43. The apparent disparity in these male/female statistics occurs because there is also fighting between women.

34   Task Force Report, p 12.

35   Bolger, op cit, p 35.

36   Langton et al, op cit, p 301. Langton's use of the term "white poison" refers to the introduction of alcohol to Aborigines by Europeans.

37   ALRC Report No 31, para 90, p 41.

38   Bolger, op cit, p 43 ff.

39   Langton et al, op cit, p 301.

40   J Atkinson, "'Stinkin Thinkin' Alcohol Violence and Government Responses" (1991) 2(51) *ALB* 4.

41   Gordon Report op cit p 105.

42   Ferrante et al, op cit, pp 35-36.

43   J Atkinson (ed), *Beyond Violence: Finding the Dream* (Office of the Status of Women, Canberra, 1990), p 146.

44   Burbank, op cit, p 61.

45   Australian Bureau of Statistics, Canberra, 1995, p 22.

46   Langton et al, op cit, p 287.

47   Ibid, pp 301-2, and Chapter 1 *"White Poison:* Aboriginal Alcohol Abuse".

48   D Bell and P Ditton, *Law: The Old and the New* (Aboriginal History, Canberra, 1980), p 13.

49   PGE Albrecht, *The Present Problem of Authority in the Aboriginal Community* (Unpublished paper, 1965) cited in EM Eggleston, *Aborigines and the Administration of Justice* (Unpublished PhD thesis, Monash University, 1966), p 430.

50   S Davis, *Above Capricorn: Aboriginal Biographies from Northern Australia* (Angus & Robertson, Sydney, 1994), pp 35-41.

51 Davis, ibid, pp 2, 113.
52 W McLennan and R Madden, *The Health and Welfare of Australia's Aboriginal and Torres Strait Islander Peoples* (Australian Bureau of Statistics, Canberra, 1997), p 31.
53 E Hunter, W Hall and R Spargo, "Alcohol Consumption and Its Correlates in a Remote Aboriginal Population" (1991) 2(51) *ALB* 8. The figures from a Kimberley survey are 46% Aboriginal women compared to 75% European women and 76% Aboriginal men compared to 87% European men.
54 ABS, op cit, p 29.
55 Langton et al, op cit, p 305.
56 Daylight and Johnstone, op cit, p 69.
57 Tangentyere Council, "What Everybody Knows About Alice" (1990), p 1, cited in Langton et al, op cit, p 304.
58 ABC Radio National, "A Day in the Life of Legal Aid-Darwin (Part 2)" *The Law Report Transcript*, 20 August 1996, pp 5-6, <http://www.abc.net.au/rn/talks/ 8.30/lawrpt/lstories/ lr200896. htm>.
59 Task Force Report, pp 10-12 and 15.
60 Ibid, p 89.
61 FTEA&R Centre (SA) Inc, *No Shame – No Violence* (Report on Proceedings, Port Lincoln, 1995), p 6.

Chapter 2

1 M Tonkinson, *Domestic Violence Among Aborigines*, A discussion paper prepared for the Domestic Violence Task Force, cited by S Gordon, K Hallahan, D Henry, *Putting the picture together: Inquiry into the Response by Government Agencies to Complaints of Family Violence and Child Abuse in Aboriginal Communities* (Dept of Premier and Cabinet, WA, 2002) (hereafter Gordon Report), p 65.
2 Ibid, p 64.
3 M Langton, "Feminism: What do Aboriginal Women gain?" *Broadside: National Foundation for Australian Women Newsletter*, 8 December 1989, p 3.
4 R Coomaraswamy, cited by H Charlesworth and C Chinkin, "Violence Against Women: A Global Issue", in J Stubbs (ed), *Women Male Violence and the Law* (AIC, Sydney, and Federation Press, Sydney, 1994), p 13.
5 Watson, L, "Sister, Black is the Colour of My Soul", in J Scutt (ed), *Different Lives* (Penguin Books, Melbourne, 1987), p 52.
6 J Huggins, "A Contemporary View of Aboriginal Women's Relationship to the White Women's Movement", in N Grieve and A Burns (eds), *Australian Women: Contemporary Feminist Thought* (Oxford University Press, Oxford, 1994), pp 70, 77 (hereafter *Contemporary View*).
7 L Behrendt, "Aboriginal Women and the White Lies of the Feminist Movement: Implications for Aboriginal Women in Rights Discourse" (1993) 1 *Australian Feminist Law Journal*, p 33.

8   G Baldini, "Rape And Sexual Abuse Within The Aboriginal Com-
    munities", Paper delivered 20 June 1996, *Balancing The Scales*, National
    Conference on Sexual Assault, Perth, 20-21 June 1996.

9   Office of the Director of Public Prosecutions, Queensland, *Indigenous
    Women within the Criminal Justice System* (Office of the Director of Public
    Prosecutions, Brisbane, 1996), p 33.

10 P Daylight and M Johnstone, *Women's Business* (Department of the Prime
    Minister and Cabinet, Office of the Status of Women, AGPS, Canberra,
    1986), p 65.

11 J Atkinson, cited by R Lincoln and P Wilson, "Aboriginal Offending:
    Patterns and Causes", in D Chappell and P Wilson, *Australian Criminal
    Justice System, the mid 1990s* (Butterworths, Sydney, 1994), p 71.

12 DPP, Qld, op cit, pp 29-41; NSW Ministry for the Status and
    Advancement of Women, *Dubay Jahli Aboriginal Women and the Law
    Report* (NSW Government, Sydney, 1994), pp 4, 5, 8, 10, 12, 13 and 18.

13 Australian Bureau of Statistics, *National Aboriginal and Torres Strait
    Islander Survey 1994: detailed findings* (Australian Bureau of Statistics,
    Canberra, 1995), p 63.

14 Ibid. The qualification is made that in the table of reasons "not reported"
    does not add up to a correct percentage total because more than one
    answer may be given. The percentages for the women not reporting inci-
    dents to the police are discussed below.

15 A Ferrante, F Morgan, D Indermaur, and R Harding, *Measuring the
    Extent of Domestic Violence* (Hawkins Press, Sydney, 1996) (hereafter
    Ferrante et al), p 36.

16 M Langton, L Ahmatt, B Moss, E Schaber, C MacKinolty, M Thomas, E
    Tilton, and L Spencer, *"Too Much Sorry Business": Report of the Royal
    Commission into Aboriginal Deaths in Custody: Vol 5 Appendix D I* (AGPS,
    Canberra, 1991), op cit, p 307 (hereafter Langton et al).

17 J Atkinson, "'Stinkin Thinkin' – Alcohol Violence and Government
    Responses" (1991) 2(51) *ALB* 5.

18 D Bell and P Ditton, *Law: The Old and the New: Aboriginal Women in
    Central Australia Speak Out* (CAALAS, Aboriginal History, Canberra,
    1980), p 36.

19 D Bell, "Women and the Land" (1979) 3(11) Nov/Dec *Identity* 28.

20 J Atkinson, "A nation is not conquered" (1996) 3(80) *ALB* 6, Gordon
    Report, p 86, 190.

21 Task Force Report, p 8.

22 Gordon Report, p 86.

23 G Baldini, "Rape and Sexual Abuse Within the Aboriginal Commu-
    nities", *Balancing the Scales: National Conference on Sexual Assault*, Perth,
    20-21 June 1996, op cit, p 2.

24 Task Force Report, p 21.

25 Ibid, pp 13, 21; L O'Donoghue, "Indigenous violence: it's everyone's
    business", *Age*, 22 October 2001, p 15.

26 Gordon Report, p 84.

27 Aboriginal Women's Legal Issues Conference Parramatta, "Background
    Paper" (1993).

28 D Bell and T Nelson, "Speaking About Rape is Everyone's Business" (1989) 12(4) *Women's Studies International Forum* 412-13.

29 ALRC Report No 31, para 321, p 218.

30 Task Force Report, p 231.

31 Bell and Ditton, op cit, p 78. For example, on one reserve to call police women had to walk a quarter of a mile in order to telephone.

32 Confidential Submission, ALRC Report No 69, Part I, p 120.

33 Ministry of the Status of Women New South Wales, op cit, p 13.

34 Bell and Ditton, op cit, p 24.

35 S Jarrett, "We Have Left it in Their Hands" (unpublished PhD Thesis, University of Adelaide, 1997), p 212.

36 Bell and Ditton, op cit, p 17.

37 "Police warn of problems on reserves", *News*, Darwin, 7 January 1974. Police can also be reluctant to enter reserves in the north because of the violence and hostility towards them which is understandable given the history of dispossession. "Police fly to melee", *West Australian*, 20 November 1976; "The village where they bash the policeman", *Morning Herald*, 12 February 1974; "Blacks stone police at "trouble station"", *Age*, 17 January 1974. In 1974 provision was made for the appointment of eight to 12 Aboriginal liaison officers to the Northern Territory police force in an effort to improve communications between Aborigines and the police. "Aboriginals "Will Act As Police Liaison Officers"", *Northern Territory News*, 29 May 1974; "Police to have Aboriginal links", *News*, 10 September 1974; but attacks on police continued being reported in newspapers. In December 1974 and January 1975 there was violent hostility between police and Aborigines including the incident at Skull Creek, near Laverton, Western Australia, which led to a Royal Commission in September 1975.

38 Aboriginal aides in police forces are known by various terms in different States: Police Liaison Officers (Queensland), Aboriginal Community Liaison Officers (NSW), Aboriginal Police Aides (WA).

39 DPP, Qld, op cit, p 30.

40 NSW Ministry for the Status and Advancement of Women, op cit, p 13.

41 DPP, Qld, op cit, pp 30-31.

42 Chief Justice's Taskforce on Gender Bias, *Report* (Chief Justice of Western Australia, 1994) (hereafter Chief Justice, WA, *Report*).

43 Jarrett, op cit, p 190.

44 (1984) 155 CLR 1.

45 (1991) 171 CLR 635.

46 (1994) 179 CLR 427.

47 Gordon Report, p 379.

48 Gordon Report, p 357.

49 E Johnston, *Royal Commission into Aboriginal Deaths in Custody, National Report: Overview and Recommendations* (AGPS, Canberra, 1991), Recommendation 106, p 54 (hereafter RCIADIC).

50 Bell and Ditton, op cit, p 44, Bell and Nelson, op cit, p 413, D Bell, "Women and the land" 1979 3(11) Identity 27.

51 Personal communications with author from a Telecom manager 1996, and from a post graduate student, 1998.

52 Gordon Report, p 182.

53 Telecom manager, personal conversation with author, July 1996.

54 Bell and Ditton, op cit, pp 106-7; I White, D Barwick and B Meehan, *Fighters and Singers* (George Allen & Unwin, Sydney, 1985), pp 64-65. Bell frequently mentions giving women transport for hunting trips or to return to their "country". See also Payne, "Inyalangka", in *Fighters and Singers*, op cit, pp 126-27; I White, "Mangakatina", in *Fighters and Singers*, op cit, p 225; V Burbank, *Fighting Women* (University of California Press, Berkeley, 1994), p 14, for other examples of the dependence of women on others for transport even to maintain their own rituals.

55 ATSIC, *Aboriginal and Torres Strait Islander Women: Part of the Solution* (ATSIC, Canberra, 1992), Recommendations, 13-16, p 8; Recommendation 32, p 10; Recommendation 50, p 12; Recommendation 62, p 13.

56 Anonymous speaker, NT, cited in Atkinson, *Beyond Violence,* op cit, p 15.

57 Bell and Ditton, op cit, p 78.

58 (1990) 96 ALR 739; (1990) 2(47) *ALB* 9.

59 Bell and Nelson, op cit, pp 412-13.

60 Jarrett, op cit, p 191.

61 Task Force Report, p 37.

62 Female worker, NT, quoted in Atkinson, *Beyond Violence,* op cit, p 15.

63 Gordon Report, p 357.

64 Task Force Report, p 232.

Chapter 3

1 Gordon Report, p 221.

2 Langton, et al, *Too much Sorry Business: Report of the Royal Commission into Aboriginal Deaths in Custody: Vol 5 Appendix D 1* (AGPS, Canberra, 1990) , p 373.

3 R Madden, *National Aboriginal and Torres Strait Islander Survey 1994: detailed findings* (ABS, Canberra, 1995), p 63.

4 A Ferrante, F Morgan, D Indermaur and RW Harding, *Measuring the Extent of Domestic Violence* (Hawkins Press, Sydney, 1996), p 70 (hereafter "Ferrante").

5 Task Force Report, p 232; J Davies, "Attack on police over Aboriginal violence", *Age,* 25 March, 2002, p 3.

6 Task Force Report, p 232.

7 Gordon Report, p 204.

8 Task Force Report, p 37.

9 Gordon Report, pp 190-91.

10 Private conversation with author.

11 J Lloyd and N Rogers, "Crossing the Last Frontier: Aboriginal Women Victims of Rape in Central Australia", in P Easteal (ed), *Without Consent: Confronting Adult Sexual Violence* (Australian Institute of Criminology, Canberra, 1993), pp 159-62.

12 T Koch, "A national disgrace", *Herald Sun,* 13 November 1998, p 19.

13 ABC Radio National, "A Day in the Life of Legal Aid-Darwin (Part 2)" *The Law Report Transcript*, 20 August 1996, p 5, <http://www.abc.net.au/rn/talks/8.30/lawrpt/lstories/ lr200896.htm>;. Atkinson, "Violence in Aboriginal Australia, Part 2", op cit, pp 8-9.

14 T Koch, "Brenda fights for a future to hide pain from the past", *Courier Mail*, Brisbane, 1 November 1997, pp 1, 2.

15 Office of the Director of Public Prosecutions, Queensland, *Indigenous Women Within the Criminal Justice System* (Office of the Director of Public Prosecutions, Brisbane, 1996).

16 R Goldfam, "Silence in Court! Problems and Prospects in Aboriginal Legal Interpreting", in D Eades (ed), *Language in Evidence* (UNSW Press, Sydney, 1995), pp 39-41.

17 HJ Steiner and P Alston, *Human Rights in Context: Law Politics and Morals*, 2nd edn (OUP, Oxford, 2000), p 168.

18 J Atkinson, *Beyond Violence: Finding the Dream* (video and booklet) (Aboriginal and Islander Sub-Program, National Domestic Violence Program, Office of the Status of Women, Canberra, 1990), p 14.

19 L Behrendt, *Aboriginal Dispute Resolution* (Federation Press, Sydney, 1995) citing comments of C Buchanen, p 44, Task Force Report, p 228.

20 "Charge on girl who was raped", *Brisbane Mail*, 15 September 1973.

21 "Gang-rape complaint sparks investigation", *Koorie Mail*, 31 August 1996, p 8; J Kiss, "A matter for regret" (1996) 31(2) *Australian Lawyer* 14.

22 M Ceresa, "Police apologise to rape victim", *Australian*, 4 June 1996, p 5.

23 Kiss, op cit.

24 *Johansen v Billing, Commissioner of Police and Police Appeal Board* (1993) (unreported, WASC, Pidgeon, Franklyn and Owen JJ, No 1744 of 1992, Hearing 17 and 18 September 1992, delivered 19 May 1993).

25 National Inquiry into Racist Violence (Australia), *Report* (AGPS, Canberra, 1991), pp 88-89.

26 Chief Justice of Western Australia, *Report of Chief Justice's Taskforce on Gender Bias* (Chief Justice of Western Australia, Perth, 1994), pp 123 and 126-29; Office of the Director of Public Prosecutions, Queensland, *Indigenous Women within the Criminal Justice System* (Office of the Director of Public Prosecutions, Brisbane, 1996), pp 29-31.

27 Office of the Status of Women and Australian Bureau of Statistics, *Australian Women's Year Book: 1995* (AGPS, Canberra, 1995) op cit, p 80.

28 P O'Shane, "Aborigines and the Criminal Justice System", in C Cunneen (ed), *Aboriginal Perspectives on Criminal Justice* (The Institute of Criminology, Sydney University Law School, Sydney, 1992), pp 3-6; G Bird, *The "Civilizing Mission": Race and the Construction of Crime* (Faculty of Law, Monash University, Clayton, Vic, 1987), p 35. The first Aboriginal Legal Service was set up in 1970 in Redfern, New South Wales. The Central Australian Aboriginal Legal Aid Service (CAALAS) and the Victorian Aboriginal Legal Service (VALS) were also established in the early 1970s.

29 G Bird, op cit, p 34; H McRae, G Nettheim, and L Beacroft, *Aboriginal Legal Issues* (Law Book Co, Sydney, 1991), pp 240-43.

30 McRae, Nettheim and Beacroft, ibid, p 287; A Bolger, *Aboriginal Women and Violence* (Australian National University, North Australian Research Unit, Darwin, 1991), p 85.

31 D Bell, and P Ditton, *Law: The Old and the New: Aboriginal Women in Central Australia Speak Out* (CAALAS, Aboriginal History, Canberra, ACT, 1980), p 30. Other Aboriginal women have had the same opinion. Chief Justice, WA, *Report*, op cit, p 121; DPP, Brisbane, op cit, pp 11, 39-40.

32 RCIADIC *National Report 3* (AGPS, Canberra, 1991), p 41.

33 RCIADIC, op cit, "Imprisonment As A Last Resort", Recommendations 90-121, pp 52-57.

34 Council for Aboriginal Reconciliation, *Going Forward: Social Justice for the First Australians*, A submission to the Commonwealth Government from the Council for Aboriginal Reconciliation (Council for Aboriginal Reconciliation, Canberra, 1995), p 54.

35 NSW Ministry for the Status and Advancement of Women, op cit, p 10; Kiss, op cit; Chief Justice, WA, *Report*, op cit, p 121; DPP, Brisbane, op cit, pp 11, 39-40.

36 J Teakle, *Australian*, 14 December 1994, p 8.

37 *R v Bowden* (unreported, Presentment No N00121841, Mildura County Court, 2000).

38 Bolger, op cit, p 85.

39 Kiss, op cit.

40 P O'Shane, "Aborigines and the Criminal Justice System", in C Cunneen (ed), *Aboriginal Perspectives on Criminal Justice* (Institute of Criminology, Sydney University Law School, Sydney, 1992), p 6.

41 J Atkinson, "Violence Against Aboriginal Women: Reconstitution of Community Law – the Way Forward" (1990) 2(46) *ALB* 7.

42 Chief Justice WA, *Report*, op cit, p 115; DPP, Qld, op cit, p 9.

43 M Wilkie, *Aboriginal Justice Programs in Western Australia: Research Report No 5* (Crime Research Centre, University of Western Australia, Perth, WA, 1991), p 20.

44 S James, "The Victorian Aboriginal Legal Service: Directions in the 90s" (1993) 1(4) *VACRO Reporter* 3; NSW Ministry for the Status and Advancement of Women, op cit, p 8.

45 NSW Ministry for the Status and Advancement of Women, op cit, p 8.

46 Ibid, p 10.

47 Office of the Status of Women and ABS, p 166.

48 James, op cit, p 3.

49 D Bell and T Nelson, "Speaking About Rape is Everyone's Business" (1989) 12(4) *Women's International Forum* Bell and Nelson, op cit, p 410; Atkinson, *Beyond Violence*, op cit, p 15.

50 ALRC Interim Report No 67, op cit, p 33.

51 NSW Ministry for the Status and Advancement of Women, *Dubay Jahli Aboriginal Women and the Law Report* (NSW Government, Sydney 1994), p 10; C Thomas, "Sexual Assault Issues for Aboriginal Women, in P Easteal (ed), *Without Consent Confronting Adult Sexual Violence* (AIC, Canberra, 1993), p 142 Lloyd and Rogers, op cit, p 153.

52 R Goldfam, "Silence in Court! Problems and Prospects in Aboriginal Legal Interpreting", in D Eades (ed), *Language in Evidence* (UNSW Press, Sydney, 1995), pp 37-38. Diana Eades is a senior lecturer in linguistics at the University of New England. Eades gave expert evidence in Robyn Kina's case.

53 Task Force Report, op cit p 87.

54 "Legal Service Policy Continues to Fail for Aboriginal Women", *Koori Mail*, 5 April 1995, 11.

55 *Koori Mail*, 5 April 1995, op cit, P Daylight and M Johnstone, *Women's Business: Report of the Aboriginal Women's Task Force* (AGPS, Canberra, 1986), p 70.

56 ALRC Report No 69 Part I, p 121; K Pringle, "R v Robyn Bella Kina" (1994) 3(67) *ALB* 14.

57 The battered woman's syndrome (BWS) was judicially recognised between Kina's trial in 1988 and her final appeal in 1993. See *Rujanjic and Kontinnen* (1991) 53 A Crim R 362 which established BWS and *Kontinnen* (unreported, SASC, Legoe J, 26-30 March 1992).

58 *Kina* (unreported, QCCA, 29 November 1993).

Chapter 4

1 D MacDonald, *Gum Boughs and Wattle Blossom* cited in R Evans, K Saunders and K Cronin, *Exclusion, Exploitation and Extermination* (Australia and New Zealand Book Co, Sydney, 1975), p 65 (hereafter Evans, Saunders and Cronin). This quotation should not be taken as implying that Aborigines have not survived to the present.

2 R Robinson, *Altjeringa and other Aboriginal Poems* (AH & AW Reed, Sydney, 1970), p 30. Robinson transcribed Aborigines' traditional stories in verse form. Robinson briefly identified Percy Mumbulla, as an "old full blood Aboriginal friend", from Wallaga Lake (where there was an Aboriginal Reserve) in southern New South Wales. However, there are a number of interesting references to a Percy Mumbler (1905/7-1991) who was an Aboriginal leader and land rights activist on the south coast in M McKenna, *Looking for Blackfellas' Point* (UNSW Press, Sydney, 2002), particularly pp 191 (photograph), 192, 195, 196-99. I like to think that they are the one person, as Mumbler obviously knew a great deal about traditional life, and Robinson quotes other of Mumbulla's verses. (Mumbulla is a local name, Mumbulla Mountain being north of Bega.) Information about Mumbulla/Mumbler (if indeed the one person) in Robinson and McKenna give respect for a courageous man who was so generous in sharing his culture.

3 C Healy, "We Know Your Mob Now" (1990) 49(3) *Meanjin* 512.

4 J Hunter and P King, in J Bach (ed), *An Historical Journal of Events at Sydney and at Sea 1787-1792* (Angus & Robertson, Sydney, 1968), pp 28, 270.

5 Private conversations with author.

6   P Sutton, "Families of Polity: Post-Classical Aboriginal Society and Native Title", discussion paper published by the national Native Title Tribunal p 6.

7   M Foucault and C Gordon, *Power and Knowledge: Selected Interviews and Other Writings: 1972-1977* (Pantheon Books, New York, 1980), p 250.

8   Evans, Saunders, and Cronin, op cit, pp 49, 50, 75 and 79, and generally for contemporary descriptions of violence to Queensland Aborigines. These excerpts are examples of a pattern of a violence which was replicated all over Australia.

9   McKenna, *Looking for Blackfellas' Point*, op cit.

10 G Taylor, "The Grand Jury of South Australia", forthcoming publication in 2004.

11 S Davis and J Prescott, *Aboriginal Frontiers and Boundaries in Australia* (Melbourne University Press, Carlton, Victoria, 1992), p 96.

12 B Hodge and V Mishra, "Aboriginal Place" in B Ashcroft, G Griffiths and H Tiffin (eds), *The post-colonial studies reader* (Routledge, London, 1995), pp 413-14.

13 D Bell, "Women and the Land" (1979) 3(11) Nov/Dec *Identity* p26, and from personal sources for 1960s information concerning Warrabri.

14 E Johnston, *Royal Commission into Deaths in Custody, National Report, Overview and Recommendations* (AGPS, Canberra, 1991), p 9.

15 C Rowley, "Who is an Aboriginal? The answer in 1967", Appendix A, *The Destruction of Aboriginal Society* (Reprinted, Pelican Books, Melbourne, 1974), pp 341-64; B Attwood, *The Making of the Aborigines* (Second Impression, Allen & Unwin, North Sydney, 1992); J Pettman, *Race and Ethnicity in Contemporary Australia* (Centre for Multicultural Education, University of London Institute of Education, London, 1986), pp 3-6. Sixty-seven legislative definitions of "Aborigine". McCorquodale, *Digest*, op cit, p xiv.

16 The principal legislation is *Aborigines Protection Act* 1869 (Vic), *Aborigines Protection and Restriction of the Sale of Opium Act* 1897 (Qld), *Aborigines Protection Act* 1890 (Vic), *Aborigines Protection Act* 1909 (NSW), *Aborigines Act* 1905 (WA), *Northern Territory Aborigines Act* 1910 (SA), *Aborigines Act* 1911 (SA), *Natives (Citizenship Rights) Act* 1944 (WA), *Native Welfare Act* 1963 (WA), *Aborigines Act* 1957 (Vic), *Aboriginal Affairs Act* 1962 (SA), *Community Welfare Act* 1972 (SA), *Aboriginal and Torres Strait Islander Affairs Act* 1965 (Qld), *Aborigines Act* 1971 (Qld), *Welfare Ordinance* 1953 (NT), *Social Welfare Ordinance* 1964 (NT), New South Wales passed *Aborigines Protection (Amendment) Acts* in 1940, 1943 and 1963, and the *Aborigines Act* 1969 (NSW).

17 P O'Shane, "Is There Any Relevance In The Women's Movement For Aboriginal Women?" (1976) 12 *Refractory Girl* 31.

18 National Committee on Violence, *Violence Directions for Australia* (AIC, Canberra, 1990), pp 165-67; E Johnston, op cit, pp 7-11.

19 D Johnston, "Native Rights as Collective Rights: A Question of Group Self-Preservation", in W Kymlicka (ed), *The Rights of Minority Cultures* (Oxford University Press, Oxford, 1995), p 190.

20 AE Woodward, *Aboriginal Land Rights Commission; First Report* (Government Printer of Australia, Canberra, 1973), pp 5-10, Council for Aboriginal Reconciliation, *Valuing Cultures* (AGPS, Canberra, 1994), pp 3-4. M Langton, *Well, I Heard It On The Radio And I Saw It On The Television ...* (Australian Film Commission, Woolloomooloo, NSW, 1993), p 27 (hereafter *Radio*).

21 D Storer (ed), *Ethnic Family Values in Australia* (Institute of Family Studies, Prentice-Hall, Sydney, 1985), p 302.

22 T Flannery, *The Future Eaters* (Reed New Holland, Sydney, reprint 2001), p 271.

23 ALRC Report No 31, paras 32-35, pp 26-31.

24 Langton, *Radio*, op cit, p 34.

25 ALRC Report No 31, para 34, p 27; R Berndt and C Berndt, "Some Points of Change in Western Australia", in A Pilling and R Waterman (eds), *Diprotodon to Detribalization* (Michigan State University Press, East Lansing, 1970), p 69.

26 ALRC Report No 31, paras 88-95, p 72.

27 *Attorney-General (Cth) v Queensland* (1990) 94 ALR 515, *Gibbs v Capewell* (1995) 126 ALR 364.

28 Langton, *Radio*, op cit, p 29.

29 163 ALR 205 at 208. For contemporary public comment see A Darby, "Landmark court decision on Aboriginality draws criticism", *Age*, 22 April 1998, p 8A. See also "Who is, and who isn't, an Aborigine", *Australian*, 21 April 1998, p 6.

Chapter 5

1 A Bolger and S Koop, "My Week", *Age*, 23 January, 1999, p 8. Angela Bolger was a Legal Aid solicitor at the Kimberley Office in 1999.

2 M Langton, *Valuing Cultures* (Council for Aboriginal Reconciliation, AGPS, Canberra, 1994), p 7 (hereafter *Valuing Cultures*); H Goodall and J Huggins, "Aboriginal Women Are Everywhere", in K Saunders and R Evans (eds), *Gender Relations in Australia* (Harcourt Brace Jovanovich, Marrickville, 1992), p 399.

3 P Sutton, "Families of Polity: Post-Classical Aboriginal Society and Native Title", Discussion Paper published by the National Native Title Tribunal, p 6.

4 Involuntary minorities whether created "from conquest or colonisation want "national liberation" – that is, some form of collective self-government, in order to ensure the continued development of their distinct culture. M Walzer, "Comment" in "Multiculturalism and the Politics of Recognition" pp 100-101, cited by W Kymlicka (ed), *The Rights of Minority Cultures* (Oxford University Press, Oxford, 1995), p 11. Apart from land rights and reconciliation some Aborigines seek political recognition of a separate Indigenous identity and culture, for instance a treaty (also broached by former Prime Minister Hawke) or Aboriginal sove-

reignty or self determination. See M Mansell, "Law Reform And The Road To Independence", in S McKillop (ed), *Aboriginal Justice Issues* (AIC, Canberra, 1993), p 11.

5   Gordon Report, pp 68-69.
6   Memmott, et al, *Violence in Indigenous Communities* (Attorney-General's Department, Canberra, 2001), p 22.
7   ALRC Report No 31, Vol 2, p 25 (fn 32).
8   E Venbrux, *A Death in the Tiwi Islands* (Cambridge University Press, Melbourne, 1995), p 16.
9   P Sutton, "The politics of suffering: Indigenous policy in Australia since the 1970s" (Politics of suffering) (2001) 11(20 November, *Anthropological Forum* pp 150, 152 ff.
10 V Burbank, *Fighting Women* (University of California Press, Berkeley, 1994), pp 33-71, 133-58.
11 A Phillip in J Bach (ed), *An Historical Journal of Events at Sydney and at Sea* (Angus and Robertson, Sydney, 1968), pp 317, 319, 333; W Tench, *Sydney's First Four Years* (Angus & Robertson, Sydney, 1961, pp 276, 290-91; M Riviere (ed), *The Governor's Noble Guest; Hyacinthe de Bougainville's account of Port Jackson 1825* (Melbourne University Press, Melbourne, 1999), pp 71, 200; and see Sutton, "Politics of Suffering" op cit, pp 152, 154, 166 for references to observations of Tench, 1793, William Collins, 1798, and Edward John Eyre.
12 Tench, op cit, pp 290-91; J Lingard, *A Narrative of the Journey to and from New South Wales* (J Taylor, Chapel-en-le Frith, England), p 29; Sutton, "Politics of suffering", op cit, p 152.
13 J Brockman (ed), *He Rode Alone* (Artlook Books, Perth, 1987), pp 155, 157; P Kaberry, *Aboriginal Woman Sacred and Profane* (George Routledge and Sons, London, 1939), pp 25, 142.
14 Sutton, "Politics of Suffering", op cit, pp 152-53.
15 This is possibly because there was less initial contact with women. Tench, op cit, pp 36, 143, 232-33.
16 Kaberry, op cit, pp 53-54; Sutton, "Politics of Suffering", op cit, p 155.
17 Julius Brockman's diaries of Kimberley life covering the 1880s to the 1890s record his discovery of the body of a blind elderly woman who was left to die: "it was apparent that she had made an effort to follow them but, losing her way, died from thirst and hunger.' At times elderly people were left by a waterhole when the band moved on. For the same reasons in dry seasons infanticide was practised, "two allowed to live out of seven born". Of twins one was killed at birth. J Brockman (ed), *He Rode Alone* (Artlook Books, Perth, 1987), pp 131-32, 146. In the 1830s in the Monaro a convict Lingard witnessed one infanticide and heard of two more." Lingard, op cit, pp 30-31. Elizabeth Eggleston recorded a mid-1960s case "where two Aboriginal women were charged with assault following the death of a child, who had been killed in accordance with tribal custom", EM Eggleston, *Aborigines and the Administration of Justice* (PhD thesis, Monash University, 1970), p 199.

18 *Kurdaitcha* shoes, literally feather foot shoes worn to conceal an executioner's tracks. C Berndt, "Mythical Women, Past and Present", in F Gale (ed), *We are Bosses Ourselves* (Australian Institute of Aboriginal Studies, Canberra, 1981), pp 18-19. Both Berndt and KS Strehlow, *Operation of fear in traditional Aboriginal society in Central Australia* (The Strehlow Foundation, Prospect, SA, 1991), p 54, note that women very rarely, "not normally", donned the *kurdaitcha* shoes. She would only do so with her husband's authority in order "to avenge some injury done … to one of her own kindred".

19 Banambi, a traditional man from Yirrkala, in M Langton et al, *'Too Much Sorry Business': Report of the Royal Commission into Aboriginal Deaths in Custody: Vol 5 Appendix D I* (AGPS, Canberra, 1991).

20 Phillip, op cit, pp 323-24, Tench, op cit, 230-31, Percy Mumbulla, "The Surprise Attack", "The Battle of Wallaga Lake", oral traditions of Wallaga Lake, South Coast of New South Wales collected by R Robinson, *Altjeringa an other Aboriginal poems* (A & AW Reed, Sydney, 1970), pp 35, 50.

21 S Davis and J Prescott, *Aboriginal Frontiers and Boundaries* (Melbourne University Press, Melbourne, 1992), pp 38, 59.

22 M Preston, "Feminism and Aboriginality: The Great Divide" (1998) 1 *Black on Black* 66.

23 Kaberry, op cit, pp 269 ff, 272.

24 F McCarthy, *Australian Aborigines Their Life and Culture* (Colorgravure Publications, Melbourne, 1957), p 102. Control was essentially wielded by "the middle aged and old men who are relentless in the discipline they impose in a community, for upon their maintenance of tribal law, established by their spiritual ancestors". P Hanks and B Keon-Cohen (eds), *Aborigines and the Law* (George Allen & Unwin, Sydney, 1984), pp 224, 227-28.

25 Mowaljarlai, "a top law man" of the Ngarinyin, describes his training and authority talking to S Lobez, "Law and culture in the West Kimberley Ngarinyin tribal lands", *The Law Report* (Radio National Transcript, 10 September 1996), pp 3-4; <http://www.abc.net.au/rn/talks/8.30/lawrpt/ lstories/lr100996.htm>.

26 Sutton, op cit, p 11.

27 D Bell, "Women and the Land" (1979) 3(11) *Identity* 26.

28 *Kirda, nimarringki* are often translated as "owner" or "boss", *kurdungurlu/jungkayi* are often translated as "worker" or "manager", P Sutton, *Oranges and lemons: Descent, Filiation and gender Politics in the Anthropology of Aboriginal Land Tenure* (Working paper for Native Title Tribunal, 1997), p 7.

29 Ibid.

30 Ibid, pp 24-25, 29.

31 C Berndt, "Mythical Women, Past and Present", in F Gale (ed), *We Are Bosses Ourselves* (Australian Institute of Aboriginal Studies, Canberra, 1983), p 18.

32 J Pettman, *Living in the Margins: racism, sexism and feminism in Australia* (Allen & Unwin, Sydney, 1992), p 25.

33 D Bell and T Nelson, "Speaking About Rape is Everyone's Business" (1989) 12(4) *Women's International Forum,* op cit, p 408.
34 Berndt, op cit, pp 18-19.
35 Burbank, op cit, pp 167, 173.
36 D Playford, "The Rose of the North Blossoms" (1978) October *Identity* 32.
37 ALRC, "Traditional Aboriginal Society and its Law", in W Edwards (ed), *Traditional Aboriginal Society* (2nd ed, Macmillan Education Australia Pty Ltd, Melbourne, 1998), pp 219-20; Hamilton, "Gender and power", op cit, p 75.
38 Elkin, op cit, pp 159-60; McCarthy, op cit, p 120; Kaberry, op cit, p 253.
39 G Ngabidj, *My Country of the Pelican Dreaming: The Life of an Australian Aborigine of the Gadjerong: Grant Ngabidj 1904-1977 (as told to Bruce Shaw)* (Australian Institute of Aboriginal Studies, Canberra, 1981), p 58.
40 K Strehlow, op cit, p 118.
41 Ngabidj, op cit, p 58.
42 Kaberry, op cit, p 152.
43 Bell and Nelson, op cit, p 408.
44 Personal Aboriginal informant.
45 Burbank, op cit, pp 152-55. Burbank found aggression can be ritualised but nonetheless women have to learn the underlying message that men's sensibilities have to be respected by women.
46 Langton et al, op cit, p 203.
47 Burbank, op cit, pp 145 ff.
48 Gordon Report, p 68.
49 G Greer, "Raiders of the Lost Art", *Age, Saturday Extra,* 6 December 1997, p 6.
50 W Edwards, *Traditional Aboriginal Society,* 2nd edn (Macmillan Educational Australia, Melbourne, 1998), pp 14-15.
51 T Strehlow, "Aboriginal Law" (1978) August *The Australasian Nurses Journal* quoted in K Strehlow, *The Operation of Fear in Traditional Aboriginal Society in Central Australia* (The Strehlow Foundation, Adelaide, nd), p 95.

Chapter 6

1 ABC Radio National, *Law Report,* <http://www.abc.net.au/rn/talks/8.30/lawrpt/lstories/lr980505.htm>.
2 J Atkinson, *Beyond Violence, Beyond Violence: Finding the Dream* (Aboriginal and Islander Sub-Program, National Domestic Violence Program, Office of the Status of Women, Canberra, 1989), p 14. Of 13 responses only two were because pressures in the community led to drinking, and one of those responses was from a researcher, not a community member.
3 Ester Illin, and Mary Butler both from Palm Island were founders in 1996 of an Aboriginal women's refuge in Townsville. Butler who was a nurse and who has worked as coordinator of the Fred Hollows trachoma program said of the abuse she has suffered and seen, "I have known the

humiliation of black eyes and bruises and seen worse cases where women lose their eyesight (because) they've been bashed about so much", L Bellamy "Breaking a community's cycle of violence", *Age News Extra* 22 December, 2001, p 4.

4   ABC Radio National, *Law Report*, op cit.

5   H McRae, G Nettheim and L Beacroft, *Aboriginal Legal Issue* (Law Book Company, Sydney, 1991), pp 215-17.

6   B Sansom, *The Camp at Wallaby Cross. Aboriginal Fringe Dwellers in Darwin* (AIAS, Canberra, 1980), pp 89-95.

7   Phillip's Journal in J Hunter, J Bach (ed), *An Historical Journal of Events at Sydney and at Sea1787-1792* (Angus and Robertson, Sydney, 1968), p 316.

8   A Hamilton, "A complex strategical situation: gender and power in Aboriginal Australia", in N Grieve and P Grimshaw (eds), *Australian Women: Feminist Perspectives* (Oxford University Press, Melbourne, 1981), p 75.

9   B Lunney, *Gone Bush* (Angus & Robertson, Sydney, 2000), pp 79-80.

10 *R v Ivan Imitja Panka* (unreported, NTSC, Muirhead J, SCC No 25 of 1980, 5 September 1980), cited in ALRC RP 6A, p 25.

11 *R v Bell* (unreported, QSCCA No 116 of 1994, 20 June 1994).

12 *Mungatopi v The Queen* (1991) 57 A Crim R 341.

13 P Kaberry, *Aboriginal Women: Sacred and Profane* (Routledge, London, 1939), p 152.

14 G Ngabidj, as told to B Shaw, *My Country of the Pelican Dreaming* (AIAS, Canberra, 1981), p 104.

15 V Burbank, *Fighting Women* (University of California Press, Berkeley, 1994), p 57, Task Force Report, p 14.

16 Burbank, op cit, pp 35-36, 57-60; R & C Berndt, *Man, Land and Myth in North Australia* (Ure Smith, Sydney, 1970), p 169.

17 Task Force Report, p 14.

18 Burbank, op cit, p 164.

19 E Eggleston, *Aborigines and the Administration of Justice* (unpublished PhD, Monash University, 1970), pp 256-57.

20 Task Force Report, pp 11, see also p 21.

21 ALRC Report No 31, op cit, p 181 (at fn 59).

22 P Francis, "Transcript of Public Hearings", La Grange, 26 March 1981, cited in ALRC RP No 11/12, *Aboriginal Customary Law and Local Justice Mechanisms: Principles, Options and Proposals* (ALRC, Sydney, 1984), p 71.

23 Task Force Report, p 21, J Teakle, *Australian*, 14 December 1994, p 8.

24 A Bolger, *Aboriginal Women and Violence* (Australian National University, North Australian Research Unit, Darwin, 1991), p 51.

25 G Macdonald, "A Wiradjuri fight story" and M Langton, "Medicine Square", in I Keen, *Being Black: Aboriginal Cultures in 'Settled' Australia* (Aboriginal Studies Press, Canberra, 1994), pp 179 ff and pp 201 ff.

26 Burbank, op cit, pp 162-67.

27 Gordon Report, p 69.

28 Task Force Report, p 17.

29 ABC Radio National, *Law Report*, op cit.

Chapter 7

1 Preliminary report of the Special Rapporteur on Violence against Women, Commission on Human Rights, 1994 in Steiner and Alston, p 204.

2 A Nannup with L Marsh and S Kinnane, *When the Pelican Laughed* (reprinted, Fremantle Arts Centre Press, South Fremantle, 1993), p 35; J Isaacs (ed), *Australian Dreaming: 40,000 years of Aboriginal History* (Landsdowne Press, Sydney, 1980), p 162.

3 I White, "Aboriginal women's status: a paradox resolved", in F Gale (ed), *Woman's Role in Aboriginal Society*, 3rd edn (AIAS, Canberra, 1978), p 36; C Berndt, "Mythical Women, Past and Present", in F Gale (ed), *We are Bosses Ourselves: The Status and Role of Aboriginal Women Today* (AIAS, Canberra, 1983), pp 18-19; A Hamilton, "A complex strategical situation: gender and power in Aboriginal Australia", in N Grieve and P Grimshaw (eds), *Australian Women: Feminist Perspectives* (OUP, Melbourne, 1981) (hereafter "Gender and power"), pp 74-75.

4 J Isaacs (ed) *Australian Dreaming: 40,000 years of Aboriginal History* (Lansdowne Press, Sydney, 1980), pp 157-58, 160-69.

5 Gordon Report, p 69.

6 P Kaberry, *Aboriginal Woman: Sacred and Profane* (Routledge, London, 1939), p 66.

7 R and C Berndt, *From Black to White in South Australia* (FW Cheshire, Melbourne, 1951), p 220 and Kaberry, op cit, p 93.

8 A Elkin, *The Australian Aborigines*, 4th edn, 1964 (Angus & Robertson, Sydney, reprinted 1966), p 159.

9 Kaberry, op cit, p 93; F McCarthy, *Australian Aborigines Their Life and Culture* (Colorgravure Publications, Melbourne, 1987), p 98.

10 K Maddock, "Law must restrain cultural cruelty", *Australian*, 10 October 2002, p 11.

11 Kaberry, op cit, p 180.

12 G Ngabidj, *My Country of the Pelican Dreaming. The life of an Australian Aborigine of the Gadjerong: Grant Ngabidj 1904-1977 (as told to Bruce Shaw)* (AIAS, Canberra, 1981), p 59.

13 R and C Berndt, *The World of the First Australians*, revised edn (Lansdowne Press, Sydney, 1981), pp 180-81; Kaberry, op cit, pp 98-99, 236.

14 K Strehlow, *Aboriginal Women: with special reference to W Lloyd Warner's "A Black Civilization": the influence of Durkheim and the local groups of Central Australia* (The Strehlow Research Foundation, Adelaide, 1989), p 118, Kaberry, op cit, p 152.

15 S Davis and J Prescott, *Aboriginal Frontiers and Boundaries* (MUP, Carlton, 1992), p 89; Kaberry, op cit, p 152, in "A tribal childhood in the Never-Never", *Australian Women's Weekly*, 11 June 1969. An Aboriginal nun, Mary Agatha, of the Brinken tribe between the Daly River and Port Keats, recounts her fear as a child when hiding from a male raiding party from another tribe.

16 J Lingard, *A Narrative of the Journey to and from New South Wales* (J Taylor, Chapel-en-le Frith, England), p 31.

17 "Black Slavery", no source, nd, specific reference is made to the *Galkama* case (Koorie Research Centre Library, Monash University).

18 S Holmes, *The Goddess and the Moon Man: The sacred Art of the Tiwi Aborigines* (Craftsman House, Roseville East, NSW, 1995), pp 73-74.

19 C Rowley, *The Destruction of Aboriginal Society* (reprinted, Penguin Books, Melbourne, 1974), p 205.

20 L Hiatt, *Arguments About Aborigines* (Cambridge University Press, Cambridge, 1996), pp 179-80.

21 ALRC 1986 RP 1, p 12.

22 R and C Berndt, *From Black to White in South Australia* (FW Cheshire, Melbourne, 1951), p 10.

23 *Hales v Jamilmira* [2003] NTCA 9, Martin CJ, at para 20).

24 A Hamilton, "The Role of Women in Aboriginal Marriage Arrangements", in Gale (ed), *Woman's Role*, op cit, p 29 (hereafter Marriage Arrangements), N Peterson, "The Importance of Women in Determining the Composition of Residential Groups in Aboriginal Australia", in F Gale (ed), *Woman's Role*, op cit, p 9; L Hercus, "Eileen McKenzie", in I White, D Barwick and B Meehan (eds), *Fighters and Singers* (George Allen & Unwin, Sydney, 1985), p 73.

25 Holmes, op cit, pp 73-74.

26 ALRC, 1986, RP 1, p 14.

27 D Bell and T Nelson, "Speaking about rape is everyone's business" (1989) 12(4) *Women's Studies International Forum* 409.

28 Kaberry, op cit, pp 100-1, 103; Hamilton, "Marriage Arrangements", op cit, p 34.

29 Lingard, op cit, p 33.

30 S Davis, *Above Capricorn* (Angus & Robertson, Sydney, 1994), p 30.

31 Nannup, op cit, p 35.

32 Hamilton, "Marriage Arrangements", op cit, p 30.

33 G Cowlishaw, cited in Hamilton, "Gender and power", op cit, p 73.

34 K Walker, "The Child Wife", in *My People* (Jacaranda Press, Milton, Queensland, 1985), p 13. Kath Walker later adopted the name Oodgeroo Noonuccal in affirmation of her Aboriginal heritage.

35 H McRae, G Nettheim, and L Beacroft, *Aboriginal Legal Issues* (Law Book Co, Sydney, 1991), p 274.

36 *Hales v Jamilmira* [2003] NTCA 9, Martin CJ, at para 12.

37 J Bowditch, "Rejected chief freed of assault", *Age*, 2 April 1970.

38 "Nola's happy to be home", *Age*, 22 September 1973.

39 Commonwealth of Australia, Parliamentary Debates, S 57, pp 1-1514, 21 August-25 October, 1973, p 723.

40 ALRC 1986 RP 1, p 7, ALRC Report 31, 1986, para 227.

41 Ibid, p 8.

42 Ibid, pp 13-14.

43 Article 6 of the Declaration on the Elimination of Discrimination against Women (1967), *Human Rights A Compilation of international Instruments* (United Nations Centre for Human Rights, New York and Geneva, 1994, Vol 1, p 145).

44 H Steiner and P Alston, *International Human Rights in Context: Law, Politics and Morals* (2nd ed OUP, Oxford, 2000), p 176.
45 P Toohey, "Victim trapped between two worlds", *Australian*, 9 October 2002, pp 1-2.
46 *Hales v Jamilmira* [2003] NTCA 9, Martin CJ, at para 6.
47 P Toohey, "Victim trapped between two worlds", *Australian*, 9 October 2002, p 1.
48 Editorial, correspondence, G Burgoyne, Groote Eylandt, NT, and K Maddock, "Law must restrain cultural cruelty", *Australian*, 10 October 2002, pp 10-11.
49 *Hales v Jamilmira* [2003] NTCA 9, Martin CJ, Mildren and Riley JJ, at para 88.
50 *Hales v Jamilmira* [2004] HCA Trans 18 (13 February 2004) Gummow, Hayne and Heydon JJ, at 7.
51 *Hales v Jamilmira* [2003] NTCA 9, Martin CJ, Mildren and Riley JJ, at para 26.
52 Gordon Report, Chapter 14, pp 367 ff.

Chapter 8

1 Task Force Report, p 21.
2 Task Force Report, p 20.
3 *DPP v Morgan* [1976] AC 182.
4 *Saragozza v The Queen* [1984] VR 187.
5 The "Griffith Code" is in force in Queensland and Western Australia, the Northern Territory has adopted it own Criminal Code. B Fisse (ed), *Howard's Criminal Law*, 5th edn (Law Book Company, Sydney, 1990), pp 25, 43.
6 W Edwards, *Traditional Aboriginal Society*, 2nd edn (Macmillan Education Australia, Melbourne, 1998), p 219.
7 J Hunter and A Phillip, P King and H Ball, *An Historical Journal of Events at Sydney and at Sea* (Angus & Robertson, Sydney, 1968), p 339.
8 W Tench, *Sydney's First Four Years* (Angus and Robertson, Sydney, 1961), pp 276, 290.
9 M Riviere (ed), *The Governor's Noble Guest* (MUP, Melbourne, 1999), pp 150, 200.
10 K Maddock, "Aboriginal Customary Law", in P Hanks and B Keon-Cohen (eds), *Aborigines and the Law* (2nd impression, George Allen & Unwin, Sydney, 1988), p 225.
11 Edwards, op cit, p 221.
12 M Lucashenko, "Violence Against Indigenous Women: Public and Private Dimensions", in S Cook and J Bessant (eds), *Women's Encounters With Violence* (Sage Publications, Thousand Oaks, California, 1997), pp 151-52.
13 H McRae, G Nettheim and L Beacroft, *Aboriginal Legal Issues* (Law Book Company, 3rd impression, 1994, Sydney), p 274.

14 "Skin" is the desert people's English language term for "classifying every member of society by one of eight sub-section terms ... Knowledge of a person's subsection affiliation, which is determined by birth". determines proper behaviour between people. D Bell, "Topsy Napurrula Nelson", in I White, D Barwick and B Meehan (eds), *Fighters and Singers* (George Allen & Unwin, Sydney, 1985), p 3.

15 K Strehlow, *Aboriginal Women: with special reference to W Lloyd Warner's "A Black Civlization": The influence of Durkheim and the local groups of Central Australia'*, 118; J Davis, *The First Born and Other Poems* (JM Dent Pty Ltd, Melbourne, 1983), p xiv.

16 D Mowaljarlai, "a full-blood initiated Ngarinyin lawman" from the West Kimberley talking to S Lobez, "National Reconciliation Week", *The Law Report* (Radio National Transcripts, 28 May 1996), <http://www.abc.net. au/rn/talks/8.30/ lawrpt/lstories/lr280501.htm>. M Young, E Munday and D Munday, *The Aboriginal People of the Monaro* (NSW National Parks and Wildlife Service, 2000), pp 202-3.

17 Tench, op cit, p 288.

18 G Eames, "Aboriginal Homicide: Customary Law Defences or Customary Lawyers' Defences", in H Strang and S-A Gerrull (eds), *Homicide: Patterns, Prevention and Control* (Australian Institute of Criminology, Canberra, 1992), p 149.

19 *R v Lane Hunt Smith* (unreported, NTSC, Gallop J, 1980) transcript, pp 99-100.

20 Law Reform Commission, *Reference on Aboriginal Customary Law Research Paper No 6A* (ALRC, Sydney, 1982), p 28; J McCorquodale, "'The Voice of the People', Aborigines, Judicial Determinism & the Criminal Justice System in Australia", in B Swanton (ed) *Aborigines and Criminal Justice* (Australian Institute of Criminology, ACT, 1984), pp 219-20.

21 ALRC *RP 6 A*, op cit, p 28.

22 J McCorquodale, *Aborigines and the Law: A Digest* (Aboriginal Studies Press, Canberra, 1987); *Forbes*, p 391; *Lane Hunt and Smith*, p 408; ALRC, op cit, p 28.

23 ALRC, RP 6A, p 23.

24 Unreported, SASC, 20 March 1991, cited in H McRae, G Nettheim and L Beacroft, *Indigenous Legal Issues: Cases and Materials*, 2nd edn (LBC Information Services, Sydney, 1997), p 380. See also *Norman Jabarula* (unreported NTSC, 23 August 1978), cited in McCorquodale, "Voice", p 218.

25 *Police v Eric Jackson* (unreported, NT Court of Summary Jurisdiction, No 267-8, 352 of 1977, 22 November 1977); *Mark Rogers and Albert Murray v The Queen* (1989) 44 A Crim R 301. Here the rapist was beaten with sticks but not around the genitals.

26 D Bell and T Nelson, "Speaking About rape is Everyone's Business' (1989) 12(4) *Women's International Law Forum* 403 at 412.

27 Australia, Senate, *Parliamentary Debates* (1969) S 42, pp 1232-33; Australia, House of Representatives, *Parliamentary Debates* (1969) HofR 65, pp 1484-86.

28 S Payne, "Aboriginal Women and the Law", in C Cunneen (ed), *Aboriginal Perspectives on Criminal Justice* (Institute of Criminology, Sydney University Law School, Sydney, 1992), pp 31-45.

29 A Bolger, *Aboriginal Women and Violence* (North Australia Research Unit, ANU, Darwin, 1991), p 98; S Payne, "Aboriginal women and the criminal justice system" (1990) 2(46) *ALB* 9.

30 E Venbrux, *A Death in the Tiwi Islands*, op cit, p 76. In *Mungatopi v The Queen* (1991) 57 A Crim R 341 at 342, a Bathurst Island case, one of the circumstances relied upon in raising the defence of provocation was that deceased wife would not stop asking gamblers for beer. The accused generally suspected the deceased of infidelity.

31 D Bell and T Nelson, "Speaking About Rape is Everyone's Business" (1989) 12(4) *Women's International Forum* 403 at 410.

32 Australian Institute of Judicial Administration, *Cross Cultural Awareness for The Judiciary* (AIJA, Melbourne, 1996), p 15.

33 J Lloyd and N Rogers, "Crossing the Last Frontier: Problems Facing Aboriginal Women Victims of Rape in Central Australia", in P Easteal (ed), *Without Consent: Confronting Adult Sexual Violence* (AIC, Canberra, 1993), p 160.

34 *R v Mark Djanjdjomeer, Morrison Naborlhborie, Laurie Nabarlambari and Benjamin Naborlhborie* (unreported, NTSC, Gallop J, SCC Nos 3-6 of 1980, 14 February 1980), in J McCorquodale, *Aborigines and the Law: A Digest* (Aboriginal Studies Press, Canberra, 1987), C264, p 387.

35 Memmott et al, *Violence in Indigenous Communities* (Crime Prevention Branch, Commonwealth Attorney General's Office, Canberra, 2001), p 7.

36 Gordon Report, p 47.

37 *R v Leering* (unreported, WASC, CCA No 127 of 1990, 21 December 1990).

38 *Mark Rogers and Albert Murray v The Queen* (1989) 44 A Crim R 301.

39 *R v Harradine* (unreported, SASC, No SCCRM 790 of 1991, S3387, 5 May 1992 at 4).

40 *R v Steven Daniel Davis* (1989) 44 A Crim R 113 and *R v Warren Charles Dinah* (unreported WASC, CCA No 75 of 1989 and No 118 of 1989, Hearing 9 August 1989, delivered 4 September 1989).

41 A number of theses cases are considered in *Mark Rogers and Albert Murray v The Queen* (1989) 44 A Crim R 301 and are *R v Charlie, Uhl and Nagamarra* (unreported, WASC, No 96 of 1987, Library No 6716, 13 May 1987); *R v Mick* (unreported, No 129 of 1988, 14 October 1988); *R v Peter* (unreported, No 108 of 1989). See also *R v Gus Forbes* (unreported, NTSC, Gallop J, SCC Nos 258, 259 of 1980, 29 August 1980) and *R v Lane, Hunt and Smith* (unreported, NTSC, Gallop J, SCC Nos 16-17, 18-19, and 20-21 of 1980, 29 May 1980), cited in McCorquodale, op cit, p 219. Atkinson writes that "Rapes are now being carried out on drunken women by groups of young boys aged 10 to 15", Atkinson, "Violence in Aboriginal Australia", *Aboriginal and Islander Health Worker*, op cit, p 10.

42 A Bolger, *Aboriginal Women and Violence* (Australian National University, Northern Australia Research Unit, Darwin, 1991).

43 Atkinson, "Violence in Aboriginal Australia", *Aboriginal and Islander Health Worker*, op cit, pp 10-11. Despite the horrific rapes endured by Aboriginal women I have found only two cases, *Jabaltjari v The Queen* (1989) 46 A Crim R 47 at 49 and *R v Anderson* (1954) NTJ 240, where the court considered the impact on the victim in the sense of taking account of a post-traumatic stress and going beyond details of physical injuries and immediate trauma. These two cases concerned Aborigines either raping, or attempting to rape, non-Aboriginal women. However, in both *Jabaltjari* and *Anderson* the judges were particularly careful to take into account Aboriginality in sentencing. They both said that principles of leniency should be applied.

44 (2000) 9 NTLR 138.

Chapter 9

1   Elder, Kowanyama, Queensland, in J Atkinson (ed), *Beyond Violence Finding the Dream* (The Aboriginal and Islander Subprogram, National Domestic Violence Education Program, Office of Status of Women, Canberra, 1990), p 8.

2   J McCorquodale, "Alcohol & Anomie: The Nature of Aboriginal Crime", in B Swanton (ed), *Aborigines and Criminal Justice* (Australian Institute of Criminology, ACT 1984), p 30.

3   Gordon Report, p 68.

4   *Australian*, 29 December 1994, p 4, report by Bernard Lane.

5   (1994) 182 CLR 45 at para 50.

6   (1980) 54 AJLR 401 at 406.

7   Unreported NTSC, O'Leary J 1984; (1985) 12 *ALB* 12 (McCorquodale, C305, p 400).

8   T Syddall, "Aborigines and the Courts" I and II cited in J McCorquodale, "'The Voice of the People': Aboriginals, Judicial Determinism and the Criminal Justice System in Australia' in B Swanton (ed), *Aborigines and Criminal Justice* (Australian Institute of Criminology, Phillip, 1984), p 136.

9   M Langton, L Ahmatt, B Moss, E Schaber, C MacKinolty, M Thomas, E Tilton, and L Spencer, *"Too Much Sorry Business": Report of the Royal Commission into Aboriginal Deaths in Custody: Vol 5 Appendix D I* (AGPS, Canberra, 1991), p 289.

10 D Solomon, "Sentencing allows for tribal payback", *Australian*, 21-22 January 1992; J Cooper, "Aborigine threatens suicide to save kin", *Australian*, 4-5 September 1993; D Humphries, "Is white law tribal injustice?", *Age*, 9 May 1992.

11 (1992) 2 NTLR 183.

12 *Pat Edwards* (unreported, NTSC, Muirhead J, 16 October 1981), ALRC RP 6A, C38, McCorquodale, C269: 5, 90

13 C Egan, "Tribal case dropped", *Australian*, 22 June 1965, p 5 (emphasis added).

14 ALRC 1986 Report No 31, Vol 1, paras 98-101, pp 77-78.

15 J Whitbourn, a Baptist Minister who had worked with the older Warlpiri and Alyawarra men at Warrabri, cited in ALRC 1986 Report No 31, Vol 1, para 103, pp 79-80.

16 Langton et al, op cit, p 287.

17 K Maddock, "Aboriginal Customary Law", in P Hanks and B Keon-Cohen (eds), *Aborigines and the Law* (2nd impression, George Allen & Unwin, North Sydney, 1998), pp 212-37.

18 ALRC 1986 Report No 31, Vol 1, para 103, p 79, para 402, p 287, para 513, p 373; Langton et al, op cit, p 365.

19 M Kriewaldt, "The Application of the Criminal Law to Aborigines of the Northern Territory of Australia" (1960-62) 5(1) *University of Western Australia Law Review* 1 at 48.

20 [1951-1976] NTJ 327 at p 330.

21 ALRC, 1986, Report No 31 (Summary Report), p 40.

22 [1951-1976] NTJ 633 at 637.

23 Ibid, p 6.

24 M Kriewaldt, "The Application of the Criminal Law to the Aborigines of the Northern Territory of Australia" (1960-1962) 5 *University of Western Australia Law Review* 1 at 10.

25 [1951-1976] NTJ 317 at 322.

26 M Langton, "Medicine Square", in I Keen (ed), *"Being Black" Aboriginal Cultures in "Settled" Australia* (Aboriginal Studies Press, Canberra, 1994), p 206.

27 V Burbank, *Fighting Women* (University of California Press, Berkeley, 1994), p 51; S Thomas, N Williams and K Coulehan, "Across two laws: Cross-cultural awareness in the Northern Territory" (1996) 31(11) *Australian Lawyer* 4-6.

28 K Strehlow, *Aboriginal Women* (Strehlow Research Foundation, Adelaide, 1989), p 135.

29 "Court told that tribe planned to kill woman", *Australian*, 26 May 1967; "Tribe 'fixed' spear death", *Sun*, 26 May 1967.

30 ALRC, "Traditional Aboriginal Society and its Law", in W Edwards (ed), *Traditional Aboriginal Society*, 2nd edn (Macmillan Education Australia, Melbourne, 1998), pp 221-22.

31 "Aborigine will not be hanged", *Australian*, 27 May 1967; "'Executioner' won't hang, says judge", *Sun*, 27 May 1967. (The actual sentence is unknown as further references to this case were not found.)

32 ALRC, 1986, Report No 31, p 308 (fn 80).

33 Unreported, NTSC, Forster CJ, 24 November 1977.

34 (1986) 25 A Crim R 155 at 158.

35 (1986) 22 A Crim R 308.

36 (1993) 117 FLR 148.

37 (1980) 22 A Crim R 308 at 311.

38 (1999) 105 A Crim R 512 at 520-22.

39 Bailey J (unreported, NTSC, Bailey J, 1997) BC9703823 at 2.

40 (1991) 57 A Crim R 341.

41 P Toohey, "Haunted by her past", *Australian*, 30 August, 2002, pp 1, 4.

Chapter 10

1   M Langton, L Ahmatt, B Moss, E Schaber, C MacKinolty, M Thomas, E Tilton and L Spencer, *"Too Much Sorry Business": Report of the Royal Commission into Aboriginal Deaths in Custody: Vol 5 Appendix D I* (AGPS, Canberra, 1991).

2   K Mahoney, "Gender bias in judicial decisions", Lecture at the Supreme Court of Western Australia, Perth, delivered on 14 August 1992, cited in Australian Institute of Judicial Administration Incorporated (AIJA) *Cross Cultural Awareness for the Judiciary* (AIJA, Melbourne, 1996), p 15.

3   Task Force Report, p 99.

4   J Atkinson, "Violence against Aboriginal Women: Reconstitution of Customary Law – the Way Forward" (1990) 2(46) *ALB* 6-7.

5   S Payne, "Aboriginal Women and the Law", in C Cunneen (ed), *Aboriginal Perspectives on Criminal Justice* (Institute of Criminology, Sydney University Law School, Sydney, 1992), p 37.

6   J Upton, "By Violence, By Silence, By Control: The Marginalisation of Aboriginal Women Under White and 'Black Law'" (1991-92) 18 *MULR* 867 at 868-69, J Scutt, "Invisible Women? Projecting White Cultural Invisibility on Black Australian Women" (1990) 2(46) *ALB* 4; P Brock (ed), *Women: Rites and Sites* (Allen & Unwin, Sydney, 1989), p xvii; D Bell, "Women's Business is Hard Work: Central Australian Aboriginal Women's Love Rituals", in M Charlesworth et al (eds), *Religion in Aboriginal Australia: An Anthology* (University of Queensland Press, Brisbane, 1984), p 349.

7   ABC, *Four Corners* program.

8   ALRC, Report No 69, Part I.

9   S Thomas, N Williams and K Coulehan, "Across two laws: Cross-cultural awareness in the Northern Territory" (1996) 31(11) *Australian Lawyer* 4-6.

10 E Eggleston, "Aborigines and the Administration of Justice" (PhD Thesis, Monash University, 1970), p 225.

11 D Bell and T Nelson, "Speaking About Rape is Everyone's Business" (1989) 12(4) *Women's International Forum* 403 ff.

12 ALRC Report No 31, Vol 1, paras 98-101, pp 77-78.

13 J Coldrey, "Aboriginals and the criminal courts", in K Hazlehurst (ed), *Ivory Scales: Black Australia and the Law* (NSW University Press in association with AIC, Sydney, 1987), p 89.

14 F Brennan, "Self-Determination: The Limits Of Allowing Aboriginal Communities To Be A law Unto Themselves" (1993) 16(1) *University of New South Wales Law Journal* 245.

15 Langton et al, op cit, pp 395-96.

Chapter 11

1   ALRC Report No 31, Vol 1, para 622, p 460.

2   R Bowden and B Bunbury, *Being Aboriginal* (ABC Enterprises, Crows Nest, 1990), p 18.

3   ALRC Report No 31, Vol 1, para 524, p 383.

4   S Thomas, N Williams, and K Coulehan, "Across two laws: cross-cultural awareness in the Northern Territory" (1996) 31(11) *Australian Lawyer* 5; P Daylight and M Johnstone, *Women's Business: Report of the Aboriginal Women's Task Force* (AGPS, Canberra, 1986), p 66; Office of the Director of Public Prosecutions, Queensland, *Indigenous Women within the Criminal Justice System* (Office of the Director of Public Prosecutions, Queensland, 1996), pp 36-37.

5   [1951-1976] NTJ 420 at 425.

6   ALRC, Report No 31, Vol 1, para 622, p 460.

7   B Attwood, "Portrait of an Aboriginal as an Artist: Sally Morgan and the Construction of Aboriginality" (1993) 25(99) *Australian Historical Studies* 309.

8   (1996) 187 CLR 1.

9   S Hawke and M Gallagher, *Noonkanbah* (Fremantle Arts Centre Press, Fremantle, 1989), p 193, cited in F Brennan, "Self-Determination: The Limits of Allowing Aboriginal Communities to be a Law unto Themselves" (1993) 16(1) *UNSW Law Journal* 245.

10 P Sutton, "The politics of suffering: Indigenous policy in Australia since the 1970s" (2001) 11(2) November, *Anthropological Forum* 160.

11 M Langton, "A Black view of history, culture", 13 February, 1981, Working Party of Aboriginal Historians 1981, "Aboriginal History and the Bicentennial volumes", *Australia 1939-1988: A Bicentennial History Bulletin.*

12 C Healy, "We Know Your Mob Now" (1990) 49(3) *Meanjin* 512; A Tucker, *Too Many Captain Cooks* (reprinted 1995, Omnibus Books, SA, 1994), p 7; D Rose, "The Saga of Captain Cook: Morality in Aboriginal and European Law" (1984) 2 *Australian Aboriginal Studies* 24. "An anthropologist was publicly attacked for referring to … the historical inaccuracy of oral traditions about a voyage of Captain Cook", Sutton, op cit, p 262.

13 For example, Banjo Woorunmurra of the Bunuba people is the senior custodian of the story of Jandammarra's land and the story should not be told without his consent. H Pedersen and B Woorunmurra, *Jandamarra and the Bunuba Resistance* (Magabala Books Aboriginal Corporation, Broome, WA, 1995), pp xi, xiii.

14 M Langton, *Well, I heard it on the radio and I saw it on the television* (Australian Film Commission, Woolloomooloo, NSW, 1993), pp 64-65.

15 I Crawford, *We Won the Victory* (Fremantle Arts Centre Press, Fremantle, 2001), p 19.

16 T Flannery, *The Future Eaters* (Reed New Holland, Sydney, 1994), pp 264-70.

17 L West, "The right to choose" (1964) December, *Smoke Signals*, p 14.

18 *Milirrpum v Nabalco Pty Ltd* (1971) 17 FLR 141 at 190-91. See also P Sutton, "Myth as history, history as myth", in I Keen (ed), *Being Black* (Aboriginal Studies Press, Canberra, 1994), p 261.

19 Sutton, op cit, pp 253-54, and see also p 256 for discussion of the difference between Aboriginal stories which are creations of Dreaming myths and those creations which incorporate and transmute European histories within Aboriginal oral traditions – for example, the "Captain Cook story", "Noah's Ark in Western Australia" and "The death and resurrection of Jesus at Nambucca Heads in New South Wales".

20 The following account of this case closely follows Roses' account in D Rose, *Dingo Makes Us Human* (Cambridge University Press, Cambridge, 1992), pp 153-64. See also H McRae, G Nettheim and L Beacroft, *Indigenous Legal Issues*, 2nd edn (LBC Information Services, Sydney, 1997), pp 105-10.

21 Ibid, p 158.

22 Ibid, 160.

23 Ibid, pp 163-64.

24 (1989) 68 NTR 26 at 28.

25 Brennan CJ, "The State of the Judicature", Opening of the 30th Australian Legal Convention, Melbourne, 19 September 1997.

26 M Langton et al, *"Too Much Sorry Business': Report of the Royal Commission into Aboriginal Deaths in Custody: Vol 5 Appendix D I* (AGPS, Canberra, 1991), p 381, Recommendation 2.7.

27 *Milirrpum v Nabalco Pty Ltd* (1971) 17 FLR 141 at 165-66.

28 H McRae, G Nettheim and L Beacroft, *Aboriginal Legal Issues* (Law Book Co, Sydney, 1991), pp 165-66. The anthropologists thought that the patriclan, *kirda* or "bosses" were the sole traditional owners, they did not appreciate the role of the *kurdungurlu* or "managers" who are the children of the female members of the patriline "thus eliminating half of the legal claimants".

29 ALRC Report No 31, para 624, p 461.

30 *Jacky Anzac Jadurin v The Queen* (1982) 44 ALR 424 at 425-26.

31 A Coombs and S Varga, *Broometime* (Hodder Headline Australia, Sydney, 2001), pp 219-25.

Chapter 12

1 Task Force Report, p 73.

2 J Cawte, *Medicine is the Law: Studies of psychiatric anthropology of Aboriginal Tribal Societies* (University Press of Hawaii, Honolulu, 1974), p 193.

3 P Wilson, *Black Death White Hands* (Allen & Unwin, Sydney, 1982), p 83, refers to the work of Terence Des Pres on concentration camp survivors in discussing the psychological dependency of Aborigines in the reserves noting that "Such psychological dependency is not unusual when one group oppresses another".

4 ALRC Report No 31, para 440, p 316.

5 Aboriginal Legal Service of Western Australia, *Telling Our Story* (Aboriginal Legal Service of Western Australia Inc, 1995), pp 49-58. (hereafter ALSWA Story).

6   S Porteous, *The Psychology of a Primitive People* (Edward Arnold, London, 1931), pp 38, 135-38; T Strehlow, *Aranda Traditions* (Melbourne University Press, Melbourne, 1947), pp 84, 172; A Elkin, *The Australian Aborigines*, 4th edn, 1964 (Angus and Robertson, Sydney, reprinted 1966), p 61.

7   A Elkin, *The Australian Aborigines*, op cit, p 55.

8   Consultations, Sir David Longlands Correctional Centre, Task Force Report, pp 75, 77.

9   *Aboriginal Deaths in Custody Overview of the Response by Governments to the Royal Commission* (AGPS, Canberra), p 5.

10 ALSWA, *Story*, pp 44-45.

11 C Rowley, *Outcasts in White Australia* (reprinted 1973, Penguin Books, Melbourne 1972), pp 52-53; "Grog" p 167, *The Remote Aborigines* (Penguin Books, Melbourne, reprinted 1974), pp 23, 31; *The Destruction of Aboriginal Society* (reprinted 1974, Penguin, Melbourne, 1972), pp 131, 280.

12 The distressing case of *Namatjira v Raabe* [1958] NTJ 608 in which the artist Albert Namatjira was convicted of supplying alcohol to Aborigines is an example of the invidious effects of prohibition.

13 *Sunday Mail*, 2 November 1975.

14 "Single sober criminal", *News* (Darwin), 22 March 1979.

15 J Cawte, quoted in Rowley, *Remote Aborigines*, op cit, p 48. Instant gratification from gin swilling was common among despairing people – William Hogarth depicted this graphically in scenes from the London slums in the late 18th century.

16 National Committee on Violence, *Violence: Directions for Australia* (AIC, Canberra, 1990), pp 169-70.

17 ALRC Report No 31, Vol 1, para 622, p 460.

18 P Sutton, "The politics of suffering: Indigenous policy in Australia since the 1970s" (2001) 11(2) November, *Anthropological Forum* 135.

19 P Wilson, *Black Death: White Hands* (Allen & Unwin, Sydney, 1982), pp 57-58.

20 E Venbrux, *A Death in the Tiwi Islands: Conflict, Ritual and Social Life in an Australian Aboriginal Community* (Cambridge University Press, Melbourne, 1995), p 16.

21 M Langton, "Medicine Square", in I Keen (ed), *Aboriginal Cultures in "Settled" Australia* (Aboriginal Studies Press, Canberra, 1994), p 212; V Burbank, *Fighting Women* (University of California Press, Berkeley, 1994), p 55.

22 M Langton et al, *"Too Much Sorry Business": Report of the Royal Commission into Aboriginal Deaths in Custody: Vol 5 Appendix D I* (AGPS, Canberra, 1991), p 287; Memmott et al, pp 26-28.

23 E Hunter, "Images of violence in Aboriginal Australia" (1990) 2(46) *ALB* 13. When the article was written Hunter was the Research Fellow at the NSW Institute of Psychiatry and the National Drug and Alcohol Research Centre.

24 Memmott et al, p 27.

25 *Tumanako v The Queen* (1992) 64 A Crim R 149 (NSWCCA).

26 (1990) 50 A Crim 31 at 34.

27 *O'Connor v The Queen* (1980) 146 CLR 64.

28 D O'Connor, and P Fairall, *Criminal Defences*, 3rd edn (Butterworths, Sydney, 1996). See Ch 12, p 226 ff, for discussion of the offence of intoxication generally.

29 ALRC, RP 6A, pp 53-63.

30 This case was *Helen Din Din Keeway* (unreported, NTSC, Forster CJ, SCC No 548 of 1980, 15 June 1981) where the accused killed her husband after years of brutal assaults upon her.

31 *Mark Rogers and Albert Murray v The Queen* (1989) 44 A Crim R 301 at 305 is a review of the following cases in which environmental factors were treated as a mitigating circumstance for alcohol consumption as one element in criminal behaviour. *Jamieson* (unreported, WASC, Library No 96, 7 April 1965); *Lee* (NTSC, SCC No 221 of 1974, 19 November 1974); *Ellen Dawn Friday* (1985) 14 A Crim 471; and *R v Charlie, Uhl and Nagamarra* (unreported, WASC, No 96 of 1987, 14 August 1987).

32 (1991) 56 A Crim R 297.

33 *R v Jerrard* (1991) 56 A Crim R 297 [CCA NSW] where Finlay J considered and followed *R v Coleman* (1990) 47 ACR 306 at 327 and *R v Sewell and Walsh* (1981) 29 SASR 12 at 14-15.

34 *Mark Rogers and Albert Murray v The Queen* (1989) 44 A Crim R 301 at 305.

35 (1997) 94 A Crim R 96 at 127.

36 Wilson, op cit, p 13.

37 J Atkinson, "Violence in Aboriginal Australia: Part 2" (1990) 14(2) *The Aboriginal and Islander Health Worker* 8, Task Force on Violence, op cit, p 16.

38 *R v Watson* (1986) 69 ALR 145.

39 *R v Watson* (1986) 69 ALR 145 at 150.

40 Wilson, op cit, p 29.

41 *R v Steward Collin Mungkuri and Simon Nyangingu (aka Peter Roger)* (1985) 12 *ALB* 11; (McCorquodale, C364, p 416).

42 "*Recommendation 52*. To help alleviate violence in aboriginal communities, alcohol and substance abuse education and rehabilitation programs currently being undertaken should be evaluated and, where appropriate, be introduced in those additional communities requiring them. Such programs should be coordinated more effectively and given appropriate government support. More emphasis needs to be given to such programs in urban areas and should include provision of better recreational facilities. *Recommendation 53*. Imaginative programs such as the Community Development Employment Program should be expanded to other communities as appropriate", National Committee on Violence, op cit, p 170.

43 Memmott et al, p 28.

44 C Egan, "Juries letting Aborigines get away with murder, says DPP", *Australian*, 15 March 2002, Nation, p 5.

Chapter 13

1 M Lucashenko, "Violence Against Indigenous Women: Public and Private Dimensions" in S Cook and J Bessant (eds), *Women's Encounters with Violence* (Sage Publications, Thousand Oaks, California, 1997), p 153.

2 Gordon Report, p 423.

3 J Pitanguy, "Preface" to Bunch and Reilly; D Otto, "Holding Up Half The Sky, But for Whose Benefit?: A Critical Analysis of the Fourth World Conference on Women" (1996) 6 *Australian Feminist Law Journal* 8.

4 Otto, op cit, pp 9, 12. The *Charter of the UN* was posited on the construction of equal rights as men's rights. Otto cites particularly arts 1(3), 8, 13(1), 55(c), 56, 62(2) and 76(c), p 9. The same allegation has been made about the UN *Declaration of Human Rights*.

5 The main United Nations documents directly concerned with women's rights are the *Convention on the Elimination of All Forms of Discrimination Against Women* (1979), entered into force 1981, United Nations, *Human Rights: A Compilation of International Instruments* (United Nations, New York, 2002), pp 112, 155, 175; *Declaration on the Elimination of Violence Against Women* (1993). See also H Charlesworth, C Chinkin and S Wright, "Feminist approaches to International Law" (1991) 85 *American Journal of International Law* 613; H Charlesworth and C Chinkin, "Violence Against Women: A Global Issue", in J Stubbs (ed), *Women, Male Violence and the Law* (Federation Press, Sydney, NSW, 1994), pp 13-27.

6 C Bunch and N Reilly, *Demanding accountability: the global campaign and Vienna Tribunal for Women's Human Rights* (Centre for Women's Global Leadership, Rutgers University, New York, 1994), p 31.

7 G Yunupingu, "A fair go for Aborigines goes with the Territory", *Australian*, 21 August 1998, p 15. Galarrwuy Yunupingu then Chair of the Northern Land Council. The article in the *Australian* was an edited text of the Vincent Lingiari Lecture which Yunupingu gave at the Northern Territory University on 20 August 1998.

8 The Declaration on the Rights of Persons Belonging to National or Ethnic, Religious and Linguistic Minorities and The Draft Declaration on the Rights of Indigenous Peoples, see M Dodson, *Indigenous Social Justice Resource Materials* (Submissions to the Parliament of the Commonwealth of Australia Social Justice Package, Aboriginal and Torres Strait Islander Social Justice Commissioner, 1995) vol 3, pp 130 ff, "Customary law and Human Rights" in Commonwealth Information Services, *Indigenous Customary Law Forum* (AGPS, Canberra, 1966), "Linking International standards with contemporary concerns of Aboriginal and Torres Strait Islander peoples", in S Pritchard (ed), *Indigenous peoples, the United Nations and Human Rights* (The Federation Press, Sydney, NSW, 1998), M Mansell, "Law Reform and the Road to Independence", in S McKillop, *Aboriginal Justice Issues* (AIC, Canberra, 1993).

9 Convention on Consent to Marriage (1962), Minimum Age for Marriage and Registration of Marriages (1965), ancillary to which are the Recommendation on Consent to Marriage, Minimum Age for Marriage and

Registration of Marriages, Declaration on the Elimination of Violence Against Women (1967) and the Convention on the Elimination of All Forms of Discrimination Against Women (1979); UN, *International Instruments,* op cit, pp 361, 364, 108 and 112.

10 L Behrendt, "Indigenous Self-Determination in the Age of Globalisation", Paper given at the "Human Rights and Global Challenges" Conference, 10-11 December, 2001, Castan Centre for Human Rights Law, Monash University.

11 I am indebted to Dr Greg Taylor, Law School, Monash University, for this information and see G Taylor, "The Grand Jury of South Australia", forthcoming 2004 publication.

12 E Eggleston, *Aborigines and the Administration of Justice* (PhD Thesis, Monash University, 1970), pp 399-420.

13 Human Rights and Equal Opportunity Commission, *Report of National Inquiry into Racist Violence* (AGPS, Canberra, 1991), p 111.

14 ALRC, 1986 Report 31, paras 533-34, pp 387-89.

15 *R v Anderson* [1954] NTJ 240 This case is singular in that it involved an attempted rape by an Aborigine of a non-Aboriginal woman.

16 ALRC, 1986, Report 31, para 533, p 388.

17 R Harding et al, *Aboriginal Contact With the Criminal Justice System and the Impact of the Royal Commission Into Aboriginal Deaths in Custody* (Hawkins Press, Sydney, 1995), pp 74-75.

18 *R v Bell* (unreported, QSC, CA No 116 of 1994, 20 June 1994).

19 Harding, op cit, pp 75-76.

20 *Juli v The Queen* (1990) 50 A Crim R 31 at 40 [WA CCA].

21 *R v Gus Forbes* (unreported, NTSC, Gallop J, 29 August 1980).

22 *R v Neil Inkamala Minor* (1992) 59 A Crim R 227 (NT CCA).

23 S Payne, "Aboriginal Women And The Law", in P Easteal and S McKillop (eds), *Women and the Law* (AIC, Canberra, 1993), p 71.

24 *R v Andy Mamarika* (favourably) (unreported, NTSC, Gallop J, 1978), *R v Gilmiri* (unfavourably) (unreported, NTSC, Muirhead J, 1979).

25 Lucashenko, op cit, p 155.

26 Langton et al, *"Too Much Sorry Business": Report of the Royal Commission into Aboriginal Deaths in Custody: Vol 5 Appendix D I* (AGPS, Canberra, 1991), pp 286, 355.

27 Jack Little – a 71-year-old Ngaringman Aborigine speaking in 2000. He was one of the first Aboriginal health workers in the Territory. M Carroll, *Ordinary People, Extraordinary Lives* (New Holland Publishers, Sydney, 2001), p 62.

28 *R v Watson* (1987) 69 ALR 145 at 149.

29 Langton et al, op cit, p 287.

30 A Rose, "Recognition of Customary Law: The Way Ahead", in *Indigenous Customary Law Forum,* op cit, p 13.

31 Model Criminal Code Officers Committee of Attorneys General, *Draft Model Criminal Code: Discussion Paper Chapter 5: Fatal Offences Against the Person* (Model Criminal Code Officers Committee, Canberra, 1998), p 143. (hereafter MCCOC, *Fatal Offences*).

32 < www.lrc.justice.wa.gov.au/Aboriginal/launch.htm>.

33 H Blagg, N Morgan and C Yavu Kama Harathunian, "Aboriginal customary law in Western Australia" (2002) 80 *Reform* 11 at 12.

34 *Koori Mail*, "Justice: Doing It", 30 October 2002, pp 34-35.

35 M Langton, "Urbanizing Aborigines: The Social Scientists' Great Deception" (1981) 2(2) *Social Alternatives* 16; L Behrendt, "Aboriginal Urban Identity: Preserving the Spirit, Protecting the Traditional in Non-Traditional Settings" (1994) 4 *Australian Feminist Law Journal* 56.

36   MCCOC, *Fatal Offences*, p 143.

37 The Universal Declaration of Human Rights (Art 18 and 19), the International Covenant on Economic, Social and Cultural Rights (Arts 1, 2, 3 and 15) and the International Covenant on Civil and Political Rights (Arts 18, 19 and 27); Merkel J, "The Right to Difference" (1998) 72 *Australian Law Journal* 939.

38 R Merkel, "The Right to Difference" (1998) 72 *Australian Law Journal* 939-40.

39 <http://www.nt.gov.au/ocm/media_releases/20021016_customlaws.html>.

40 Elizabeth Eggleston quoted in ALRC Report 31 (1986) vol 2, p 109, see also Justice Blackburn in *Milirrpum v Nabalco Pty Ltd* (1971) 17 FLR 141.

41 D Bell, "Aboriginal Women and the Recognition of Customary Law in Australia", in B Morse and G Woodman (eds), *Indigenous Law and the State* (Foris Publications, Dordrecht, Holland, 1988), p 310. Bell's work has mainly been with Aboriginal women.

42 *Australian*, 4 November 1994, p 3.

43 Office of the Director of Public Prosecutions, Queensland, *Indigenous women within the criminal justice system* (DPP, Qld, 1996), p 17.

44 F Brennan, "Self-Determination: The Limits of Allowing Aboriginal Communities to be a Law unto Themselves" (1993) 16(1) *University of New South Wales Law Journal* 244 at 247.

Chapter 14

1 This title is taken from the British Columbia Book Task Force on Family Violence, *Is Anybody Listening?* (Victoria BC: Minister of Women's Equality, 1992) quoted in Task Force Report, p 3.

2 Women, Queensland, in J Atkinson (ed), *Beyond Violence: Finding The Dream* (Office of the Status of Women, Canberra, 1990), p 6 (hereafter *Beyond Violence*).

3 P O'Shane, "A Tall Order", *Age*, News Extra, p 5.

4 *Beyond Violence: Finding the Dream* (video and booklet) (Aboriginal and Islander Sub-Program, National Domestic Violence Program, Office of the Status of Women, Canberra, 1989); "'Stinkin thinkin' violence" (1991) 2(51) *ALB* 4-6; "A Nation is not Conquered" (1996) 3(80) *ALB* 4-9. Marcia Langton's opposition to intra-communal violence is discussed below. J Pettman, *Living in the margins: racism, sexism and feminism in Australia* (Allen & Unwin, Sydney, NSW, 1992), p 71 (hereafter *Margin'*). Pat

O'Shane, addressed this issue at a Violence in Australia Conference, *Australian*, 30 October 1996, p 12.

5 ATSIC *Please Explain: A Summary of ATSIC's report to the UN Committee on the Elimination of Racial Discrimination* (ATSIC, February, 1999) B Hocking (ed), *International Law and Aboriginal Human Rights* (Law Book Co, Sydney, 1988); M Mansell, "Treaty Proposal Aboriginal Sovereignty" (1989) 2(37) *ALB* 4.

6 N Pearson, "On the Human Right to Misery, Mass Incarceration and Early Death" (2001) December, *Quadrant* p 10.

7 Pearson, ibid, p 18.

8 M Langton, "Senses of Place" (2002) 166 *overland* 75.

9 N Pearson, "Don't disempower blacks", *Australian*, 28 April 2003, p 9.

10 <http://www.onlineopinion.com.au/2002/Nov02/Dodson.htm>; M Shaw, "Aborigines let down by leaders: Dodson" *Age*, 12 June 2003, p 6.

11 Task Force Report, op cit, p x.

12 ALRC, Report No 31 SR, p 14. The Law Reform Commission failed to tackle the issues of, for example, "sacred rape", and as discussed below; it affirmed traditional marriage and did not really address its inequities from women's point of view save for saying that it was essential that each party consent. Only one member, Professor JR Crawford, recommended that traditional marriage not be recognised for legal purposes if a party was below the general minimum marriageable age (16 for boys, 14 for girls) in Australian law. Ibid, p 25. The Law Reform Commission recommended that "traditional marriage should be recognised for the purposes of carnal knowledge charges, provided that *the other party is shown to have consented*" (emphasis added). Ibid, p 22. In saying this the Commission ignored both the difficulty faced by Aboriginal women giving evidence in court, especially the situation of a young girl in such a matter (discussed in Chapter 2) and the control exerted by male elders in the community over what evidence may be presented in court (discussed in Chapter 5). The Commission itself admitted that there was an "initial failure adequately to seek the views of Aboriginal women", which omission had to be rectified later. Ibid, p 3.

13 ALRC, Report No 69, Part I, pp 28, 119, 122-23 for following references.

14 Recommendation 5.2, ALRC, Report No 69, Part I, p xxv.

15 Recommendation 12.2, ALRC, Report No 69, Part I, p xxxiv.

16 Migrant women also suffer particularly high rates of domestic violence (ALRC, Report No 69 Part I, pp 27-28) and like Aboriginal women, can occupy a particularly disadvantaged place in Australian society. See Recommendation 9.7, ibid, p xxvii, s 10, "Violence against women and immigration law", ibid, p xxx, and s 11, "Violence and women's refugee status", ibid, p xxxii.

17 ALRC, Report No 69, Part I, pp 117-20.

18 [1999] 2 AC 629.

19 (2002) 187 ALR 574.

20 Personal communication to author.

21 M Lucashenko, "Violence Against Indigenous Women: Public and Private Dimensions", in S Cook and J Bessant (eds), *Women's Encounters with Violence: Australian Experiences* (Sage Publications, Thousand Oaks, California, 1997), p 157.

22 D Jopson, "O'Shane slams black leaders", *Age*, 22 June, 2001, News, p 6.

23 Hansard, Senate, 25 August, 1999, pp 7774, 7782.

24 K Taylor, "ATSIC says that it acted on abuse", *Age*, 20 June, 2001.

25 B Birnbauer, J-A Davies and C Saltau, "Black violence, Black Despair", *Age*, 23 June, 2001, p 5.

26 M Langton, "Feminism: What do Aboriginal Women Gain?", op cit, p 3.

27 Task Force Report, p 57.

28 L O'Donoghue "Indigenous violence: it's everyone's business", *Age* 22 October, 2001, p 15.

29 E Scott, "Black women's burden", *Age*, 20 June 2001; E Scott, "O'Shane's words could destroy decades of progress", *Sydney Morning Herald*, 20 June 2001.

30 <www.aifs.gov.au/acssa/pubs/newsletter/n2html>.

31 Jopson, op cit.

32 Langton, op cit, p 87.

33 "Aboriginal women need to be able to make an informed decision. That is, whether they choose to use the law or whether they choose not to use the law. In most instances, the choice has been taken away from them by the legal system's inability to provide a culturally appropriate and sensitive legal service", Aboriginal Women's Legal Issues Group, Sydney, *Submission*, ALRC, Report No 69, Part I, p 127.

34 "This leads to problems for Aboriginal women attempting to exercise their rights under the non-Aboriginal legal system which is male dominated and usually does not have procedures for dealing with Aboriginal women's business in a culturally appropriate way". Confidential Submission, ALRC Report No 69, Part I, pp 120, 122.

35 C Thomas, "Sexual Assault Issues for Aboriginal Women', in P Easteal (ed), *Without Consent: Confronting Adult Sexual Violence* (Australian Institute of Criminology, Canberra, 1993), pp 144-47.

36 J Lloyd and N Rogers, "Crossing the Last Frontier: Problems Facing Aboriginal Women Victims of Rape In Central Australia", in P Easteal (ed), *Without Consent Confronting Adult Sexual Violence* (AIC, Canberra, 1993), pp 162-63.

37 E Alvares, "A Women's Refuge for Bourke: A Community Initiative", in S McKillop (ed), *Aboriginal Justice Issues* (AIC, Canberra, 1993), p 179.

38 ALRC, Interim Report No 67, p 124 (fn 9).

39 D Curtis, "Julalikari Council's Community Night Patrol", in S McKillop (ed), *Aboriginal Justice Issues* (AIC, Canberra, 1993), p 73.

40 Lloyd and Rogers, op cit, p 162.

41 Payne, op cit, p 72.

42 P Daylight and M Johnstone, *Women's business: report of the Aboriginal Women's task force* (AGPS, Canberra, 1986), p 67.

43 Alvares, op cit, p 183.

44 There has been conflict between Aboriginal women and non-Aboriginal women over control of action on behalf of, or by, Aboriginal women since the 1930s, and Jackie Huggins believes that another expression of this cultural dichotomy caused Aboriginal women to reject the Australian feminist movement, H Goodall and J Huggins, "Aboriginal Women are Everywhere: Contemporary Struggles", in K Saunders and R Evans (eds), *Gender Relations in Australia: Domination and Negotiation* (Harcourt Brace Jovanovich, 1992), pp 400-2 and the powerful role which Aboriginal can play as "the interface" between their people and bureaucracy, p 412.

45 Goodall and Huggins instance the tensions with funding bodies over funding to the Mygunyah Committee for Aboriginal women in Dubbo and Bourke. Non-Aboriginal women see the preferable solution to family violence as moving away while Aboriginal women wish to remain within their community and rather seek temporary shelter. Goodall and Huggins, op cit, pp 411-12.

46 The Women's Legal Resource Group, Melbourne, is one of the few legal services in Australia which is specific to the needs of women.

47 Human Rights and Equal Opportunity Commission, *Report of the National Inquiry into Racist Violence in Australia* (AGPS, Canberra, 1991).

48 AIJA, *Annual Report* (AIJA, Melbourne, 1997), pp 13-14, and author's conversation with Ms Ann Wallace, Executive Secretary of the AIJA.

49 Gordon Report, p 323.

50 Aboriginal and Torres Strait Islander Commission, *Second ATSIC National Women's Conference Report* (ATSIC, September, 1994), p 17.

51 Women's Commission for Refugee Women and Children, "UNHCR Policy on Refugee Women and Guidelines on Their Protection: An Assessment of Ten Years of Implementation", May 2002, cited in an unpublished paper by S Kneebone, "Women Within the Refugee Construct: At the Margin of Non-Citizenship" (Castan Centre for Human Rights, Monash University Law School, October, 2003), p 7.

52 Task Force Report, p 15.

Select bibliography

Aboriginal and Torres Strait Islander Commission, *Aboriginal and Torres Strait Islander Women: Part of the Solution – National Conference* (ATSIC, Canberra, April, 1992)

Aboriginal and Torres Strait Islander Commission, *Evaluation of the Effectiveness of ATSIC Programs in Meeting the Needs of Aboriginal Women and Torres Strait Islander Women: Final Report* (Office of Evaluation and Audit, ATSIC, August, 1995)

Aboriginal and Torres Strait Islander Commission, *Please Explain: A Summary of ATSIC's report to the UN Committee on the Elimination of Racial Discrimination* (ATSIC, February, 1999)

Aboriginal and Torres Strait Islander Commission, *Second ATSIC National Women's Conference Report* (ATSIC, September, 1994)

Aboriginal and Torres Strait Islander Social Justice Commissioner, *Second Report* (AGPS, Canberra, 1994)

Aboriginal and Torres Strait Islander Social Justice Commissioner, *Indigenous Social Justice: Strategies and Recommendations* (Office of the Aboriginal and Torres Strait Islander Social Justice Commissioner, Sydney, 1995)

Aboriginal Deaths in Custody: Overview of the Response by Governments to the Royal Commission (AGPS, Canberra, 1992)

Aboriginal Legal Service of Western Australia, *Telling Our Story* (Aboriginal Legal Service of Western Australia Inc, 1995)

Aboriginal Women's Legal Issues Conference, Parramatta, *Background Paper* (1993)

Atkinson, J (ed), *Beyond Violence: Finding the Dream* (Office of the Status of Women, Canberra, 1990)

Atkinson, J, "Violence Against Aboriginal Women: Reconstitution of Community Law – the Way Forward" (1990) 2(46) *ALB* 6

Atkinson, J, "Violence in Aboriginal Australia: Colonisation and Gender" (1990) 14(2) *The Aboriginal and Islander Health Worker* 5

Atkinson, J, "Violence in Aboriginal Australia: Part 2" (1990) 14(3) *Aboriginal and Islander Health Worker* 4.

Atkinson, J, "'Stinkin Thinkin" – Alcohol, Violence and Government Responses" (1991) 2(51) *ALB* 4

Atkinson, J, "A Nation is not Conquered" (1996) 3(80) *ALB* 6

Attwood, B, *The Making of the Aborigines* (Allen & Unwin, North Sydney, 1992)

Attwood, B and Arnold, J (eds), *Power, Knowledge and Aborigines* (La Trobe University Press, Melbourne, 1992)

Attwood, B and Markus, A, *The 1967 Referendum or When Aborigines Didn't Get the Vote* (Australian Institute of Aboriginal and Torres Strait Islander Studies, Canberra, 1997)

Australian Bureau of Statistics, *Australian Women's Year Book 1995* (Office of the Status of Women and Australian Bureau of Statistics, AGPS, Canberra, 1995)

Australian Bureau of Statistics, *National Aboriginal and Torres Strait Islander Survey 1994: detailed findings* (Australian Bureau of Statistics, Canberra, 1995)

Australian Council of Churches, *Justice for Aboriginal Australians* (Australian Council of Churches, Sydney, 1981)

Australian Institute of Judicial Administration Inc, *Aboriginal Cultural Awareness Programme* (Australian Institute of Judicial Administration, Melbourne, 1993)

Australian Institute of Judicial Administration Inc, *Annual Reports*, 1995, 1996, 1997, 1998 (Australian Institute of Judicial Administration, Melbourne)

Australian Institute of Judicial Administration Inc, *Cross Cultural Awareness for the Judiciary: Final Report to the Australian Institute of Judicial Administration* Australian Institute of Judicial Administration, Melbourne, 1996)

Australian Law Reform Commission, *Reference on Aboriginal Customary Law: Promised Marriage in Aboriginal Society: Research Paper 1* (Law Reform Commission, Sydney, 1982)

Australian Law Reform Commission, *Reference on Aboriginal Customary Law: Aboriginal Customary Law and the Substantive Criminal Law: Research Paper No 6* (Law Reform Commission, Sydney, 1982)

Australian Law Reform Commission, *Reference on Aboriginal Customary Law: Appendix: Cases on Traditional Punishment and Sentencing Research Paper No 6A* (Law Reform Commission, Sydney, 1982)

Australian Law Reform Commission, *The Recognition of Aboriginal Customary Laws: Report No 31* (AGPS, Canberra, 1986)

Australian Law Reform Commission, *The Recognition of Aboriginal Customary Laws: Summary Report* (AGPS, Canberra, 1986)

Australian Law Reform Commission, *Equality Before the Law: Justice for Women – Report No 69 Part I* (Law Reform Commission, Sydney, 1994)

Australian Law Reform Commission, *Equality before the Law: Women's Equality: Interim Report No 69 Part II* (Law Reform Commission, Sydney, 1994)

Australian Law Reform Commission, *Equality Before the Law: Women's Access to the Legal System: Interim Report No 67* (Law Reform Commission, Sydney, 1994)

SELECT BIBLIOGRAPHY

Baldini, G, "Rape and Sexual Abuse Within the Aboriginal Communities", *Balancing the Scales: National Conference on Sexual Assault* (Perth, 20-21 June 1996)

Behrendt, L, *Aboriginal Dispute Resolution* (Federation Press, Sydney, NSW, 1995)

Bell, D, *Daughters of the Dreaming* (McPhee Gribble, George Allen & Unwin, Melbourne, 1983)

Bell, D and Ditton, P, *Law: The Old and the New: Aboriginal Women in Central Australia Speak Out* (CAALAS, Aboriginal History, Canberra, 1980)

Bell, D and Nelson, TT, 'Speaking About Rape is Everyone's Business" (1989) 12(4) *Women's International Forum* 403

Berndt, RM, *Australian Aboriginal Religion* (EJ Brill, Leiden, 1974)

Berndt, RM and Berndt, CH, *Aborigines of the West: their Past and their Present* (University of Western Australia Press, Perth, 1980)

Berndt, RM and Berndt, CH, *From Black to White in South Australia* (FW Cheshire, Melbourne, 1951)

Berndt, RM and Berndt, CH, *Man, Land and Myth in North Australia* (Ure Smith, Sydney, 1970)

Berndt, RM and Berndt, CH, *The World of the First Australians*, revised edn (Lansdowne Press, Sydney, 1981)

Berndt, R and Berndt, C, *End of an Era: Aboriginal Labour in the Northern Territory* (AIAS, Canberra, 1987)

Brennan, G, "Self-Determination: The Limits Of Allowing Aboriginal Communities to be a Law Unto Themselves" (1993) 16(1) *University of New South Wales Law Journal* 245

Bolger, A, *Aboriginal Women and Violence* (Australian National University, North Australian Research Unit, Darwin, 1991)

Brock, P (ed), *Women, Rites and Sites* (Allen & Unwin, Sydney, 1989)

Brock, P, *Outback Ghettos* (Cambridge University Press, Cambridge, 1993)

Brockman, J (ed), *He Rode Alone* (Artlook Books, Perth, 1987)

Bunch, C and Reilly, N, *Demanding accountability: The global campaign and Vienna Tribunal for Women's Human Rights* (Centre for Women's Global Leadership, Rutgers University, New York, 1994)

Burbank, VK, *Fighting Women* (University of California Press, Berkeley, 1994)

Cawte, J, *Medicine is the Law: Studies of Psychiatric Anthropology in Australian Tribal Societies* (University Press of Hawaii, Honolulu, 1974)

Ceresa, M, "Police Apologise to Rape Victim", *Australian*, 4 June 1996, A5

Charlesworth, M, Morphy, H, Bell, D and Maddock, K, *Religion in Aboriginal Australia: An Anthology* (University of Queensland Press, Brisbane, 1984)

Chappell, D and Wilson, P, *The Australian Criminal Justice System: the mid 1990s* (Butterworths, Sydney, 1994)

Chief Justice of Western Australia, *Report of Chief Justice's Taskforce on Gender Bias* (Chief Justice of Western Australia, Perth, 1994)

Cohen, P and Somerville, M, *Ingelba and the Five Black Matriarchs* (Allen & Unwin, Sydney, 1990)

Commonwealth Information Services, *Indigenous Customary Law Forum* (AGPS, Canberra, 1996)

Cook, S and Bessant, J (eds), *Women's Encounters with Violence* (Sage Publications, Thousand Oaks, California, 1997)

Coombs, HC, *Issues in Dispute: Aborigines Working for Autonomy* (North Australia Research Unit, Australian National University, Darwin, 1993)

Council for Aboriginal Reconciliation, *Addressing the Key Issues of Reconciliation* (AGPS, Canberra, reprinted 1994)

Council for Aboriginal Reconciliation, *Controlling Destinies* (AGPS, Canberra, 1994)

Council for Aboriginal Reconciliation, *Valuing Cultures* (AGPS, Canberra, 1994)

Council for Aboriginal Reconciliation, *Going Forward: Social Justice for the First Australians: A Submission to the Commonwealth Government from the Council for Aboriginal Reconciliation* (Council for Aboriginal Reconciliation, Canberra, 1995)

Cousins, M and Hussain, A, *Michel Foucault* (Macmillan, London, 1984)

Criminal Justice Commission, Queensland, *Aboriginal Witnesses in Queensland's Criminal Courts* (Criminal Justice Commission, Brisbane, 1996)

Cummings, E, "Customs and Culture: the Current Situation in Relation to Violence against Aboriginal Women" (1993) 17(6) *Aboriginal and Islander Health Worker* 15

Cunneen, C (ed), *Aboriginal Perspectives on Criminal Justice* (Institute of Criminology, Sydney University Law School, Sydney, 1992)

Daylight, P and Johnstone, M, *Women's Business: Report of the Aboriginal Women's Task Force* (Office of the Status of Women, AGPS, Canberra, 1986)

Dodson, M, "Customary Law and Human Rights", in Commonwealth Information Services, *Indigenous Customary Law Forum* (AGPS, Canberra, 1996)

Dodson, M, *Indigenous Social Justice Strategies and Recommendations: Indigenous Social Justice Regional Agreements* and *Indigenous Social Justice Source Materials* (Submissions to the Parliament of the Commonwealth of Australia Social Justice Package, Vols 1-3, Aboriginal and Torres Strait Islander Social Justice Commissioner, 1995)

Eades, D (ed), *Language in Evidence: Issues Confronting Aboriginal and Multicultural Australia* (University of NSW Press, Sydney, 1995)

Easteal, P (ed), *Without Consent: Confronting Adult Sexual Violence* (Australian Institute of Criminology, Canberra, 1993)

Easteal, P and McKillop, S (eds), *Women and the Law* (AIC, Canberra, 1993)

Edwards, WH (ed) *Traditional Aboriginal Society*, 2nd edn (Macmillan Education Australia, Melbourne, 1998)

Eggleston, EM, *Aborigines and the Administration of Justice* (PhD Thesis, Monash University, 1970)

Elkin, AP, *The Australian Aborigines*, 4th edn (1964, Angus and Robertson, Sydney, reprinted 1966)

Ferrante, A, Morgan, F, Indermaur, D and Harding, RW, *Measuring the Extent of Domestic Violence* (Hawkins Press, Sydney, 1996)

FTEA&R Centre (SA) Inc, *No Shame No Violence: Report* (FTEA&R Centre (SA) Inc, Port Lincoln, SA, 1995)

Gale, F (ed), *We Are Bosses Ourselves* (Australian Institute of Aboriginal Studies, Canberra, 1983)

Gale, F (ed), *Woman's Role in Aboriginal Society* (Australian Institute of Aboriginal Studies, Canberra, 1978)

Gilbert, K (ed), *Inside Black Australia* (Penguin Books Ltd, Melbourne, 1988)

Gordon, S, Hallahan, K and Henry, D, *Putting the picture together, Inquiry into the Response by Government Agencies to Complaints of Family Violence and Child Abuse in Aboriginal Communities* (Department of Premier and Cabinet, Western Australia, 2002)

Grieve, N and Burns, A (eds), *Australian Women Contemporary Feminist Thought* (Oxford University Press, Melbourne, 1994)

Grieve, N and Grimshaw, P (eds), *Australian Women: Feminist Perspectives* (Oxford University Press, Melbourne, 1983)

Hanks, P and Keon-Cohen, B (eds), *Aborigines and the Law* (George Allen & Unwin, Sydney, 1984)

Harding, RW, Broadhurst, R, Ferrante, A and Loh, N, *Aboriginal Contact with the Criminal Justice System and the Impact of the Royal Commission into Aboriginal Deaths in Custody* (Hawkins Press, Sydney, 1995)

Hawke, S and Gallagher, M, *Noonkanbah* (Fremantle Arts Centre Press, Fremantle, WA, 1989)

Hazlehurst, K, *Ivory Scales, Black Australia and the Law* (University of NSW Press, Sydney, 1987)

Hiatt, LR, *Arguments About Aborigines* (Cambridge University Press, Cambridge, 1966)

Hiatt, LR (ed), *Australian Aboriginal Mythology* (Australian Institute of Aboriginal Studies, Canberra, 1975)

Hocking, B (ed), *International Law and Aboriginal Human Rights* (Law Book Co, Sydney, 1988)

Huggins, J, "Always Was Always Will Be" (1992) 25(100) *Australian Historical Studies* 459

Huggins, J, Huggins, R and Jacobs, JM, "Kooramindanjie: Place and the Post-Colonial" (1995) 39 *History Workshop Journal* 166

Huggins, R and Huggins, J, *Auntie Rita* (Aboriginal Studies Press, Canberra, 1994)

Human Rights and Equal Opportunity Commission, *Report of the National Inquiry into Racist Violence in Australia* (AGPS, Canberra, 1991)

Isaacs, J (ed), *Australian Dreaming: 40,000 years of Aboriginal history* (Lansdowne Press, Sydney, 1980)

Johnston, E, *Royal Commission into Aboriginal Deaths in Custody National Report: Overview and Recommendations* (AGPS, Canberra, 1991)

Kaberry, P, *Aboriginal Women: Sacred and Profane* (Routledge, London, 1939)

Keen, I (ed), *Being Black: Aboriginal cultures in "settled" Australia* (Aboriginal Studies Press, Canberra, 1994)

Kenny, C, *Women's Business* (Duffy and Snellgrove, Sydney, 1996)

Kidd, R, *The Way We Civilise* (University of Queensland Press, Brisbane, 1997)

Kimberley Aboriginal Law and Culture Centre, *Yirra Land Law And Language* (KALACC, Fitzroy Crossing, Western Australia 1996)

Koch, T, "A National Disgrace", *Herald Sun*, 13 November 1998, p 19

Kriewaldt, MC, "The Application of the Criminal Law to Aborigines of the Northern Territory of Australia" (1960-62) 5(1) *University of Western Australia Law Review* 1

Langton, M, "Feminism: What do Aboriginal Women Gain?" (8 December 1989) *Broadside: National Foundation for Australian Women Newsletter* 3

Langton, M, "Urbanizing Aborigines: The Social Scientists" Great Deception" (1981) 2(2) *Social Alternatives* 16

Langton, M, *Well, I heard it on the radio and I saw it on the television ...* (Australian Film Commission, Sydney, 1993)

Langton, M, Ahmatt, L, Moss, B, Schaber, E, MacKinolty, C, Thomas, M, Tilton, E and Spencer, L, *"Too Much Sorry Business": Report of the Royal Commission into Aboriginal Deaths in Custody: Vol 5 Appendix D I* (AGPS, Canberra, 1991)

Madden, R, *National Aboriginal and Torres Strait Islander Survey 1994: detailed findings* (Australian Bureau of Statistics, Canberra, 1995)

Maddock, K, *The Australian Aborigines: A Portrait of their Society*, 2nd edn (Penguin Books, Melbourne, 1974)

Malinkowski, B, *The Family Among the Australian Aborigines: A Sociological Study* (Schocken Books, New York, 1963)

Markus, A, *Governing Savages* (Allen & Unwin, Sydney, 1990)

McCarthy, F, *Australian Aborigines Their Life and Culture* (Colorgravure Publications, Melbourne, 1957)

McCorquodale, J, *Aborigines and the Law: A Digest* (Aboriginal Studies Press, Canberra, 1987)

McKenna, M, *Looking for Blackfellas' Point* (UNSW Press, Sydney, 2002)

McKillop, S (ed), *Aboriginal Justice Issues* (AIC, Canberra, 1993)

McNamara, L, *Aboriginal Human Rights, The Criminal Justice System and the Search for Solutions: A Case for Self Determination: Discussion Paper No 19* (Australian National University, Northern Australian Research Unit, Casuarina, NT, 1993)

McRae, H, Nettheim, G and Beacroft, L, with McNamara, L, *Indigenous Legal Issues*, 2nd edn (LBC Information Services, Sydney, 1997)

Memmott, P, Stacy, R, Chambers, C and Keys, C, *Violence in Indigenous Communities* (Crime Prevention Branch, Commonwealth Attorney General's Department, Canberra, 2001)

Model Criminal Code Officers Committee of Attorneys General, *Draft Model Criminal Code: Discussion Paper Chapter 5: Fatal Offences Against the Person* (Model Criminal Code Officers Committee, Canberra, 1998)

Morse, BW and Woodman, GR (eds), *Indigenous Law and the State* (Foris Publications, Dordrecht, Holland, 1988)

National Committee on Violence, *Violence: Directions for Australia* (AIC, Canberra, 1990)

National Inquiry into Racist Violence (Australia), *Report* (AGPS, Canberra, 1991)

New South Wales Ministry for the Status and Advancement of Women, *Dubay Jahli: Aboriginal Women and the Law Report* (New South Wales Government, Sydney, 1994)

Ngabidj, G, *My Country of the Pelican Dreaming: The Life of an Australian Aborigine of the Gadjerong: Grant Ngabidj 1904-1977 (as told to Bruce Shaw)* (Australian Institute of Aboriginal Studies, Canberra, 1981)

Noongar Alcohol & Substance Abuse Service, *The Strong Speak Out* (Noongar Alcohol & Abuse Substance Service, Perth, 1993)

NSW Ministry for the Status and Advancement of Women, *Dubay Jahli Aboriginal Women and the Law Report* (NSW Government, Sydney, 1994)

Office of the Director of Public Prosecutions, Queensland, *Indigenous Women within the Criminal Justice System* (Office of the Director of Public Prosecutions, Brisbane, 1996)

Office of the Status of Women and Australian Bureau of Statistics, *Australian Women's Year Book: 1995* (AGPS, Canberra, 1995)

O'Shane, P, "Is there any Relevance in the Women's Movement for Aboriginal Women?" (September 1976) 12 *Refractory Girl* 31

Pettman, J, *Race and Ethnicity in Contemporary Australia* (Centre for Multicultural Education, University of London Institute of Education, London, 1986)

Pettman, J, *Whose Country is It Anyway? Cultural Politics, Racism and the Construction of Being Australian* (Research School of Pacific Studies, Australian National University, Canberra, 1988)

Pettman, J, *Living in the Margins: racism, sexism and feminism in Australia* (Allen & Unwin, Sydney, NSW, 1992)

Pettman, J, *Women, Nationalism and the State: International Feminist Perspective* (Gender and Development Studies Unit, Asian Institute of Technology, Bangkok, 1992)

Pritchard, S (ed), *Indigenous Peoples, the United Nations and Human Rights* (Federation Press, Sydney, 1998)

Reynolds, H, *The Other Side of the Frontier* (Penguin Books, Melbourne, 1982)

Reynolds, H, *Dispossession* (Allen & Unwin, Sydney, 1989)

Reynolds, H, *Fate of a Free People* (Penguin Books, Melbourne, 1995)

Reynolds, H, *This Whispering in our Hearts* (Allen & Unwin, Sydney, 1998)

Rintoul, S, *The Wailing: A National Black Oral History* (William Heinemann, Port Melbourne, 1993)

Robertson, B (ed), *Aboriginal and Torres Strait Islander Women's Task Force on Violence* (State of Queensland, 2000)

Rose, D, *Dingo Makes Us Human* (Cambridge University Press, Cambridge, 1992)

Rose, D, "The Saga of Captain Cook: Morality in Aboriginal and European Law" (1984) 2 *Australian Aboriginal Studies* 24

Rose, D, "A Case of Murder", cited in McRae, H, Nettheim, G and Beacroft, L, *Indigenous Legal Issues*, 2nd edn (LBC Information Services, Sydney, 1997)

Rowley, CD, *Outcasts in White Australia* (Penguin Books, Melbourne, reprinted 1973)

Rowley, CD, *The Remote Aborigines* (Penguin Books, Melbourne, reprinted 1974)

Rowley, CD, *The Destruction of Aboriginal Society* (Penguin Books, Melbourne, reprinted 1976)

Rowley, CD, *A Matter of Justice* (Australian National University Press, Canberra, 1978)

Royal Commission into Aboriginal Deaths in Custody (APGS, Canberra, 1991)

Sam, M, *Through Black Eyes: A handbook of family violence in Aboriginal and Torres Strait Islander Communities* (Secretariat of National Aboriginal and Islander Childcare, Canberra, 1992)

Saunders, K and Evans, R (eds), *Gender Relations in Australia: Domination and Negotiation* (Harcourt Brace Jovanovich, Sydney, 1992)

Scutt, J (ed), *Different Lives* (Penguin Books, Melbourne, 1987)

Strang, H and Gerrull, S-A (eds), *Homicide: Patterns, Prevention and Control* (Australian Institute of Criminology, Canberra, 1992)

Strehlow, K, *Aboriginal Women: with special reference to W Lloyd Warner's "A Black Civilization": the influence of Durkheim and the local groups of Central Australia* (The Strehlow Research Foundation, Adelaide, 1989)

Strehlow, KS, *Operation of fear in traditional Aboriginal society in Central Australia* (The Strehlow Foundation, Adelaide, 1991)

Strehlow, TG, *Aranda Traditions* (Melbourne University Press, Melbourne, 1947)

Strang, H and Gerrull S-A (eds), *Homicide: Patterns, Prevention and Control* (Australian Institute of Criminology, Canberra, 1992)

Stubbs, J (ed), *Women, Male Violence and the Law* (The Institute of Criminology, Sydney, and Federation Press, Sydney, 1994)

Sullivan, J, *Banggaiyerri: The Story of Jack Sullivan as told to Bruce Shaw* (Australian Institute of Aboriginal Studies, Canberra, 1983)

Sutton, P, "The politics of suffering: Indigenous policy in Australia since the 1970s" (2001) 11(2) *Anthropological Forum* 125

Swanton, B (ed), *Aborigines and Criminal Justice* (Australian Institute of Criminology, Canberra 1984)

Upton, JCR, "By Violence, By Silence, By Control: The Marginalisation of Aboriginal Women Under White and 'Black Law'" (1992) 18 *Melbourne University Law Review* 867

Towers, K, "Report to Slate State over Cell Deaths", *Australian*, 11 July 1992, 2

Venbrux, E, *A Death in the Tiwi Islands: Conflict, Ritual and Social life in an Australian Aboriginal Community* (Cambridge University Press, Melbourne, 1995)

White, I, Barwick D and Meehan, B, *Fighters and Singers* (George Allen & Unwin, Sydney, 1985)

Wilkie, M, *Aboriginal Justice Programs in Western Australia: Research Report No 5* (Crime Research Centre, University of Western Australia, Perth, 1991)

Williams, NM, "Phyllis Kaberry in East Kimberley: 'she was the first one ...'" (1988) 12(1) *Aboriginal History* 91.

Wilson, P, *Black Death: White Hands* (Allen & Unwin, Sydney, 1982)

Worgan, G, *Journal of a First Fleet Surgeon* (Library Council of New South Wales, Sydney, 1978)

Table of Cases

Cases on intra-communal Aboriginal violence to women have frequently been unreported. Of unreported cases all older cases and some recent cases are unavailable electronically. The only avenue for obtaining transcripts of these cases is through the particular court registries and some court libraries. Hence when cases are unreported references to more accessible sources have been included, namely the ALRC 1986 Law Reform Commission Report into Aboriginal Customary Law (Commonwealth of Australia, 1986), the preliminary ALRC Research Paper 6A (ALRC, 1982) and J McCorquodale, *Aborigines and the Law: A Digest* (Aboriginal Studies Press, 1987). Nearly all case references in these sources have been included as one account might supplement another. Because of scanty reporting contemporary newspaper reports and the *Aboriginal Law Bulletin (ALB)* have been used for some cases not covered elsewhere.

TABLE OF CASES

Jamieson (unreported, WASC, Library No 96, 7 April 1965): 191

Jamilmira (Jackie Pascoe) see Hales v Jamilmira : 63, 64, 65, 66, 67, 69, 72, 74

Jerrard (1991) 56 A Crim R 297: 130, 192

Johansen v Billing, Commissioner of Police and Police Appeal Board (unreported, WASC, Pidgeon, Franklyn and Owen JJ, Hearing 17 and 18 September 1992, delivered 19 May 1993): 28, 166

Juli(1990) 50 A Crim R 31: 15, 128, 130, 194

Jungala (Old Barney) (unreported, NTSC, Muirhead J, 8 February 1978), ALRC Report No 31, p 308 (fn 81), McCorquodale, C317: 98

Jungarai, Joseph Murphy, bail application reported (1981) 9 NTR 30; reasons for sentence, unreported, 2 November, 1981 (NTSC, Muirhead J), appeal from sentence, unreported, 4 June 1982 (FCAFC, Toohey, McGregor, Sheppard JJ), ALRC 1986 Report 31, para 495: 121

Keeway (Helen Din Din) (unreported, NTSC, Forster CJ, SCC No 548 of 1980, 15 June 1981): 191

Kina (Robyn Bella) (unreported, QSC, CCA, 29 November 1993): 32, 33, 169

Kontinnen (unreported, SASC, Legoe J, 26-30 March 1992): 169

Kunoth, (Allan) [1957] NTJ 420: 108, 111

Lane (Burt) Hunt (Ronald) and Smith (Reggie) (unreported, NTSC, Gallop J, 29 May 1980), McCorquodale, C333: 77, 182, 184

Lee (Benny) (unreported, NTSC, Forster J, 19 November 1974), ALRC RP 6A, C2: 97, 99, 191

Leering (Andrew) (unreported, WASC, CCA, Hearing 13 November 1990, delivered 21 December 1990): 82, 183

Lowe (1984) 58 CLR 414: 139

Mabo v Queensland [No 2] (1992) 175 CLR 1: 9, 88, 143

Mamarika (Andy) (unreported, NTSC, Gallop J, 9 August 1978), ALRC 1986 Report No 31, paras 510, 625, McCorquodale, C 349: 119, 194

Mamarika (Moses) (1982) 42 ALR 94: 121

Mangukala (Lazarus) (unreported, NTSC, Forster J, No 313 of 1974, 18 April 1975); ALRC RP 6A; C5, McCorquodale, C 352: 64, 74

Mick (unreported No 129 of 1988, 14 October 1988): 184

Minor (Neil Inkamala) (1992) 59 A Crim R 227: 90, 139, 194

Milirrpum v Nabalco Pty Ltd (1971) 17 FLR 141: 114, 121, 189, 196

Moffa (1997) 138 CLR 601: 94

Muddarubba (Aboriginal) [1956] NTJ 317: 94, 95, 96

Mulparinga (Aboriginal Charlie) [1953] NTJ 219: 96, 98

Mungatopi (1991) 57 A Crim R 341: 60, 62, 102, 177, 183

Mungkilli, Martin and Mintuma (unreported, SASC, 20 March 1991), H McRae, G Nettheim and L Beacroft, Indigenous Legal Issues, Commentaries and Materials (2nd ed, LBC Information Services, Sydney, 1997), p 380: 80

Index

INDEX